Microsoft®

S0-FEQ-708

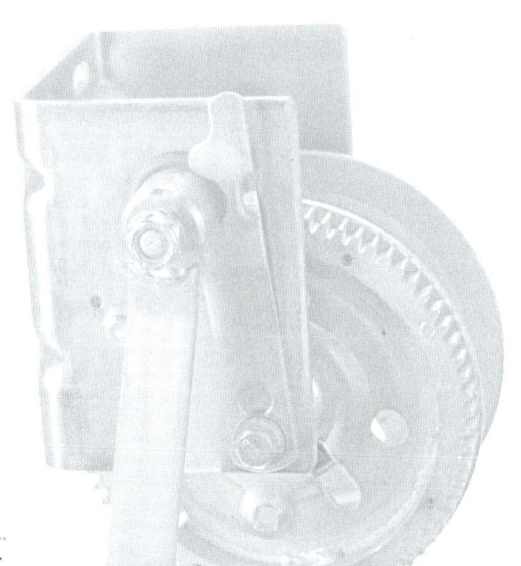

Microsoft
INTERNET SECURITY
and **ACCELERATION (ISA)**
SERVER 2000

Jason Ballard
Bud Ratliff

PUBLISHED BY
Microsoft Press
A Division of Microsoft Corporation
One Microsoft Way
Redmond, Washington 98052-6399

Copyright © 2003 by Jason Ballard, Bud Ratliff

All rights reserved. No part of the contents of this book may be reproduced or transmitted in any form or by any means without the written permission of the publisher.

Library of Congress Cataloging-in-Publication Data
Ballard, Jason 1974-
        Microsoft Internet Security and Acceleration (ISA) Server 2000 Administrator's Pocket Consultant / Jason Ballard, Bud Ratliff.
        p. cm.
        Includes bibliographical references and index.
        ISBN 0-7356-1442-3
        1. Computer networks--Security measures--Software. 2. Computer security--Software. 3. Internet--Security measures--Software. I. Ratliff, Bud, 1970- II. Title.

QA76.9.A25B355   2003
005.8--dc21   2003050977

Printed and bound in the United States of America.

1 2 3 4 5 6 7 8 9   QWE   8 7 6 5 4 3

Distributed in Canada by H.B. Fenn and Company Ltd.

A CIP catalogue record for this book is available from the British Library.

Microsoft Press books are available through booksellers and distributors worldwide. For further information about international editions, contact your local Microsoft Corporation office or contact Microsoft Press International directly at fax (425) 936-7329. Visit our Web site at www.microsoft.com/mspress. Send comments to *mspinput@microsoft.com*.

Microsoft, Microsoft Press, NetMeeting, Visual Basic, Windows, Windows NT, and Windows Server are either registered trademarks or trademarks of Microsoft Corporation in the United States and/or other countries. Other product and company names mentioned herein may be the trademarks of their respective owners.

The example companies, organizations, products, domain names, e-mail addresses, logos, people, places, and events depicted herein are fictitious. No association with any real company, organization, product, domain name, e-mail address, logo, person, place, or event is intended or should be inferred.

Microsoft Press
Acquisitions Editor: Martin DelRe
Project Editor: Valerie Woolley

nSight, Inc.
Project Manager: Tempe Goodhue
Copyeditor: Joe Gustaitis
Technical Editor: Tony Northrup
Layout Artist: Patty Fagan
Proofreaders: Jennifer Carr, Rob Saley
Indexer: Jack Lewis

Body Part No. X08-77655

Contents at a Glance

Part I
Microsoft ISA Server 2000 Administrator's Fundamentals

1. Overview of Microsoft ISA Server 2000 Administration   3
2. Installing and Configuring Microsoft ISA Server 2000   21
3. Installing and Configuring Microsoft ISA Server 2000 Clients   45
4. Configuring ISA Server on Small Business Server Installations   59
5. Migrating from Microsoft Proxy Server 2.0   73
6. Monitoring and Reporting   83

Part II
Microsoft ISA Server 2000 Policy Management and Publishing Services

7. Configuring ISA Policy Elements   103
8. Configuring ISA Access Policy   119
9. Publishing Fundamentals   147
10. Common Web and Server Publishing Scenarios   171

Part III
Microsoft ISA Server 2000 and Enterprise Systems Administration

11. Managing ISA Server and Windows Active Directory   201
12. Using Enterprise and Array Policies   211
13. Working with Enterprise Technologies and ISA Server 2000   223

Part IV
Microsoft ISA Server 2000 Security Management
- 14 Microsoft ISA Server 2000 and Perimeter Networks   253
- 15 Securing ISA Server 2000   269

Table of Contents

Acknowledgments xxvii
Introduction xxix

Part I
Microsoft ISA Server 2000 Administrator's Fundamentals

1   **Overview of Microsoft ISA Server 2000 Administration**   3
    How ISA Server Operates as a Caching
    and Firewall Server   3
      Firewall: The Secure Server   4
      Caching: The Acceleration Server   4
    ISA Server Product Editions   5
      Quick Comparison of ISA Product Editions   5
        Operating System Compatibility   6
        Basic Hardware and Server Requirements
        for ISA Server   7
      Detailed Comparison of ISA Server Implementations   8
        Small Business Server 2000   8
        ISA Server 2000 Standard Edition   10
        ISA Server 2000 Enterprise Edition   11
    Using Common ISA Server Tools and Utilities   12
      Using the ISA Management Console   12
        Console View Options   13
        Working with ISA Management Nodes   14
      ISA Server Wizards   17
      Commonly Used MMCs   17
      Command-Line Utilities   18
      ISA Community   18
      Add-Ons for ISA Server   18

Administering ISA Server Remotely		19
ISA Management Console		19
Terminal Services		19
Third-Party Products		20
Additional Resources		20
2	**Installing and Configuring Microsoft ISA Server 2000**	**21**
Installing ISA Server 2000		21
Before You Begin		21
Installing ISA Server on Windows Server 2003		26
Installing ISA Server Service Pack 1		26
Modifying the Role of ISA Server: Enabling Array Membership		26
Joining ISA Server to a Domain		27
Running the Enterprise Initialization Tool		27
Configuring Enterprise Policy Settings		28
Verifying Schema Extensions		29
Promoting a Stand-Alone Server to an Array Member		29
Configuring ISA Server		30
Configuring the Local Address Table (LAT)		31
Manually Creating a New Local Address Table (LAT) Entry		31
Automatically Constructing the Local Address Table (LAT)		31
Modifying a LAT Entry		32
Deleting a LAT Entry		32
Configuring the Local Domain Table (LDT)		32
Creating a New LDT Entry		33
Modifying an LDT Entry		33
Deleting an LDT Entry		33
Configuring Automatic Discovery		33
Enabling Automatic Discovery		33

Configuring the ISA Server Cache 35
　Setting the Size of the Cache 36
　Configuring the Cache Properties 36
　Determining the Load Factor 38
　Configuring the Intra-Array Address 38
　Configuring Scheduled Content Downloads 39
　Installing ISA Server Feature Pack 1 40
　Uninstalling ISA Server Feature Pack 1 41
Uninstalling ISA Server 42
　Performing an Uninstall with Add/Remove Programs 42
　Performing an Uninstall with Rmisa.exe 42
Additional Resources 43

3 Installing and Configuring Microsoft ISA Server 2000 Clients 45

Working with the SecureNAT Client 46
　Installation 46
　　Simple Network vs. Complex Network 47
　Configuration 47
　　Configuring the HTTP Redirector Filter 47
Working with the Web Proxy Client 48
　Installation 49
　Configuration 49
Working with the Firewall Client 51
　Installation 51
　　UNC-Based Installation 51
　　IIS Web-Based Installation 52
　　Group Policy–Based Installation 53
　　Silent Installations 54
　Configuration 55
　　Firewall Client Configuration 56
　　Firewall Client Configuration Properties in the ISA Management Console 56
　　Configuring a Workstation with All Clients 57

Client Dependencies on the Infrastructure 57
　DNS Requirements and Considerations 57
　　Configure a Protocol Rule to Allow DNS Lookups 57
　　DHCP Services 58
Additional Resources 58

4 Configuring ISA Server on Small Business Server Installations 59

Limitations and Differences of ISA Server with SBS 59
　Installation 60
　Configuration 63
　　Small Business Server Internet Connection Wizard 63
Common Procedures and Troubleshooting Steps 68
　Internet Connection Wizard Doesn't Start 68
　ISA Server Services Won't Start If Network Address Translation (NAT) is Enabled 68
　Use Only the Dial-Up Connection Specified in ISA Server to Connect to the Internet 69
　Dynamic DNS Services for Small Businesses 69
　Can't Renew DHCP Assigned IP Address on External ISA Interface 69
　Disabling ICW for Dial-Up Connections 69
　Manually Assigning Fax Server Privileges 70
　Logging User Activity 70
　Problems with ISA Server and IIS on the Same Computer 71
　Removing ISA Server from SBS 71
Additional Resources 71

5 Migrating from Microsoft Proxy Server 2.0 73

Prerequisites to Upgrading Proxy Server 2.0 to ISA Server 73
Upgrading the Proxy Server from Windows NT 4 to Windows 2000 74
　Backing Up the Proxy 2.0 Server 75
　Uninstalling Proxy Server 2.0 75
　Upgrading the Operating System to Windows 2000 75

Installing the Microsoft Proxy Server 2.0
Update for Windows 2000 76
Restoring the Proxy Server 2.0 Configuration 76
Performing an Upgrade to ISA Server 2000 76
Stopping Proxy 2.0 Server Services 77
Removing a Proxy 2.0 Server from an Array 77
Installing ISA Server to Upgrade Proxy Server 2.0 78
Differences Between Proxy Server
and ISA Server 80
Configure the Outbound Web Requests Listener 80
Be Aware of Differences Between the Winsock Client
and the ISA Firewall Client 80
Configure Published Servers as SecureNAT
Clients for Convenience 81
Reconfigure IIS After Installing ISA Server 81
Additional Resources 81

6 **Monitoring and Reporting 83**
Services 83
Monitoring ISA Server Services 83
Service Monitoring in ISA Management Console 84
Services Console 84
Command-Line Service Management 85
Sessions 85
Monitoring Sessions 85
Determining Session Type 86
Aborting Sessions 86
Events 87
Monitoring Events 87
Analyzing Events 88
Alerts 88
Creating an Alert 88
Sending an E-Mail Message 89
Running a Program 90

Reporting the Event to a Windows 2000 Event Log   90
Stopping Selected ISA Server Services   90
Starting Selected ISA Server Services   90
Configuring an Alert   91
Viewing Alerts   92
Resetting Alerts   93
Reporting with ISA Server   93
Generating Reports   93
Reporting Job Properties   93
Creating a Report   94
Report Types   95
Viewing Reports   95
Saving Reports   96
Logging Transactions in ISA Server   96
ISA Log Components   96
Configuring Logs   97
Logging to a File   98
Logging to a Database   98
Executing SQL Scripts   98
Defining an ODBC System DSN   99
Configuring ISA to Log to an ODBC Database   99
Additional Resources   100

Part II
Microsoft ISA Server 2000 Policy Management and Publishing Services

7 Configuring ISA Policy Elements   103
Policy Elements Explained   103
Serving Multiple Purposes   104
Enterprise Policies and Policy Elements   105
Schedules   105
Creating New Schedules   105
Deleting Schedules   106
Adjusting Existing Schedules   106

Destination Sets	107
Creating New Destination Sets	107
Deleting Destination Sets	108
Configuring Destination Sets	108
Client Address Sets	109
Creating Client Address Sets	109
Deleting Client Address Sets	109
Configuring Client Address Sets	110
User Manager	110
Protocol Definitions	110
Creating Protocol Definitions	111
Deleting Protocol Definitions	111
Configuring Protocol Definitions	112
Content Groups	112
Creating Content Groups	113
Deleting Content Groups	113
Configuring Content Groups	114
Dial-Up Entries	114
Configuring a Network Dial-Up Connection on Windows 2000 Server	114
Configuring a Network Dial-Up Connection on Windows Server 2003	115
Creating Dial-Up Entries	116
Deleting Dial-Up Entries	116
Configuring Dial-Up Entries	117
Bandwidth Priorities	117
Creating Bandwidth Priority Entries	117
Deleting Bandwidth Priority Entries	118
Configuring Bandwidth Priorities	118
Additional Resources	118

8 Configuring ISA Access Policy 119

Processing Outgoing Requests	119
Primary Access Policy Components	120

Site and Content Rules	120
Creating a Site and Content Rule	121
Deleting a Site and Content Rule	122
Configuring a Site and Content Rule	123
Enabling and Disabling a Site and Content Rule	123
Protocol Rules	123
Creating a Protocol Rule	124
Deleting a Protocol Rule	125
Configuring a Protocol Rule	125
IP Packet Filters	126
Creating an IP Packet Filter	126
Deleting an IP Packet Filter	127
Configuring an IP Packet Filter	128
Ancillary Access Policy Components	128
Bandwidth Rules	128
Creating a Bandwidth Rule	129
Deleting a Bandwidth Rule	129
Modifying a Bandwidth Rule	130
Modifying Bandwidth Rule Processing Order	131
Routing Rules	131
Creating a Routing Rule	131
Deleting a Routing Rule	133
Configuring a Routing Rule	133
Firewall Chaining	134
Outgoing Web Requests	135
Creating an Outgoing Listener	135
Configuring and Deleting an Outgoing Listener	137
Configuring Outgoing Authentication	137
Resolving Requests Within an Array	138
Altering the Outgoing Web Requests Port Values	138

Table of Contents | xiii

    Modifying Outgoing Web Requests
    Connection Settings 139
    Optimizing Server Performance 140
ISA Server Extensions 140
    Application Filters 140
        Enabling/Disabling an Application Filter 141
        FTP Access Filter 141
        HTTP Redirector Filter 142
        SOCKS V4 Filter 143
        Streaming Media Filter 143
    Web Filters 144
    Additional Resources 145

9 Publishing Fundamentals 147
    Installation Modes 147
    Processing Incoming Requests 148
    Web Publishing 148
        Prerequisites 149
        Incoming Web Requests 149
            Creating an Incoming Listener 150
            Configuring and Deleting an Incoming Listener 151
            Configuring Incoming Authentication 152
            Resolving Requests Within an Array 152
            Altering the Incoming Web Requests Port Values 152
            Modifying Incoming Web Requests
            Connection Settings 153
        Creating a Web Publishing Rule 154
        Deleting a Web Publishing Rule 155
        Configuring a Web Publishing Rule 155
        Enabling/Disabling a Web Publishing Rule 156
        Adjusting the Rule Processing Order 156
        Accessing Secured Sites 157
            Web Publishing and SSL Bridging 157
            Server Publishing and SSL Tunneling 158

Table of Contents

Web Filters for Inbound Access	158
Using Link Translation	158
Server Publishing	161
Limitations	161
Prerequisites	162
Creating a Server Publishing Rule	162
Deleting a Server Publishing Rule	163
Configuring a Server Publishing Rule	163
Enabling/Disabling a Server Publishing Rule	164
Routing and IP Packet Filters	164
Enabling Packet Filtering	165
Enabling IP Routing	166
Application Filters for Inbound Access	166
DNS Intrusion Detection Filter	166
H.323 Filter	167
POP Intrusion Detection Filter	168
RPC Filter	168
SMTP Filter	168
Additional Resources	169
10 Common Web and Server Publishing Scenarios 171	
Common Prerequisites	171
Configuring the LAT	172
Configuring DNS Resolution	172
Routing	172
Disabling Socket Pooling	172
Publishing Web Server	174
Publishing a Web Site Behind the ISA Server	174
Creating a Destination Set	174
Creating a Web Listener for Incoming Web Requests	175
Creating a Web Publishing Rule	175

Publishing a Web Site on the ISA Server	176
Modifying Web Site Properties in IIS	176
Creating a Web Publishing Rule	176
Publishing Secured Web Site (HTTPS)	176
Web Server Certificate	177
Creating an Incoming Listener	177
Using the Predefined HTTPS Protocol Definition	177
Creating an HTTPS (SSL) Server Publishing Rule	177
Publishing FTP Server	178
Using Packet Filters to Provide FTP Services	179
Configuring FTP Packet Filters to Allow PASV Clients	180
Publishing FTP Using ISA Server	180
Disabling Socket Pooling	180
Configuring FTP Server to Listen on the Internal Interface	181
Disabling Port Attack Mechanism	181
Configuring the Server Publishing Rule	181
Enabling the FTP Access Filter	182
Publishing Exchange Server	182
Publishing a Mail Server Located Behind ISA Server	183
Configuring DNS Resolution	183
Configuring Server Client Type	183
Creating Client Address Sets	183
Creating Protocol Definitions	184
Running the Secure Mail Publishing Wizard	184
Publishing Exchange Using the RPC Publishing Wizard for Outlook Clients	185
Configuring DNS Resolution Configure Server Client Type	185
Creating a Site and Content Rule	185
Configuring Client Address Sets	186

Creating Protocol Rules	186
Enabling Client Authentication	186
Creating a Server Publishing Rule	186
Configuring the Outlook Clients	186
Enabling Access to Exchange Servers Outside ISA Server	187
Publishing an OWA Server	187
Prerequisites	187
Using a Web Publishing Rule	188
Using the OWA Web Publishing Wizard	189
Publishing SQL Server	189
Creating an Incoming Listener	189
Using the Predefined Protocol Definition	190
Creating a SQL Server Publishing Rule	190
Publishing Remote Desktop or a Terminal Server	191
Creating an RDP Protocol Definition	191
Creating a RDP Publishing Rule	192
Publishing a Citrix Server	192
Configuring the Citrix Server as a SecureNAT Client	193
Creating a Citrix ICA Protocol Definition	193
Creating a Citrix Server Publishing Rule	193
Configuring the Citrix Server	194
Configuring the Citrix Clients	194
Publishing a DNS Server	194
Publishing a Public DNS Server Located Behind an ISA Server	195
Creating an Incoming Listener	195
Using the Predefined Protocol Definition	195
Creating a DNS Server Publishing Rule	195
Publishing a Public DNS Server on the ISA Server	196
Using the Predefined DNS Query Packet Filter	196
Creating Two DNS Server Packet Filters	197

Table of Contents | xvii

Additional Resources 198
General Scenario-Based References 198
Microsoft Knowledge Base References 198

Part III
Microsoft ISA Server 2000 and Enterprise Systems Administration

11 Managing ISA Server and Windows Active Directory 201
Stand-Alone Versus Array Members 201
Characteristics of a Stand-Alone ISA Server 201
Characteristics of an ISA Server Array Member 202
Active Directory Interoperability 202
Creating and Configuring ISA Server Arrays 202
ISA Server Array Criteria 203
Administrative Requirements for ISA Server Arrays 203
Creating the Array Environment 203
Creating a New Array 204
Adding or Removing Array Members 205
Moving an ISA Array Member to a Different Array 206
Configuring Array Permissions 207
ISA Server 2000 and Domain Integration 207
Managing a Multidomain Configuration and Trust Relationships 207
ISA Server and Windows NT 4.0 domains 207
ISA Server and Windows 2000 and Windows Server 2003 Domains 208
Additional Resources 209

12 Using Enterprise and Array Policies 211
Enterprise and Array Policies Explained 211
Enterprise and Array Decisions 212
Configuring Enterprise Policy Settings 213

Enterprise Policy Administration — 213
    Creating Enterprise Policies — 214
    Configuring Enterprise Policies — 214
    Backing Up and Restoring an Enterprise Configuration — 215
    Deleting Enterprise Policies — 216
    Enterprise Administration and Permissions — 216
    Connecting to Remote Enterprise and Arrays — 217
    Applying an Enterprise Policy to Selective Arrays — 217
    Setting a Default Enterprise Policy — 218
Array Policy Administration — 218
    Allowing Array Policies — 218
    Configuring Array Policies — 219
        Forcing Packet Filtering for an Array — 219
        Allowing Publishing Rules in an Array — 219
    Configuring Enterprise Policy Settings for an Array — 219
    Backing Up, Restoring and Deleting an Array Configuration — 220
Additional Resources — 221

13 Working with Enterprise Technologies and ISA Server 2000 — 223

Cache Array Routing Protocol (CARP) — 223
    Enabling CARP for Outgoing and Incoming Web Requests — 224
    Configuring Intra-Array Communication — 225
    Configuring the CARP Load Factor — 225
    CARP and Scheduled Content Download — 226
Network Load Balancing — 226
    Prerequisites — 227
        Installing and Configuring Network Load Balancing — 227
        Additional Configuration for ISA Server and Network Load Balancing — 229
        Server Publishing and Network Load Balancing — 230
        Using DNS Round Robin — 230

Table of Contents | xix

Virtual Private Networks (VPNs)	231
Using ISA Server as a VPN Server	231
Configuring a Gateway-to-Gateway VPN	231
Configuring the Local VPN Server	231
Configuring the Remote VPN Server	233
Confirming the Gateway-to-Gateway Configuration	234
Connecting Remote Clients Using VPN	234
Configuring a Client Virtual Private Network (VPN)	234
Configuring a VPN Connectoid	236
Configuring VPN Pass-Through	237
Manually Configuring the VPN	238
H.323 Gatekeeper	241
Prerequisites	241
Create a DNS Service Record for the H.323 Gatekeeper	241
Defining Access to the H.323 Protocol	242
Installing and Configuring the H.323 Gatekeeper	243
Installing the H.323 Gatekeeper Service Management Console	243
Enabling the H.323 Filter	244
Adding an H.323 Gatekeeper	244
Configuring H.323 Gatekeeper Properties	244
Configuring H.323 Gatekeeper Permissions	245
Enable IP Routing to Improve H.323 Performance	245
Configure Call Routing Rules	245
Creating a Call Routing Rule	245
Configuring an Internal NetMeeting Client to Use an H.323 Gatekeeper	248
Configuring an External NetMeeting Client to Use an H.323 Gatekeeper	249
Additional Resources	249

Part IV
Microsoft ISA Server 2000 Security Management

14 Microsoft ISA Server 2000 and Perimeter Networks   253
- Perimeter Networks Explained   253
- Trihomed ISA Server Perimeter Networks   254
  - Configuring the Trihomed ISA Server Network Interfaces   254
  - Configuring the Trihomed Perimeter Network   255
  - Limitations of a Trihomed Perimeter Network   256
- Back-to-Back ISA Server Perimeter Networks   256
  - Configuring the Back-to-Back ISA Servers   257
  - Configuring Back-to-Back Perimeter Networks   258
    - Configuring a Private Address Perimeter Network   259
    - Configuring a Public Address Perimeter Network   260
- Limitations of Perimeter Networks   263
- Publishing Services in Perimeter Networks   263
  - Publishing Web Servers   264
    - Configuring the Web Server In a Trihomed Perimeter Network   264
    - Configuring the Web Server In a Back-to-Back Perimeter Network   264
  - Publishing FTP Services   265
    - Configuring the PORT Mode FTP Server in a Trihomed Perimeter Network   265
    - Configuring the PASV Mode FTP Server in a Trihomed Perimeter Network   266
    - Configuring FTP in a Back-to-Back Perimeter Network   266
  - Publishing SMTP Services in a Trihomed Perimeter Network   267
- Additional Resources   268

15 Securing ISA Server 2000   269
- Trustworthy Computing   269
  - Common Types of Attacks and Best Prevention Practices   270

Intrusion Detection	271
Configuring Intrusion Detection	272
Intrusion Detection Alerts and Actions	275
ISA Server Security Wizards	275
Security Templates	276
Optimizing ISA Server Security	278
Checklist for Securing ISA Server 2000	278
Securing the Network Interface Adapters	279
Disabling Services	281
Running ISA Server on a Dedicated Server	282
URLScan 2.5 for ISA Server	282
Installing URLScan 2.5	283
Disabling the URLScan Web Filter	284
Configuring the Urlscan.ini File	284
A Look at Web Authentication with RSA SecurID	285
Installing the RSA SecurID Web Filter	286
Additional Resources	286
Security References	286
Trustworthy Computing	287
Securing ISA Server 2000	287

Tables

1
- 1-1. Feature Comparison by Product Edition — 5
- 1-2. Memory and Processor Support for the Windows Server Platform — 6
- 1-3. ISA Server Forward Caching Minimum Requirements — 7
- 1-4. ISA Server Reverse Caching (or Publishing) Minimum Requirements — 8
- 1-5. System Requirements for Microsoft Small Business Server 2000 — 9
- 1-6. Hardware and Software Requirements — 10
- 1-7. MMCs Commonly Used with ISA Server — 17
- 1-8. Command Prompts to Retrieve Common Utilities — 18

2
- 2-1. ISA Server 2000 Modes Feature Comparison — 24
- 2-2. Enterprise Policy Settings — 29
- 2-3. Steps Required to Configure a Newly Installed ISA Server — 30
- 2-4. Caching Configuration Properties — 37

3
- 3-1. ISA Server 2000 Clients and Their Functionality — 45
- 3-2. Firewall Client Configuration — 56

5
- 5-1. Comparing ISA Server and Proxy Server 2.0 Terminology — 74

6
- 6-1. Column Information Provided for Monitoring Services — 84
- 6-2. ISA Server Services Executable Names — 85
- 6-3. Session Information — 86
- 6-4. Alert Configuration Options — 91
- 6-5. Configurable Report Properties — 94
- 6-6. Built-In Report Categories and Descriptions — 95
- 6-7. ISA Server Log Types — 96
- 6-8. ISA Server Log File Formats — 97
- 6-9. SQL Server Scripts for Creating Log Tables — 98

7
- 7-1. Policy Element Definitions — 104
- 7-2. Destination Set Properties and Explanations — 107
- 7-3. Uses of the Client Address Set — 109
- 7-4. Protocol Definitions — 111

8
- 8-1. Order of Evaluation for Outgoing Requests — 119
- 8-2. Rule Configuration Page Properties — 121

xxiv | Tables

8-3.	Controlling Access Based on Destination Sets	122
8-4.	Configuring a Site and Content Rule	123
8-5.	Protocols Available in Protocol Rules	124
8-6.	Configurable Properties for Protocol Rules	125
8-7.	Filter Settings	127
8-8.	Configure IP Packet Filter Options	128
8-9.	Property Settings for Bandwidth Rules	130
8-10.	Authentication Types	132
8-11.	Routing Rule Configuration Properties	133
8-12.	Authentication Options for a Listener	136
8-13.	Application Filters Explained	141
8-14.	Understanding the HTTP Redirector Options	142
8-15.	Configuring Live Stream Splitting	144

9
9-1.	Order of Evaluation for Incoming Requests	148
9-2.	Authentication Options for a Listener	151
9-3.	Controlling Access Based on Destination Sets	154
9-4.	Rule Action Page Properties	155
9-5.	Configuring a Web Publishing Rule	156
9-6.	Configuring a Server Publishing Rule	164
9-7.	Configuring H.323 Call Control Options	167
9-8.	Configuring SMTP Filter Keyword Options	168
9-9.	Configuring SMTP Filter Attachment Options	169

10
10-1.	Protocol Rules Required for Exchange POP3 and IMAP Communications	184
10-2.	DNS Query Packet Filter Settings	197
10-3.	DNS Zone Transfer Packet Filter Settings	197

11
11-1.	Administrative Requirements for Stand-Alone Servers and Array Members	203
11-2.	Enterprise Policy Options	204

12
12-1.	Comparing Enterprise and Array Policies	212
12-2.	Configurable Options in Enterprise and Array Policies	212
12-3.	Default Enterprise Policy Settings	214
12-4.	ISA Server Array Backup Configuration	220

13
13-1.	Configuring the Cluster Parameters	227
13-2.	Configuring the Host Parameters	228
13-3.	ISA Server VPN Wizards Explained	231
13-4.	H.323 Gatekeeper Properties	244

	13-5.	Options for Changing a Phone Number	247
	13-6.	Advanced Calling Options for Internal NetMeeting Clients	249
14	14-1.	Trihomed Perimeter Network IP Packet Filter Configuration Settings	256
	14-2.	Configuration for a Private Address Back-to-Back Perimeter Network	259
	14-3.	Configuration for a Public Address Back-to-Back Perimeter Network	261
	14-4.	Limitations of Back-to-Back Perimeter Networks	263
	14-5.	IP Packet Filter Settings for Publishing Web Services in a Trihomed Perimeter Network	264
	14-6.	IP Packet Filter Settings for Publishing a PORT Mode FTP Server in a Trihomed Perimeter Network (Allowing Inbound Access to Port 21)	265
	14-7.	IP Packet Filter Settings for Publishing a PORT Mode FTP Server in a Trihomed Perimeter Network (Allowing Outbound Requests From Anyone From Port 20)	265
	14-8.	IP Packet Filter Settings for Publishing a PASV Mode FTP Server in a Trihomed Perimeter Network (Allowing External Clients to Connect to a High Port)	266
	14-9.	IP Packet Filter Settings for Publishing an SMTP Server in a Trihomed Perimeter Network	267
15	15-1.	Microsoft Trustworthy Computing Initiatives	269
	15-2.	Intrusion Attacks Explained	272
	15-3.	Application Level DNS Attacks Explained	274
	15-4.	Security Configuration Wizard Levels and Templates	276

Acknowledgments

The process of writing *Microsoft Internet Security and Acceleration Server 2000 Administrator's Pocket Consultant* resulted from an abundant harvest and would not have been possible without the combined effort of some fantastic people.

The book started with the seed of an idea that Stephen Legler of Microsoft Consulting Services helped plant. Juliana Aldous, our acquisitions editor, watered it and helped to repot it a few times to keep it alive. Martin DelRe transplanted us to our final home (bless him) and introduced us to Valerie Woolley. As our project editor, Valerie helped to coordinate the detailed editorial process that provides you, the reader, with a much higher quality book than we could ever have achieved on our own.

Tony Northrup—our technical editor and a fine author (and photographer) in his own right—provided masterful oversight technically and clarified many a procedure, especially as we were working with the not-yet-released Windows Server 2003. Tempe Goodhue, project manager at nSight, Inc., valiantly weeded to ensure that the format for the book came out just right. Copy editor Joe Gustaitis pruned the wild branches of our prose, corrected our typos, and trimmed the number of passive constructions that were strewn (sorry, Joe) throughout the book.

The staunch support and insightful suggestions of Adina Hagege of the ISA Server team provided the incentive to help publish this book. Of course, we must thank the pillars of the ISA Server community: the übermeister of ISA Server, Tom Shinder, for his tireless efforts in the ISA Server newsgroups to continue exploring the possibilities for using ISA Server and for the comprehensive books that he and his wife—Debra Littlejohn Shinder—published; Jim Harrison, administrator of isatools.org, for his contributions to the ISA Server community and his sharp wit; as well as other folks who have provided significant contributions to the ISA Server community, like Zach Gutt, Joern Wettern, and others too countless to name.

Most especially, our families deserve high praise for putting up with what amounted to abandonment during the entire time we were writing and consulting and running races. Jason wishes to thank his wife, son, and family for their tremendous support throughout the entire book. Bud wishes to thank his family, friends, and clients for their understanding and encouragement. He is eternally grateful to his wife, Fran, for her patience and support during those nights and weekends when he was locked away in his room.

Introduction

Microsoft Internet Security and Acceleration Server 2000 Administrator's Pocket Consultant provides a specific resource for administrators of ISA Server—those people who use the product on a day-to-day basis. With this book you don't need to wade through the theory behind how ISA Server could or should work in different environments; instead, you can quickly find information that concisely explains how to conduct a specific activity.

With the increase in the number of viruses, threats from hackers, and the increased need for protecting data (because so much more proprietary company information is exposed these days than in the past), your need for a well-tuned ISA Server increases daily. An incorrectly configured firewall is worse than no firewall at all in many cases because it gives a false sense of security.

Many of the books on ISA Server on the market today provide a wealth of information but can't be neatly tucked under your arm while you're rushing to troubleshoot this hour's crisis. With the lack of time and resources available in most companies, administrators need a practical reference guide that provides fast and accurate answers to the most basic questions about how to install, configure, and operate ISA Server 2000.

This "survival manual" provides you with a quick and easy-to-access set of answers for common ISA Server configuration and operations questions. It focuses on the most common tasks you need to perform—such as installing ISA Server, publishing a Web server, or setting up a virtual private network (VPN). This book won't, of course, provide an answer for every question, but it gives clear and useful instructions for the most common scenarios in use today and offers references that direct you to more comprehensive resources.

Conventions Used in This Book

A variety of elements are used to help keep the text clear and easy to follow. You'll find code terms and listings in monospace type, except when we tell you to actually type a command. In that case, the command appears in **bold** type. New terms introduced and defined are in *italics*. Other conventions include:

Notes To provide additional details on a particular point that needs emphasis.

Cautions To warn you when there are potential problems you should look out for.

More Info To point you to more information on a subject.

 Tips To offer helpful hints or additional information.

Support

Every effort has been made to ensure the accuracy of this book. Microsoft Press provides corrections for books through the World Wide Web at the following address:

http://mspress.microsoft.com/support/

If you have comments, questions, or ideas regarding this book or the companion disc, please send them to Microsoft Press using either of the following methods:

Postal Mail:

>Microsoft Press
>Attn: *Microsoft® Internet Security and Acceleration (ISA) Server 2000 Administrator's Pocket Consultant* Editor
>One Microsoft Way
>Redmond, WA 98052-6399

E-mail:

>*msinput@microsoft.com*

Please note that product support isn't offered through the above addresses. For support information, visit Microsoft's Web site at *http://support.microsoft.com*.

Part I

Microsoft ISA Server 2000 Administrator's Fundamentals

Part I covers the fundamental tasks you need to administer Microsoft ISA Server 2000. Chapter 1 provides an overview of ISA Server concepts, versions, types, and tools. Chapter 2 covers the most common installation and post-installation procedures for ISA Server. Chapter 3 focuses solely on how to install, configure, and use the three types of ISA Server clients. Chapter 4 explores differences and limitations when ISA Server is used in conjunction with Microsoft Small Business Server 2000. Chapter 5 provides steps for migrating Proxy Server 2.0 to ISA Server. Chapter 6 explains how to configure reports, alerts, logs, and other ways to monitor your ISA server.

Chapter 1

Overview of Microsoft ISA Server 2000 Administration

This chapter introduces the basic functions that Microsoft Internet Security and Acceleration Server 2000 performs, explaining how it can function as either a caching or firewall product, or both. We then compare the available ISA Server product editions, describe the fundamental ISA Server tools and utilities, and conclude with a brief description of how to administer an ISA Server remotely.

Note Throughout this book, Internet Security and Acceleration Server 2000 will be referred to as "ISA Server" to denote the product. When you see "ISA server" with the lowercase s in *server*, be aware we're referencing the physical server itself and not the ISA Server 2000 product. Unless otherwise noted, we assume that ISA Server SP1 is installed in your environment. If it's not, please see Chapter 2, "Installing and Configuring Microsoft ISA Server 2000," for instructions on how to install service packs.

How ISA Server Operates as a Caching and Firewall Server

ISA Server provides companies of all shapes and sizes with two major components: a true multilayer firewall and scalable Web cache.

ISA Server can be installed in any of three modes: caching, firewall, or integrated. Caching and firewall modes provide only the services for which they're named; integrated mode provides both caching and firewall functionality. Although both functions have many complex aspects, it's important to understand some of the more widely used functions of each.

Firewall: The Secure Server

As a firewall, ISA Server stands between your internal computers and the Internet; it protects your internal resources from external attacks and can prevent internal computers from accessing certain external sites. ISA Server received the International Computer Security Association (ICSA) Labs certification, the de facto standard for products seeking the secure firewall label. The key firewall benefits of ISA Server include

- **Integrated intrusion detection** There are several preconfigured conditions that, when met, will trigger alerts that inform an administrator of attempts to breach the firewall. These attacks include the following: generic ports scan attack, enumerated port scan attack, Internet Protocol (IP) half scan attack, land attack, ping of death attack, User Datagram Protocol (UDP) bomb attack, and Windows out of band attack. ISA Server also contains application filters that help to identify and prevent common Domain Name System (DNS) and Post Office Protocol 3 (POP3) attacks. See Chapter 8, "Configuring ISA Access Policy," for more information.

Note A description of each of the named attacks will be covered in detail in Chapter 6, "Monitoring and Reporting."

- **Secure publishing** This function makes internal resources, like a Microsoft Exchange server, safely available to clients connecting across the Internet. External clients use the public IP address of the ISA Server to access content. The transaction is checked and delivered to the internal server only if the right conditions are met. The internal servers are never directly exposed to the Internet, making them much more secure. See Chapter 9, "Publishing Fundamentals," for more information about publishing.

- **Packet, circuit, and application-level filtering** Filters make explicitly allowed resources available to specified applications, computers and users only when needed. See Chapter 9 for more information.

Note By default, no traffic is allowed through your ISA Server installation. You must set up a protocol rule to enable communication between the internal clients and the Internet.

Caching: The Acceleration Server

ISA Server functioning as a caching server allows Internet content, such as images on a Web page, to be stored (cached) to a place located on your internal network. When content is requested a subsequent time, the Web content provided to the requestor comes from an internal server rather than retrieving the content from a more distant Internet location. This improves the speed at which Web content can be served, because the files can be retrieved at the speed of your local network instead of the much slower speed of your Internet connection. ISA Server configured as a Web-caching server brings many improvements over earlier versions of the software, Proxy Server 1.0 and 2.0. ISA Server's caching features include

- **High-performance Web cache** Cached objects can be stored not only on disk, but also in the server's RAM, which significantly improves the speed at which the ISA server can provide content to requesting clients. The cache is now in a single, indexed file on each ISA server, which allows for quicker and more efficient searches of cached content.
- **Active caching** This feature, when enabled, helps to ensure the extent to which content will remain fresh when it's configured. It's normally used when an Internet connection has excess capacity and a flat billing rate, because active caching requires more bandwidth to proactively access and pull down Internet content.
- **Scheduled Download Service** When clients access certain popular and quickly changing Web content, such as CNN's home page, you can schedule ISA Server to go out and download content on a regular basis (for example, every 15 minutes). This service allows only certain sites to be updated on a regular basis, rather than updating all sites more frequently, as is the case with Active Caching.
- **Distributed and Hierarchical caching** Rather than duplicating Web content on all servers, ISA Server allows Web content to be distributed across the enterprise. Certain servers are responsible for certain sites and content, making more efficient use of space on internal servers and leveraging the higher-speed access of the local area network (LAN) to share Internet content. Distributed caching is available only in the Enterprise edition.

ISA Server Product Editions

ISA Server ships in two versions: Standard Edition and Enterprise Edition. It also comes packaged with Microsoft Small Business Server 2000 (SBS). In the following section we provide an overview of the three different editions.

Quick Comparison of ISA Product Editions

Table 1-1 lists the features that differ among editions.

Table 1-1. Feature Comparison by Product Edition

Features	ISA with Small Business Server	ISA Server Standard Edition	ISA Server Enterprise Edition
Scalability	Very limited	Limited	Full
Distributed and Hierarchical Caching	None	Hierarchical only	Both
Active Directory Integration	Limited	Limited	Full
Tiered policy	No	No	Yes
Multiserver Management	No	No	Yes

More Info Just after the Table of Contents, you'll find an index of tables that will help you quickly find useful information in this Administrator's Pocket Consultant.

SBS also includes a Standard Edition version of ISA Server, along with Microsoft Windows 2000 Server Service Pack 1, Microsoft SQL Server 2000, and Exchange 2000 Server. When Microsoft SBS is installed, there are some limitations inherit in its use. For example, it can support only up to 50 clients, and it has very limited scalability because all products must reside on the same machine. For more information on SBS and ISA integration, refer to Chapter 4, "Configuring ISA in Small Business Server Installations" and also *http://www.microsoft.com/sbserver/*.

ISA Server Standard Edition is designed to meet the needs of workgroups and small to medium-size company environments. The Standard Edition can be installed only as a stand-alone server, must use local policies (which are stored in the registry), and has a physical limitation in that it supports only four processors.

ISA Server Enterprise Edition is designed for companies looking to integrate ISA Server with Active Directory directory service, establish arrays of servers for streamlined caching, or for those requiring multiserver management capabilities. Enterprise Edition can be installed as a stand-alone server or as an array (a collection of ISA servers that share the same cache), supports Enterprise and Array level policies, has no restrictions of processors supported, and must be installed on Windows 2000 Server or Windows 2000 Advanced Server with Service Pack 1, Windows 2000 Datacenter Server, or Windows Server 2003, Standard Edition or the 32-bit version of Windows Server 2003 Enterprise Edition.

Note ISA Server 2000 isn't supported with Windows Server 2003 Web Edition, the 64-bit version of Windows Server 2003 Enterprise Edition, or Windows Server 2003 Datacenter Edition.

Operating System Compatibility

Although you can install ISA Server on either the Windows 2000 Server platform or the Windows Server 2003 platform, there are some differences in the respective capabilities. Table 1-2 displays the amount of memory and number of processors supported for each Server platform.

Table 1-2. Memory and Processor Support for the Windows Server Platform

Server Platform	Memory	Processor
Windows 2000 Server	4 GB of RAM	4 CPUs
Windows 2000 Advanced Server	8 GB of RAM	8 CPUs
Windows Server 2003 Standard Edition	4 GB of RAM	4 CPUs
Windows Server 2003 Enterprise Edition	32 GB of RAM	8 CPUs

Service Pack Level Before installing ISA Server on a Windows 2000 Server or Advanced Server, a minimum of Service Pack 1 for Windows is required. No Service Packs are required to install ISA Server on Windows 2000 Datacenter Server. Microsoft has already released a Service Pack for ISA Server, Service Pack 1. ISA Server Service Pack 1 is a minimum requirement when installing ISA Server on a Windows Server 2003, Standard Edition or Enterprise Edition server.

Follow these steps to determine if ISA Server Service Pack 1 has been installed:

1. On the Start menu, choose Programs, choose Microsoft ISA Server, and then click ISA Management to start the ISA Management MMC (Microsoft Management Console) plug-in.
2. Click to expand Internet Security And Acceleration Server, then Servers And Arrays, and then click the name of your ISA server.
3. Select Computer.
4. Right-click the name of your ISA server in the list in the right pane and then click Properties on the shortcut menu. The ISA Server version section of the dialog box shows the current version number.

Basic Hardware and Server Requirements for ISA Server

The following basic hardware is recommended for any installation of ISA Server:

- Pentium II 300 Mhz or higher processor
- Minimum 256 MB of RAM
- At least one NTFS file system (NTFS) partition
- At least 20 MB of available hard disk space for the program files
- A Windows 2000/Windows Server 2003–compatible network interface card (NIC) or modem connection, or both

Forward Caching Requirements When using ISA Server 2000 to provide caching services to internal clients, use the requirements shown in Table 1-3 to guide your configuration.

Table 1-3. ISA Server Forward Caching Minimum Requirements

Number of Users	ISA Server Computer	RAM (in MB)	Disk Space Allocated for Caching
Up to 500	Single ISA Server computer with Pentium II, 300 MHz processor	256	2-4 Gigabytes (GB)
500–1000	Single ISA Server computer with two Pentium III, 550 MHz processors	256	10 GB
In excess of 1000	Two or more ISA Server computers, each with Pentium III, 550 MHz processors	256 for each server	10 GB for each server

Reverse Caching (or Publishing) Requirements If you plan to use ISA Server 2000 to publish any internal servers, such as a Web site, then you can predict your hardware requirements by measuring the traffic your site generates. Table 1-4 outlines these hardware requirements according to traffic volume.

Table 1-4. ISA Server Reverse Caching (or Publishing) Minimum Requirements

Hits per Second	ISA Server computer
Fewer than 100	Single ISA Server computer with Pentium II, 300 MHz processor
As many as 250	Single ISA Server computer with Pentium III, 450 MHz processor
In excess of 250	ISA Server computer with Pentium III, 550 MHz processor Additional ISA Server computer for each 250 hits per second. You can also use Performance Monitor to determine bottlenecks and then add servers or stronger hardware, as necessary.

Note Allocate enough RAM for your ISA Server to accommodate all published content. ISA Server uses RAM to store the cache, which will increase speed by eliminating any content being read from page files on the disk.

Detailed Comparison of ISA Server Implementations

The following section describes in more detail some of the differences between the implementations of ISA Server mentioned earlier in the chapter.

Small Business Server 2000

SBS is targeted toward companies that have fewer than 50 clients and is very limited in its ability to scale out. Keep in mind that SBS must be installed on a single machine, is limited to no more than 50 connections at one time, can't trust other domains, and—although it can have additional domain controllers—can't share information with other domains. ISA Server 2000 is integrated with several other Microsoft Server products for reduced cost, as well as ease of installation, configuration, and administration. The hardware requirements and licensing information reflected below are for the entire Microsoft Small Business Server 2000 product and not just for ISA Server 2000.

Scalability The most obvious drawback to using SBS is the inability to expand beyond 50 clients. If your company will grow in the near future, you should consider moving to a more traditional Windows 2000/Windows Server 2003 domain structure with a separate ISA Server installation. Alternatively, Microsoft offers a Small Business Server Migration Pack, which allows an upgrade to individually licensed copies of the SBS components. See the link at http://www.microsoft.com/sbserver/techinfo/deployment/2000/MigrationPack.asp for more information.

Hardware and Software Table 1-5 shows both the minimum and recommended requirements for SBS.

Table 1-5. System Requirements for Microsoft Small Business Server 2000

Minimum	Recommended
Pentium II 300 megahertz (MHz) or compatible processor	Pentium III 500 MHz, Dual Pentium II 300 MHz, or compatible processor or higher, depending on your system configuration
128 MB of RAM	256 MB of RAM or higher, depending on your system configuration
4 gigabyte (GB) available hard disk space	Two or more mirrored 4-GB hard disks, depending on your system configuration
No modem	Two modems, one for Shared Fax Service and one for Remote Access Service, Shared Modem Service, and, of course, Internet Security and Acceleration Server dial-up service
CD-ROM drive	CD-ROM drive
One network adapter card	Ensure that your network adapter is configured to operate at its highest available capacity so that it doesn't function as a bottleneck.
Video graphics adapter capable of 256 colors and 800 by 600 pixels	Video graphics adapter capable of 256 colors and 800 by 600 pixels

Best practices call for at least 20 MB of available space for your ISA Server program files and approximately 100 MB plus .5 MB of cache for each user.

Licensing To find the most current information regarding Small Business Server product licensing, visit the Microsoft Small Business Server Web site at *http://www.microsoft.com/sbserver/howtobuy/*.

A basic Small Business Server license comes with five Client Access Licenses (CALs), which allow clients to connect to the SBS machine. You can add CALs by purchasing Client Add Packs, which are 3.5-inch disks that function as both license and license activation media. Client Add Packs are available in 5-user or 20-user increments.

Note Small Business Server 2000 allows an unlimited number of user accounts but restricts the number of computer connections to 50.

More Info For more information regarding using ISA Server with SBS, refer to Chapter 4, "Configuring ISA in Small Business Server Installations." Other references include the Small Business Server Resource Kit. See especially Chapter 11, "ISP Connectivity Tasks," Chapter 19, "E-Mail and Internet Connectivity Options," and Chapter 21, "Firewall Security and Web Caching with ISA Server."

ISA Server 2000 Standard Edition

The Standard Edition of ISA Server 2000 meets the needs of most organizations that have between 50 and 500 users and don't wish to use centralized policies or arrays.

Scalability ISA Server Standard Edition has a greater ability to scale than Small Business Server (which includes the Standard Edition of ISA Server) only because its connections are not limited to 50 clients. Standard Edition can't take advantage of server arrays or enterprise policies. If your company plans to use server arrays or enterprise policies in the future, you must have Active Directory and use ISA Server Enterprise Edition. If your organization plans to grow to accommodate a large number of users who are located in different facilities or to a number of users who might overwhelm the server, you should consider using ISA Server Enterprise Edition. Refer to Chapter 6, "Monitoring and Reporting," for more information about monitoring your ISA server's performance.

With ISA Server 2000 Standard Edition, the basic trade-off is between capital cost for the licensing and administrative restrictions. The inability to centrally configure enterprise policies and arrays requires much more configuration time by administrators if several ISA servers will be used in the organization.

Table 1-6 shows both the minimum and recommended hardware and software requirements for ISA Server Standard Edition.

Table 1-6. Hardware and Software Requirements

Component	Minimum	Recommended
CPU	Pentium II 300 megahertz (MHz) or compatible processor	Pentium III 500 MHz / Dual Pentium II 550 MHz or higher processors for every 500 users. Note: you'll be limited to only four processors.
Memory	256 MB of RAM	RAM should equal the amount of cacheable content being published.
Hard Disk Space	20 MB for ISA Server program files 2 GB on a NTFS partition for cache	Best practices call for at least 20 MB of available space for your ISA Server program files and 100 MB plus .5 MB of cache for each user.
Operating System	Windows 2000 Server with Service Pack 1; Windows 2000 Advanced Server with Service Pack 1; Windows 2000 Datacenter Server; Windows Server 2003, Standard Edition; Windows Server 2003, Enterprise Edition	Always apply the most current operating system service pack.

Table 1-6. Hardware and Software Requirements

Component	Minimum	Recommended
ISA Service Packs	ISA Server Service Pack 1 is required for operation on Windows Server 2003, Standard and Enterprise editions	Always apply the most current ISA Server patches and hot fixes to ensure the greatest stability.
Networking	One Windows 2000/Windows Server 2003–compatible NIC and an additional Windows 2000/Windows Server 2003–compatible NIC, modem, or ISDN adapter for connecting to the Internet or another ISA server.	Ensure that your network adapter is configured to operate at its highest available capacity so that it doesn't function as a bottleneck.

Licensing Microsoft ISA Server 2000 Standard Edition requires a license for each processor in use. For that reason, it may be more cost effective to upgrade existing processors to higher speed processors rather than add processors to multiprocessor-capable systems.

ISA Server 2000 Enterprise Edition

ISA Server 2000 Enterprise Edition provides the same functionality as Standard Edition but adds features that improve your ISA Server environment's management and redundancy.

Scalability If you have a large or widely distributed organization, cost savings result from being able to centrally manage multiple ISA servers (grouped in what are known as arrays) from a single management console. These servers can provide fault tolerance by picking up the work of any members that fail. In addition, all servers can be governed by a single Enterprise policy, which is stored in Active Directory. Consider the amount of time it would take one administrator to configure 25 different servers with the same access policy. With enterprise and array policies, one administrator can configure all 25 servers with the same policy using a central management console.

By default, the Domain Admins group of the forest root domain and any members of the Enterprise Admins group have the ability to manage enterprise policies. They, in turn, grant administrative rights for array policies.

Enterprise and array policies provide consistent administration for managing ISA servers across one's entire organization. They provide the highest level of control, overriding any array policies. Enterprise policies are stored in Active Directory and can apply across the entire forest.

Because arrays are limited to a single site or domain, array policies have the same limitations. Enterprise policies provide the base level of access available to an array. An array policy can further restrict access to items from the enterprise policy baseline.

Note An array policy can only further restrict access; it can't open up access limited by an enterprise policy.

Hardware and Software The hardware requirements for ISA Server 2000 Enterprise Edition are the same as those for the Standard Edition listed above, with just a few important distinctions:

- Whereas Standard Edition restricts the number of processors utilized to four, there's no limit under an Enterprise Edition installation.

- The Enterprise Edition requires a modification to the Active Directory schema, which you accomplish by running the ISA Enterprise Initialization Tool found on the ISA Server 2000 CD.

Note When you install ISA Server 2000 Enterprise Edition, you'll need to modify the schema of your Windows 2000 or Windows Server 2003 Active Directory, a significant change. Only a member of the Schema Admins group can make this modification. Once it's made, the change can't be reversed, only disabled. Plan for this change well in advance, contacting the appropriate people in your organization to obtain their support.

Licensing A Microsoft ISA Server 2000 Enterprise Edition requires a license for each processor in use. For that reason, it may be more cost effective to upgrade existing processors to higher speed processors, rather than adding additional processors to multiprocessor-capable systems.

Using Common ISA Server Tools and Utilities

Microsoft ISA Server includes several tools and wizards that help to make administration easier. In this section we discuss the ISA Management Console and its components and then briefly explain the wizards available to help automate tasks. Finally, we describe other commonly used MMCs, command line utilities, and third-party add-ons that extend the functionality of ISA Server.

Using the ISA Management Console

The ISA Management Console controls almost all aspects of ISA Server Management, so you'll want to be very familiar with its structure, components, and options. We will provide a brief overview of all the components. The MMC for the SBS, Standard, and Enterprise Editions of ISA contain a Server and Arrays node, but (fittingly) only the Enterprise Edition contains an Enterprise node, which allows management of Enterprise Policies.

Chapter 1 Overview of Microsoft ISA Server 2000 Administration | 13

To launch the ISA Management Console, complete the following steps:
1. Click the Start button, choose Programs, and then choose Microsoft ISA Server.
2. Click on the ISA Management icon. You'll see the default view of the ISA Management Console, as shown in Figure 1-1.

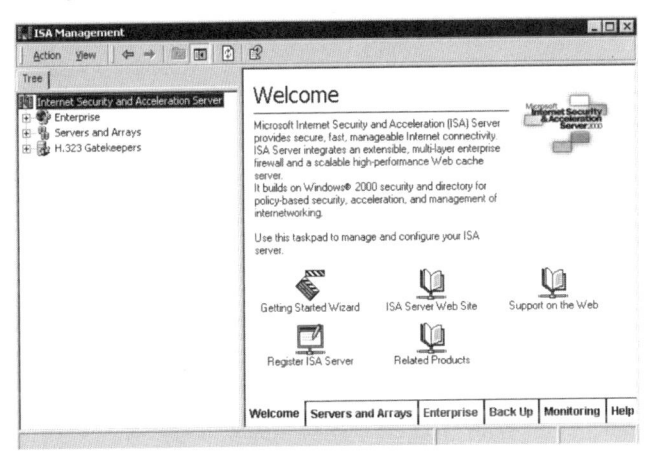

Figure 1-1. *The left-hand pane displays the console tree, which displays all components of your ISA Server installation. The right-hand pane shows the detail for the node selected in the left pane.*

Console View Options

Throughout this book we describe the steps involved with performing daily tasks using ISA Server. As we discuss the steps, we also demonstrate them using the Advanced view within the ISA Management Console. The console supports either the Taskpad or Advanced view, but most administrators tend to use Advanced view. The Taskpad view is much more graphically oriented and wizard-driven; however, some elements of administration don't appear when using this view. To switch to the Advanced View, click on the ISA Management Console's View menu and then choose Advanced.

You can customize the contents of the MMC by clicking the View menu and then choosing Customize. You'll be able to add or remove components of the view. Configure your MMC as shown in Figure 1-2 on the following page.

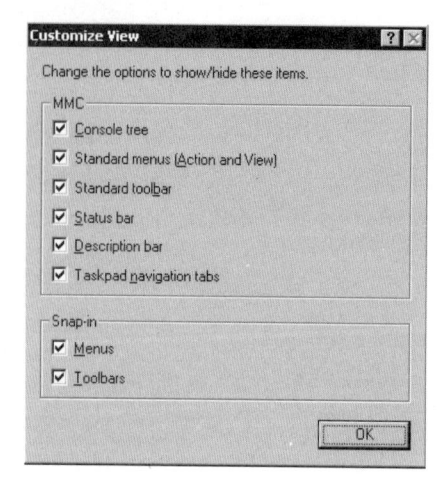

Figure 1-2. *The Customize View dialog box allows you to add or remove items such as toolbars from the ISA Management Console.*

Working with ISA Management Nodes

The ISA Management Console contains several administrative nodes. This section describes those nodes from a very general perspective. Subsequent chapters provide more detail, and we explain their use with step-by-step instructions.

Monitoring This folder contains information about four aspects of your ISA Server installation:

- **Alerts** Shows the actual output generated by alerts configured in the Monitoring Configuration node below

- **Services** Shows the main ISA services running on the ISA Server machine and provides the ability to start and stop these services

- **Sessions** Shows all sessions currently running against the Web proxy or firewall service

- **Reports** Stores the reports created by report jobs, which are configured in the Monitoring Configuration node below

Computers The Computers folder lists all the ISA servers in your environment. It also shows useful information about each server, such as the load factor and the server's primary domain controller.

Access Policy The Access Policy folder is central to controlling access through the firewall, and contains three folders:

- **Site and Content Rules** Allow or deny access to the Internet based on destination sets

- **Protocol Rules** Determine which protocols (like Hypertext Transfer Protocol [HTTP] or File Transfer Protocol [FTP]) can access the Internet

- **IP Packet Filters** Enable the ISA Server to block or allow packets destined for certain computers on the internal network

Publishing The Publishing folder is used to configure the publication of Web and other servers (like Exchange) to external clients and is separated into two folders:

- **Web Publishing Rules** Determine how Web-based content (HTTP) is intercepted and routed by the ISA server to internal Web servers.
- **Server Publishing Rules** Determine how information destined for and sent from servers that have been published (made available to Internet clients through the ISA Server) is routed internally.

Bandwidth Rules The Bandwidth Rules folder allows the creation and administration of rules governing the priority of specified connections. The New Bandwidth Rule Wizard allows you to easily configure a new rule that defines the protocol, schedule, client address sets, destination sets, and content groups to which you want the bandwidth priority rule to apply.

Policy Elements Policy Elements are subdivided into seven categories: Schedules, Bandwidth Priorities, Destination Sets, Client Address Sets, Protocol Definitions, Content Groups, and Dial-Up Entries. Each element is a building block of the policies created to manage the flow of information in and out of the network.

- *Schedules* define the hours that a particular rule will be in effect. ISA Server has two preconfigured schedules: Weekends, which provide access all day Saturday and Sunday; and Work Hours, which provide access from 9:00 A.M. to 5:00 P.M., Monday through Friday.
- *Bandwidth Priorities* let you define a priority that consists of a number from 1 to 200. A lower number has a correspondingly lower priority.
- *Destination Sets* consist of domain names (like *.northwindtraders.com), or IP addresses (like 10.0.0.1 to 10.0.0.255), which designate a computer or set of computers to which you want to allow or restrict access. You can also limit or enable access to a specific path or folder on a computer using destination sets.
- *Client Address Sets* specify a range of IP addresses that designate certain clients to which you want to limit or allow access.
- *Protocol Definitions* specify a protocol by specifying a port number (1 through 65535), a protocol type (Transmission Control Protocol [TCP] or UDP), and direction (for UDP protocol: Send Only, Receive Only, Send Receive, Receive Send; and for TCP protocol: Inbound, Outbound). ISA Server comes with a large number of commonly used protocols, such as HTTP, Hypertext Transfer Protocol Secure (HTTPS), FTP, and so on.
- *Content Groups* apply only to HTTP and FTP traffic that's processed through the Web Proxy service. These groups define certain application files based on their Multipurpose Internet Mail Extensions (MIME) type or application extensions. For example, you can create a Content Group called BasicOfficeDocs that includes all files that contain the extensions .doc, .ppt, .xls, and .mdb.

- *Dial-Up Entries* allow you to configure the Dial-Up Connection and user account information necessary to dial out from the ISA server using a modem.

Cache Configuration Cache configuration controls the cache's drives and properties and contains two folders, as follows:

- **Scheduled Content Download Jobs** Allows you to update the Internet content stored in your ISA Server cache on a schedule. You can configure a new job for each site that requires updating.
- **Drives** Allows you to configure the drives on which the cache is stored.

Monitoring Configuration This section controls the jobs that produce the alerts and report jobs stored in the Monitoring node, as well as the logs created by each of the services:

- **Alerts** Allow you to specify a certain action that should take place when an event occurs. For example, when ISA Server detects IP spoofing, the default alert makes an entry in the Event Log. You can configure that event to then send an e-mail message to the local administrator.
- **Logs** Capture information about the Packet filters, Firewall service, and the Web proxy server to be logged in a central location. This section provides the ability to enable/disable logging, specify the content to be logged, and specify the location of the log itself.
- **Report Jobs** Provide the ability to schedule reports to run that show Web Usage, Application Usage, Traffic & Utilization, and Security information.

Extensions Application Filters and Web Filters, the two folders in this section, contain the filters that help to protect and manage content coming across the ISA Server functioning as a firewall.

- **Application Filters** Preconfigured filters that examine certain types of content (like HTTP, FTP, and Simple Mail Transfer Protocol [SMTP] traffic) and specify certain actions to perform upon that traffic. For example, the HTTP Redirector Filter will redirect HTTP traffic sent by Secure Network Address Translation (NAT) and firewall clients to the Web Proxy service or it can send the request directly to the specified Web server, depending on how you configure the filter.
- **Web Filters** Preconfigured and third-party filters that examine and perform actions on Web-based content.

Network Configuration This area is where very important basic networking information is viewed and configured for ISA Server.

- **Routing** Allows defined clients to take certain actions when defined sites are accessed.
- **Local Address Table (LAT)** Defines what are considered to be internal IP addresses (for example, 10.0.0.1 to 10.0.0.255).
- **Local Domain Table (LDT)** Defines all the domains that are considered to be internal (for example, internal.northwindtraders.local).

Chapter 1 Overview of Microsoft ISA Server 2000 Administration | 17

Client Configuration This section controls the configuration of both the Web Proxy and firewall clients and will be examined further in Chapter 3, "Installing and Configuring Microsoft ISA Server 2000."

- **Web Browser** Allows the automatic configuration of Web browsers in the environment.
- **Firewall Client** Allows the automatic configuration of firewall clients in the environment.

ISA Server Wizards

With ISA Server, Microsoft simplified many procedures by creating step-by-step wizards for administrators to use. For instance, at the end of installing ISA Server, you're prompted to launch the Getting Started Wizard, a friendly graphical tool that steps an administrator through all of the important configurable options necessary to install and configure ISA Server and enable clients to browse the Internet.

The wizards that you'll use the most include

- **Getting Started Wizard** Guides you through the configuration steps for ISA Server.
- **VPN Client Wizard** Step-by-step wizard for allowing external virtual private network (VPN) clients to dial into the ISA server.
- **Web Publishing Wizard** Guides you through publishing an internal Web server to the Internet.
- **Server Publishing Wizard** Guides you through publishing an internal server (non-Web server) to the Internet.

Commonly Used MMCs

In addition to the ISA Management Console, you'll use other MMCs to effectively administer, manage, and troubleshoot ISA Server. The Windows 2000 operating system provides many Administration Tools for managing key services. Table 1-7 highlights and defines the other common MMCs you'll most likely need when administering ISA Server.

Table 1-7. MMCs Commonly Used with ISA Server

Administrative Tool	Purpose
Event Viewer	Manage events and logs
Services	Manage interaction of services with the operating system
Terminal Services Manager	Manage connections to the Terminal Server
ISA Server Performance Monitor	Monitor ISA Server performance

Command-Line Utilities

Although you perform most administration within the ISA Management Console, sometimes you must rely on other tools. When administering ISA Server, many command-line utilities come in handy. Table 1-8 lists several commonly used commands.

Table 1-8. Command Prompts to Retrieve Common Utilities

Command Prompt	Utility
Ping	Used to check the availability of IP-based network resources by sending out a packet and requesting a response
Tracer	Traces the number of hops that a packet must travel to reach a network resource
Telnet	Tool used to connect to TCP ports on the ISA Server in order to determine if the ports are configured correctly
Netst	Command-line utility used to determine port availability on the ISA Server
Route Add	Adds static routes to Windows 2000/Windows Server 2003 machines and is used when configuring the LAT
Chkwsp32	Command-line utility for firewall clients, allowing you to verify that the firewall client has established connectivity to the specified ISA Server

ISA Community

Since the release of ISA Server in 2001, the interest in, and support of, the product has grown quickly. Many Web sites are dedicated to the product and help to make the day-to-day administration of ISA Server that much simpler.

Refer to the following Web sites for a rich set of detailed information and tools:

- http://www.microsoft.com/isaserver
- http://www.microsoft.com/technet
- http://www.isaserver.org
- http://www.isatools.org

Add-Ons for ISA Server

There are many add-on products for ISA Server that focus on various elements found in the product. For instance, software is available for handling intrusion detection, providing access control, monitoring traffic and events, reporting on logged content, and maintaining high availability (load balancing).

For a complete listing of the add-ons for ISA Server, visit http://www.microsoft.com/isaserver/partners/default.asp.

Administering ISA Server Remotely

There are several ways to administer ISA Server remotely. The following methods are the most common that you'll use:

- ISA Management Console
- Terminal Service
- Third-Party Remote Control Applications

ISA Management Console

MMC is the framework that allows snap-ins to be configured. Snap-ins like the ISA Management Console provide the graphical user interface for performing day-to-day administrative tasks. Approximately all of the administration performed in ISA Server is done within the ISA Management Console. To install the console on a remote computer, perform the following steps:

1. Insert the ISA Server CD into the computer.
2. After the Microsoft ISA Server Setup launches, click Install ISA Server.
3. Click Continue.
4. Enter the ISA Server CD key and then click OK.
5. Click OK to verify the product ID number.
6. Click I Agree to accept the End User License Agreement.
7. Click Custom Installation.
8. Clear the ISA Services check box. Highlight Administration Tools and click Change Option. Select the ISA Management check box, click OK, and then click Continue.
9. Clear Start ISA Server Getting Started Wizard and click OK.
10. Click OK to complete the installation of the ISA Management Console.

Terminal Services

Windows 2000 and Windows Server 2003 include Terminal Services, a component that you can install during the installation of the operating system, as well as from the Add/Remove Programs utility in the Control Panel.

When selecting to install Terminal Services, you can deploy it in one of two modes: application server or remote administration.

Application mode is appropriate if you'll be installing applications on the Terminal Server and configuring the server to provide server-based computing. Using application mode, you're required to license the terminal service clients that will be connecting to the Terminal Server. The appropriate mode for Terminal Services on an ISA Server is remote administration mode. Remote administration mode doesn't require the purchase of terminal service client licenses, and it allows for two concurrent connections to the Terminal Server. Considering that the main purpose of remote administration mode is remote administration, two concurrent connections are appropriate. Only members of the Administrators group can connect to the Terminal Server in remote administration mode.

Third-Party Products

A variety of other tools on the market allow you to perform administration from a remote computer. Some products are freeware, others cost hundreds of dollars. Listed below are three cost-effective remote administration tools that you could use to administer ISA Server when choosing not to use Terminal Services or the ISA Management Console.

- **VNC** Otherwise known as Virtual Network Computing, a remote display system that allows connectivity from almost anywhere. This product is freeware and can be downloaded from *http://www.uk.research.att.com/vnc/*.

- **NetMeeting** Microsoft's collaboration utility for whiteboarding, video conferencing, and desktop sharing. It ships with Windows 2000 and is a very handy, integrated solution for remote desktop connectivity. An administrator must configure the Remote Desktop Sharing service, which requires a reboot of the server. NetMeeting 3.0 ships with the operating system but can be downloaded separately from *http://www.microsoft.com/netmeeting/*.

- **PCAnywhere** A Symantec product that's been around for many years. The product is a very stable remote control application and has a rich feature set, but it's costlier than the options listed above. See *http://www.symantec.com/pcanywhere/* for more information.

Additional Resources

For more information on topics covered in this chapter, consult the following:

- "Caching with ISA Server 2000" at *http://www.microsoft.com/isaserver/techinfo/planning/cachingwp.asp*
- "Deployment of ISA Server 2000 at Microsoft" at *http://www.microsoft.com/isaserver/techinfo/planning/2000/wp_deploymentatmicrosoft.asp*
- "ISA Server Architecture Overview" at *http://www.microsoft.com/isaserver/techinfo/deployment/2000/wp_architecturaloverview.asp*
- Microsoft Knowledge Base article "ISA Microsoft Management Console Is Slow to Open" at *http://support.microsoft.com/?kbid=313328*
- Shinder, Thomas. *Configuring ISA Server 2000* (Syngress: Rockland, MA. 2001)

Chapter 2

Installing and Configuring Microsoft ISA Server 2000

Before you can start administering Microsoft ISA Server 2000, you have to know how to perform the typical ISA Server installation and post-installation tasks. This chapter explains how to install ISA Server and its Service Pack on Microsoft Windows 2000 and Microsoft Windows Server 2003 and how to modify roles to allow your ISA Server to function as either a stand-alone or array member server. It also walks through the steps to configure the basics of a newly installed ISA Server.

Installing ISA Server 2000

The Microsoft ISA Server Getting Started Wizard guides you through most steps in setting up your ISA Server; this section helps to provide additional clarification for installing and configuring your ISA Server in a stand-alone configuration.

Note These procedures assume a Windows 2000-based installation. See the section of this chapter entitled "Installing ISA Server on Windows Server 2003" for tips on installing ISA on the Windows Server 2003 platform.

Before You Begin

Before beginning your installation, ensure that the hardware and software of the computer on which you'll install ISA Server is configured with the appropriate elements:

- **Network adapters** You'll need two network connections: one for connecting to your internal network and the other for connecting to the external network. The exception to this rule would be when ISA Server is installed in cache mode; in that case only one network adapter is required.

- **Transmission Control Protocol/Internet Protocol (TCP/IP) settings** Confirm that the Internet Protocol (IP) addresses assigned to your network adapters are static and not assigned by Dynamic Host Configuration Protocol (DHCP).

- **Modem or Integrated Services Digital Network (ISDN) adapter** If your server requires a modem or an ISDN adapter to connect to the external network, ensure that the dial-up connection has been created and that your ISDN adapter's channels are configured so that ISA Server can utilize all relevant channels through your Internet service provider (ISP).

- **Windows 2000 routing table** When ISA Server is installed, it can't have a default gateway set on its internal network interface. Therefore, you must ensure that the local server's routing table is configured with static routes for all relevant internal networks. Use the ROUTE ADD command to add these routes.

> **More Info** Refer to the Installation Guide included on the ISA Server 2000 CD by clicking the Read Installation Guide option on the ISA Server Setup menu or by navigating to the \ISA\isastart.htm page on the ISA Server install media.

To install ISA Server as a stand-alone server, complete the following steps.

1. Insert the ISA Server CD and click the Install ISA Server icon on the Microsoft ISA Server Setup screen (see Figure 2-1). Ensure that you have the proper ISA Server Edition of the CD or the setup files available on a network location.

> **Note** If autorun is disabled, double-click the file ISAautorun.exe to launch the Microsoft ISA Server setup program.

Figure 2-1. *To install ISA Server as a stand-alone server, begin with the Microsoft ISA Server Setup screen.*

Chapter 2 Installing and Configuring Microsoft ISA Server 2000 | 23

2. Click Continue to move beyond the Copyright Law And International Treaties warning.
3. Type in your 10-digit CD key number and then click OK.
4. Review and then click OK to accept your Microsoft Product ID number.
5. Click I Agree to accept the End User License Agreement (EULA).
6. You are now presented with the types of installation (Typical, Custom, Full) you can choose from and where you'd like the ISA Server program files to be located. The three installation types to choose from are:

    - **Typical** ISA Server installs commonly used components (ISA Services and the ISA Management console).

    - **Custom** This option allows you to specify each component you wish to install (for example, Custom installation would allow you to choose to install only the ISA Management console on a workstation for performing remote administration of ISA Server).

    - **Full** This option includes the components selected in a typical installation, plus the selection of add-in services (H.323 Gatekeeper Service and Message Screener) and Administration Tools (the H.323 Gatekeeper Administration Tool).

7. Click Change Folder to change the default installation path if necessary, and then click your preferred installation type to continue.

Note The default location for the ISA Server program files is C:\Program Files\Microsoft ISA Server.

8. If you selected Custom in the previous step, select the options to install and click Continue.
9. Choose whether you wish the server to be a stand-alone or array member server. After you choose, ISA Server setup will stop some services. You should click OK when prompted to continue.

    - If you're installing the first ISA Server on your network or if the system isn't participating in Active Directory, you'll receive a message indicating that the computer will be installed as a stand-alone server. There's no choice in this situation: you must click Yes to install ISA Server as a stand-alone server; you can later upgrade the stand-alone server to an array, if you choose.

More Info For more information on upgrading a stand-alone server to an array, see the section of this chapter entitled "Promoting a Stand-Alone Server to an Array Member."

   - If an array already exists, however, you'll receive the message shown in Figure 2-2. If you choose Yes, you'll need to either select the array you wish to join or create a new array.

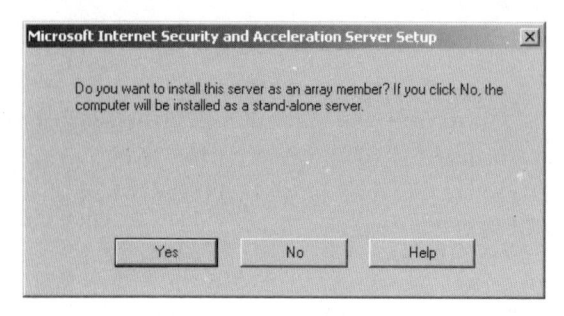

Figure 2-2. *ISA Server setup will prompt you to add the new server to an existing array.*

> **Note** If you're installing ISA Server into an existing array, you won't have a choice of mode; it will be determined by the array

10. Determine in which of the three available modes your ISA server will run: firewall, cache, or integrated. Whereas firewall mode provides only security features and cache mode provides only Web content acceleration features, integrated mode provides all features. See Table 2-1 for a comparison of features:

Table 2-1. ISA Server 2000 Modes Feature Comparison

Feature	Firewall Mode	Cache Mode	Integrated Mode
Access policy	Yes	Yes (Hypertext Transfer Protocol [HTTP] and Hypertext Transfer Protocol Secure [HTTPS] only)	Yes
Application filters	Yes	No	Yes
Cache configuration	No	Yes	Yes
Enterprise policy	Yes	Yes	Yes
Firewall and SecureNAT client support	Yes	No	Yes
Packet filtering	Yes	No	Yes
Real-time monitoring	Yes	Yes	Yes
Reports	Yes	Yes	Yes
Server publishing	Yes	No	Yes
Virtual private networking	Yes	No	Yes
Web filters	Yes	Yes	Yes
Web publishing	Yes	Yes	Yes
Web Proxy client support	Yes	Yes	Yes

Chapter 2 Installing and Configuring Microsoft ISA Server 2000 | 25

11. Select the mode you require and then click Continue.

Note If you choose either firewall or cache mode, some of the steps listed below will not appear in your installation. If this is the case, simply skip the irrelevant steps.

12. The installation sets the default size of the cache to 100 MB and places it on a local, Windows NT file system (NTFS) formatted drive; the ISA Server cache file must reside on an NTFS formatted partition. To change the default location or adjust the size of the cache, follow these steps:
    - Click the appropriate drive displayed by the setup wizard.
    - Type in the preferred size, in megabytes, in the Cache Size field.
    - Click Set.
    - When you are satisfied with the cache size setting, click OK to continue.

Note Later in this chapter you'll learn how to adjust the ISA Server cache file's size by using the ISA Management console.

13. Configure the Local Address Table (LAT).
    - If you know all internal network segments utilized by your workplace, type the beginning and ending IP addresses in the From and To dialog boxes and click Add. Repeat this procedure for each unique, internal network segment.
    - If you've already confirmed or configured the server's routing table with all internal network routes, click Construct Table. This selection lets the ISA Server installation automatically add well-known and specified private ranges to the LAT based on the local server's routing table. To add network address ranges based on the routing table, check the appropriate network adapter and click OK. Click OK again to confirm the warning message.
14. Once you've added all the unique internal network segments to the LAT by using either of the above procedures, click OK to continue.
15. If you elected to install the Message Screener by choosing a Custom or Full installation type in Step 6, you'll be presented with a warning that the Simple Mail Transfer Protocol (SMTP) service is needed on the ISA Server. Click OK to continue.
16. The installation begins copying files, updating the system, and starting and stopping services. The Launch ISA Management Tool window appears. Clear the check box if you don't wish to launch the Getting Started Wizard after installation is complete. Click OK to continue.
17. Click OK to complete the ISA Server installation.

Installing ISA Server on Windows Server 2003

You can install ISA Server 2000 on the Windows Server 2003 platform, but there are some additional requirements:

- When you begin the installation of ISA Server, a warning message appears informing you that ISA Server Service Pack 1 is required before the product will function correctly and that you can ignore any messages received during the installation until installation of ISA Server SP1 completes.
- At the end of the installation, another warning states that errors were received and services failed to start. Installing ISA Server SP 1 fixes this problem.
- Read through the most current information about running ISA Server on Windows Server 2003 by visiting *http://www.microsoft.com/isaserver/setupserver2003.asp*.

Installing ISA Server Service Pack 1

Microsoft ISA Server Service Pack 1 is a recommended installation for all who have implemented ISA Server 2000. The installation procedures are identical whether ISA Server is installed on the Windows 2000 platform or the Windows Server 2003 platform. To begin the installation ensure that you have the either the CD or setup files available locally or on a network location.

> **Tip** Windows 2000 Server and Windows 2000 Advanced Server must have Windows 2000 Service Pack 2 or higher applied before ISA Server Service Pack 1 will install.

Follow these steps to install ISA Service Pack 1:

1. Download the ISA Service Pack from *http://www.microsoft.com/isaserver/downloads/*.
2. Double-click the file Isasp1.exe to begin the installation.
3. Click I Agree to accept the EULA. Updated ISA Server program files are copied to the server. Click OK to complete the installation of SP 1 and restart the ISA server.

> **Tip** To keep your ISA Server healthy, be sure to check for and apply additional hotfixes and service packs at *http://www.microsoft.com/isaserver/downloads/* as they're released.

Modifying the Role of ISA Server: Enabling Array Membership

As noted in the previous section, "Installing ISA Server 2000," an ISA Server functions in one of two roles: stand-alone or array member. This section explains the prerequisites for installing an ISA server as an array member.

Joining ISA Server to a Domain

To join a server running the Windows 2000 Server platform to a domain, complete the following steps:

1. Right-click the My Computer icon on the desktop and then click Properties.
2. Click the Network Identification tab and then click Properties.

Caution If you're following this procedure on the Windows Server 2003 platform, in step 2 select the Computer Name tab and click Change. This is the only step that differs from the procedures provided.

3. Click Domain, type in your domain name, and then click OK.
4. When presented with an authentication dialog box, provide an account and password with Domain Admin privileges to join the server to the domain. You'll have to reboot the server to complete joining the domain.

More Info For detailed step-by-step explanations of server administration, see *Microsoft Windows 2000 Administrator's Pocket Consultant* or *Microsoft Windows Server 2003 Administrator's Pocket Consultant*, both published by Microsoft Press and written by William R. Stanek.

Running the Enterprise Initialization Tool

The Enterprise Initialization Tool provided on the ISA Server 2000 CD allows you to modify the Active Directory schema to include specific ISA Server classes and properties. Performing this extension to the schema enables ISA Server to integrate into your Active Directory directory service.

An Active Directory schema modification requires certain domain-level rights for the user performing the extension: the domain user must be a member of the Schema Admins global group and the Domain Admins global group.

Caution Attempting to execute the Enterprise Initialization Tool with a domain user account lacking the necessary domain-level rights can yield unexpected results, including the possibility of corrupting the directory. Take extreme care when performing this procedure.

You can view the extensions the ISA Enterprise Initialization Tool will make before you pull the trigger: look at two files located on the ISA Server 2000 CD in the ISA folder—Schema.ldif and Schemaup.ldif—which are the actual Lightweight Directory Access Protocol (LDAP) Data Interchange Format files that alter the Active Directory schema.

To run the Enterprise Initialization Tool, obtain the ISA Server setup files and complete the following steps:

> **Note** If autorun is disabled, double-click the file ISAautorun.exe to launch the Microsoft ISA Server setup program.

1. Click Run ISA Server Enterprise Initialization.
2. Click Yes to accept the message informing you that the ISA Server schema will be installed to Active Directory.
3. When adding the ISA Server classes and properties to the Active Directory schema, you have the ability to convert the ISA server to an array member. See Table 2-1 for an explanation of the options. Click OK when you've made the appropriate selections.
4. Setup now modifies the Active Directory schema. This step can take a few minutes to complete, so be patient and don't cancel the process while it's executing.
5. Click OK to complete the inclusion of the ISA Server classes and properties in the Active Directory schema.

Allow replication to occur between all domain controllers before attempting to promote your ISA Server from a stand-alone server to an array member.

Configuring Enterprise Policy Settings

As an array member, enterprise policies can be implemented to control rules centrally across all ISA servers in your workplace. Figure 2-3 shows the ISA Enterprise Initialization dialog box, and Table 2-2 explains the options.

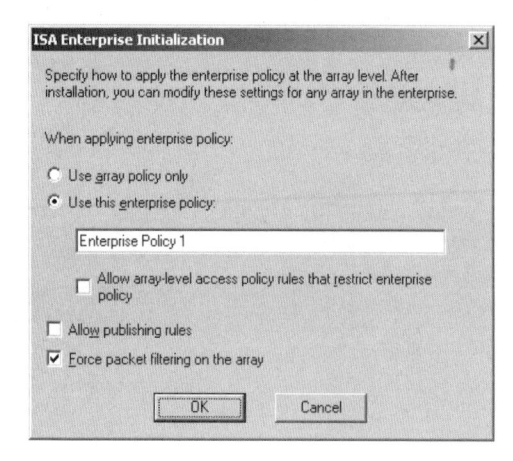

Figure 2-3. *When upgrading to an array, configure enterprise policy settings.*

Table 2-2. Enterprise Policy Settings

Policy Setting	Description
Use Array Policy Only	This option frees this array from any enterprise-level rules.
Use This Enterprise Policy	This option allows you to choose a specific Enterprise Policy to apply to this array.
Allow Array-Level Access Policy Rules That Restrict Enterprise Policy	When this box is checked, administrators can further restrict the enterprise policy at the array level.
Allow Publishing Rules	When checked, this box allows internal servers to be made available to external users through publishing configured at the array level.
Force Packet Filtering On The Array	When checked, this box requires that packet filtering be enabled at the array level.

Verifying Schema Extensions

To confirm that the ISA Server extensions were added to the schema, complete the following steps:

1. Open the Active Directory Schema console.

Tip If you've never opened the Active Directory Schema console, you must register the Schmmgmt.dll on a domain controller to access the Microsoft Management Console (MMC). You can perform this action for the command line by typing **regsvr32 schmmgmt.dll** and pressing Enter. Then launch the MMC by clicking Start, Run, typing **MMC**, and then clicking OK. When the MMC console launches, select Add/Remove Snap-In from the Console menu. In the Add/Remove Snap-In dialog box, click the Add button. In the Add Standalone Snap-In dialog box, select Active Directory Schema, and click Add. Click Close, and then click OK to return to the console.

2. In the left pane, expand the Active Directory Schema node and then the Classes node, and search for classes that begin with msFPC.

Promoting a Stand-Alone Server to an Array Member

After a successful modification to the Active Directory schema, you can promote an ISA Server from a stand-alone server to an array member. Promoting an ISA server to an array member allows the ISA Server configuration data to be stored in Active Directory, a central location for the data that's replicated across all of your domain controllers.

Caution Before promoting a stand-alone server to an array member, consider carefully that the process can't be reversed. An array member can't be converted back to a stand-alone server without completely uninstalling and reinstalling ISA Server; even then, the entries for the array member remain in Active Directory

To promote a stand-alone server to an array member, complete the following steps:

1. Open the ISA Management console and then, in the left pane, right-click the server node (the name of your ISA server) and then click Promote.
2. Click Yes to promote the server to an array member.
3. On the Enterprise Policy Settings page, you can control how enterprise policies are enabled for the array. Click OK when you've made the appropriate selections.

More Info See Table 2-2 for an explanation of the choices under Use Custom Enterprise Policy Settings. More detailed coverage on Enterprise and array policies is covered in Chapter 11, "Managing ISA Server and Windows Active Directory."

4. The server is promoted to an array member and array configuration is stored in Active Directory. This process might take a few minutes. When it's done, click OK.
5. To establish the connection to the newly created array, in the left pane right-click Internet Security And Acceleration Server and then click Connect To....
6. Click Connect To Enterprise And Arrays and then click OK. A new Enterprise node appears in the left pane above the Servers And Arrays node.

Configuring ISA Server

Once your ISA Server is installed, you must perform some additional steps before it will work completely. For an ISA Server in integrated mode (which includes both firewall and caching functionality), you must complete the steps shown in Table 2-3.

Table 2-3. Steps Required to Configure a Newly Installed ISA Server

Action	Procedure Location
Configure the LAT, Local Domain Table (LDT), and Autodiscovery	Chapter 2 (next section)
Configure the cache	Chapter 2
Configure policy elements	Chapter 7
Configure access policy (site and content rules, protocol rules, and packet filtering)	Chapter 8

Configuring the Local Address Table (LAT)

The LAT defines what are considered to be internal IP addresses (for example, 10.0.0.1 to 10.0.0.255). Although the LAT can be automatically configured during installation based on the local server's routing table, it's a good practice to confirm the LAT entries to ensure that all local networks are listed. From a security standpoint, it's even more important to verify that no external networks are included.

Caution If any external IP addresses or ranges show up in your LAT, you have a security vulnerability. The LAT defines what is considered "internal" to your network, so having an external IP address is a lot like a fortress leaving a door open in one of its walls.

The following sections describe how to configure the LAT.

Manually Creating a New Local Address Table (LAT) Entry

If you choose to manually create your LAT, follow these steps:

1. Open ISA Management and, in the left pane, click the plus sign (+) next to the Network Configuration node. Typically, you'd expand Servers And Arrays and then the server node (the name of your ISA server).
2. Right-click Local Address Table (LAT) and choose New and then LAT Entry from the shortcut menu.
3. On the New LAT Entry page, type in the beginning and ending IP addresses for an internal address range in the From and To dialog boxes. Optionally, you can provide a description for the LAT entry.
4. Click OK to close.

Automatically Constructing the Local Address Table (LAT)

If you're working in a typical environment, use the built-in features that help to automatically construct your LAT:

1. Open ISA Management and, in the left pane, click the plus sign (+) next to the Network Configuration node. Typically, you'd expand Servers And Arrays and then the server node (the name of your ISA server).
2. Right-click Local Address Table (LAT) and choose Construct LAT....

Tip In addition to step 2, you can also right-click Local Address Table (LAT) from the MMC, choose All Tasks, and then click the Construct LAT button.

3. You can choose to construct the LAT by adding the private address ranges defined in Request for Comments (RFC) 1918 (10.x.x.x, 172.16.x.x–172.31.x.x, and 192.168.x.x) or by adding IP address ranges based on the ISA server's routing table, or both. If you're going to use the routing table, you must check the applicable network adapter to determine the IP address ranges added to the LAT. Select the appropriate check boxes and then click OK.

> **Note** If you select the check box to add address ranges based on the selected computer's Windows 2000 routing table, you must choose one of the associated network adapters before you can click OK to close.

Modifying a LAT Entry

Once you've configured the LAT, you may need to modify at some point in the future. Use these steps to perform an update:

1. Open ISA Management and, in the left pane, click the plus sign (+) next to the Network Configuration node and then click Local Address Table (LAT). Typically, you'd expand Servers And Arrays and then the server node (the name of your ISA server).

2. In the right-hand pane, right-click the applicable LAT entry and then click Properties.

3. Modify the IP address range by typing the beginning and ending IP addresses in the From and To dialog boxes. Optionally, update the description for the modified LAT entry.

4. Click OK to close.

Deleting a LAT Entry

At some point you may want to delete a LAT entry. Follow these steps to remove an IP address or range of IP addresses from the LAT:

1. Open ISA Management. In the left pane, click the plus sign (+) next to the Network Configuration node and then click Local Address Table (LAT). Typically, you'd expand Servers And Arrays and then the server node (the name of your ISA server).

2. In the right-hand pane, right-click the applicable LAT entry and click Delete.

3. Click Yes to confirm the deletion.

Configuring the Local Domain Table (LDT)

The LDT is used only by firewall clients. It specifies all the domain names (like *northwindtraders.local*) that are internal to the network and routes all name resolution requests to an internal Domain Name System (DNS) server, rather than routing resolution requests to an external DNS server.

Creating a New LDT Entry

To create a new LDT table, follow these steps:

1. Open the ISA Management console and, in the left pane, click the plus sign (+) next to the server node, click the plus sign (+) next to the Network Configuration node, and then click Local Domain Table (LDT).
2. Right-click Local Domain Table (LDT), choose New, and then choose LDT Entry.
3. On the New LDT Entry page, type the name of a local domain name in your organization. Optionally, type a description and click OK. Repeat for each unique local domain name in your workplace.

Modifying an LDT Entry

Follow these steps when you want to modify an LDT entry:

1. In the right-hand pane, right-click the applicable LDT entry and then click Properties.
2. In the Local Domain dialog box, type in a different local domain name or click Browse to select from a list of available domain names. Optionally, type a description.
3. Click OK to close the LDT entry properties page.

Deleting an LDT Entry

To delete an LDT entry, follow these steps:

1. In the right-hand pane, right-click the applicable LDT entry and then click Delete.
2. Click Yes to confirm the deletion.

Configuring Automatic Discovery

Automatic discovery allows all Firewall and Web Proxy clients to update themselves with their intended ISA Server using the Web Proxy Autodiscovery Protocol (WPAD). This section describes how to enable Automatic Discovery for Firewall and Web Proxy clients, and how to configure WPAD on your DNS or DHCP servers.

Enabling Automatic Discovery

If you want to enable Automatic Discovery, follow these steps.

1. Open ISA Management console. In the left pane, right-click your ISA server node and then click Properties.
2. Select the Auto Discovery tab.
3. Select the Publish Automatic Discovery Information check box, and, optionally, you can change the port automatic that discovery utilizes for incoming Web requests by typing in a new port number.
4. Click OK to close.

5. When prompted by an ISA Server Warning, you can choose to select either Save The Changes, But Don't Restart The Service(s) or Save The Changes, And Restart The Service(s). Click OK to close.

Automatic Discovery for Firewall Clients If you want to enable Automatic Discovery for Firewall clients, follow these steps.

1. Open ISA Management. In the left pane, click the Client Configuration node. Typically, you'd expand Servers And Arrays and then the server node (the name of your ISA server).
2. In the right-hand pane, right-click Firewall Client and then click Properties.
3. In the General tab, specify by DNS name or IP address how firewall clients should connect to your ISA server.
4. Check the Enable ISA Firewall Automatic Discovery In Firewall Client check box.
5. Click OK to close.

Automatic Discovery for Web Proxy Clients If you want to enable Automatic Discovery for Web Proxy clients, follow these steps.

1. Open ISA Management and, in the left pane, click the Client Configuration node. Typically, you'd expand Servers And Arrays and then the server node (the name of your ISA server).
2. In the right-hand pane, right-click Web Browser and click Properties.
3. In the General tab, ensure that the check box Configure Web Browser During Firewall Client Setup is selected. Ensure that your ISA server's correct name is specified in the DNS Name dialog box.

> **Note** You can't modify the port from the properties of the firewall client. The port is determined by the Outgoing Web Requests tab on your ISA server node's property page.

4. Select the following check boxes to configure automatic discovery for Web Proxy clients:
   - **Automatically Discover Settings** When this box is selected, the Web Proxy service searches for ISA servers. This function is valid only on Microsoft Internet Explorer versions 5 and later.
   - **Set Web Browsers To Use Automatic Configuration Script** When this option is enabled, the browsers use the automatic configuration script to update their proxy information. The default script is located at *http://yourISAserver:8080/array.dll?Get.Routing.Script*, but administrators can specify a custom URL if needed.

> **Tip** These settings are only valid during the firewall client setup.

5. Click OK to close.

Configuring a WPAD Entry in DNS and DHCP To configure a WPAD entry in DNS, follow these steps.

1. Open the DNS Management console by clicking Start and then choosing Programs. Click Administrative Tools and then DNS.
2. In the left pane, click the plus sign (+) next to your DNS server, click the plus sign (+) next to Forward Lookup Zones, right-click the applicable forward lookup zone where the WPAD entry will be created, and, finally, click New Alias.
3. In the Alias name, type **WPAD**.
4. In the Fully Qualified Name For Target Host, type the fully qualified domain name of the ISA server or ISA array.
5. Click OK, and close the DNS console.

To configure a WPAD entry in DHCP, follow these steps.

1. Open the DHCP Management console by clicking Start and then choosing Programs. Click Administrative Tools and then DHCP.
2. In the left pane, click the plus sign (+) next to your DHCP server, right-click your DHCP server, and then click Set Predefined Options.
3. Click Add and provide the following information:
   - Name: type **WPAD**
   - Date Type: select String
   - Code: type **252**
4. Click OK.
5. In String, type **http://*yourISAserver:Autodiscoveryportnumber*/wpad.dat** (where *yourISAserver* is the name of your ISA server and *Autodiscoveryportnumber* is the port on which automatic discovery information is being published).

Tip Port 80 is designated for Automatic Discovery of incoming Web requests.

6. In the left pane, select Server Options. Right-click Server Options and then click Configure Options.
7. Confirm that the option 252 WPAD check box is selected and then click OK.
8. Close the DHCP console.

Configuring the ISA Server Cache

The ISA Server cache enables the caching of Web content. It's important to set up the cache's location and configuration correctly to ensure that the cache is located in the appropriate place and that the settings allow quick and timely retrieval of information.

Setting the Size of the Cache

Follow these steps to set the size of the cache:

1. Open the ISA Management console. In the left pane, click the plus sign (+) next to the Cache Configuration node, and then select Drives. Expand Servers And Arrays and then the server node (the name of your ISA server).
2. In the right-hand pane, right-click your ISA server's cache file and then click Properties.
3. Highlight the NTFS partition where you'd like to set the cache file.
4. In the Maximum Cache Size (MB) dialog box, type the maximum size in MB that you care to allocate to the cache and then click Set.
5. On the highlighted partition, the Cache Size column should now display the value set in Step 4.
6. Click OK to close.
7. When prompted by an ISA Server Warning, you can choose to click either Save The Changes, But Don't Restart The Service(s) or Save The Changes, And Restart The Service(s). Click OK to close.

Configuring the Cache Properties

The Caching Configuration Properties tab has one descriptive tab and four configurable tabs. Open the dialog box by right-clicking the Cache Configuration node in the ISA Management console and then click Properties (see Figure 2-4).

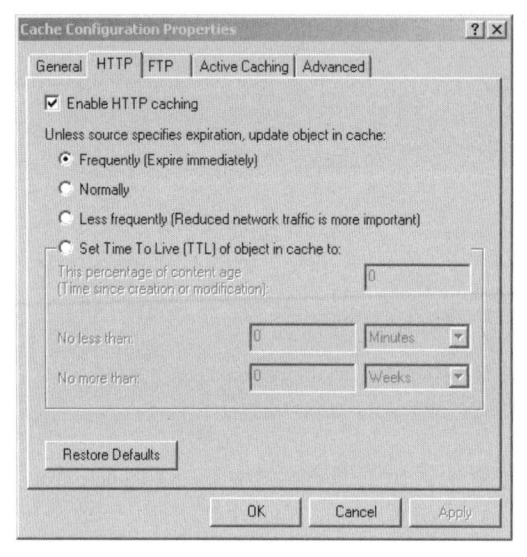

Figure 2-4. *To configure the cache properties, use the Cache Configuration Properties dialog box.*

Chapter 2 Installing and Configuring Microsoft ISA Server 2000

Table 2-4 describes the different cache properties for each of the tabs in the Cache Configuration Properties dialog box.

Table 2-4. Caching Configuration Properties

Tab	Option	Description
General	N/A	This tab displays the total cache size of all servers in the array.
HTTP	Enable HTTP Caching	This option enables or disables the caching of HTTP content on the ISA Server.
	Frequently	Requires the ISA Server to refresh the HTTP content frequently, which keeps the information timely but requires more network bandwidth to the Internet.
	Normally	This default option balances the currency of applications in the cache with network bandwidth, requiring less frequent updates.
	Less Frequently	Network traffic is kept to a minimum, but objects in the cache aren't as current.
	Set Time To Live	This option allows you to specify the time that objects will be kept in the cache based on their TTL. This option is useful for maintaining cached content indefinitely, if desired.
FTP	Enable FTP Caching	Determines the time desired to retain FTP objects in the cache. The default time is one day or 1440 minutes.
Active Caching	Enable Active Caching	When checked, this option enables the most currently accessed content in the cache to be automatically updated during low-use periods on the server. See the Microsoft Knowledge Base article 301231: "Description of the Active Caching Feature" for more information about how active caching works.
Advanced	Do Not Cache Objects Larger Than...	Allows you to specify the maximum file size—in kilobytes, megabytes, or gigabytes—of content that will be cached.
	Cache Objects That Have An Unspecified Last Modification Time	Objects that don't have a header that contains dates and times usually aren't cached. This option allows such objects to be cached.
	Cache Objects Even If They Do Not Have An HTTP Status Code Of 200	ISA doesn't, by default, cache any content that doesn't have a success code of 200. Checking this option allows ISA to cache error messages (which have other status codes, such as 401—Access Denied).

(continued)

Table 2-4. Caching Configuration Properties *(continued)*

Tab	Option	Description
	Cache Dynamic Content	Most Web search or query results are usually valid only for highly individualized queries and return a URL that contains a question mark. Selecting this box allows such pages to be cached.
	Maximum Size of URL Cached In Memory	This limits the size of the URL string that's cached in memory.
	If Web Site of Expired Object Cannot Be Reached	When an expired object's Web site can't be reached, you can choose to either return an error message or set parameters that will allow you to return the expired content.
	Percentage Of Free Memory To Use for Caching	Cache content is stored in RAM to improve performance. By default, 50 percent of the memory is allocated for this purpose. This option allows you to change this setting.

Determining the Load Factor

To determine the load factor for a server in an array, complete the following steps:

1. Open ISA Management and, in the left pane, select the Computer node. Typically, you'd expand Servers And Arrays and then the server node (the name of your ISA server).
2. In the right-hand pane, right-click the object representing your ISA server and then click Properties.
3. Select the Array Membership tab.
4. In the Load Factor dialog box, specify the load factor for this ISA server.
5. Click OK to close.

Configuring the Intra-Array Address

To configure the intra-array address for a server in an array, complete the following steps:

1. Open ISA Management and, in the left pane, click the Computer node. Typically, you'd expand Servers And Arrays and then the server node (the name of your ISA server).
2. In the right-hand pane, right-click the object representing your ISA server and then click Properties.
3. Select the Array Membership tab.
4. In the Intra-Array Communication dialog box, type the internal IP address to be used for intra-array communication. Optionally, you can click Find, click the applicable internal IP address, and then click OK.

Tip The intra-array IP address chosen for communication must be defined in the LAT.

5. Click OK to close.

Configuring Scheduled Content Downloads

To configure schedule content downloads, complete the following steps:

1. Open ISA Management. In the left pane, expand Servers And Arrays, your server node (the name of your ISA server), and, finally, expand the Cache Configuration node.
2. Right-click Scheduled Content Download Jobs, click New, and then choose Job.
3. Type a name to be given to the Scheduled Content Download and then click Next.
4. On the Start Time page, specify the date and time for this job to start downloading the content. Click Next.
5. On the Frequency page, click to download content Once, Daily, or Weekly On. If you click Weekly On, you must select the days of the week on you wish to download content. Click Next to continue.
6. On the Content page, as shown in Figure 2-5 type in the URL of the site you wish to download. Optionally, you can choose to download content only from the URL domain supplied and to cache dynamic content. Click Next to continue.

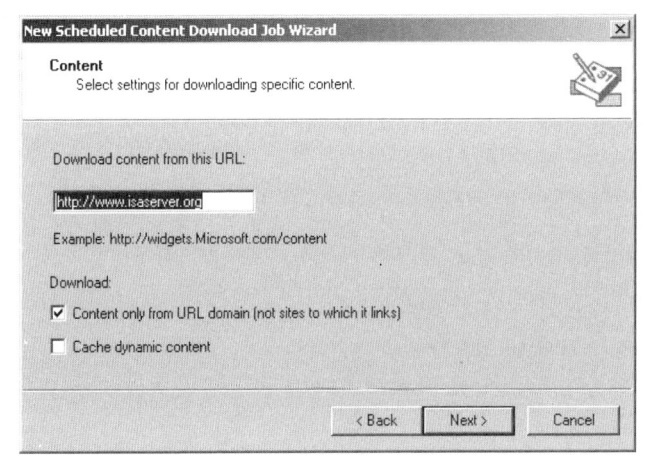

Figure 2-5. *The Content page specifies the URL of the site that will be downloaded on a schedule.*

7. On the Links And Downloaded Objects page (see Figure 2-6), you can choose options to control the content's TTL, the depth of the links this job should crawl, and the maximum number of cached objects. Click Next to continue.

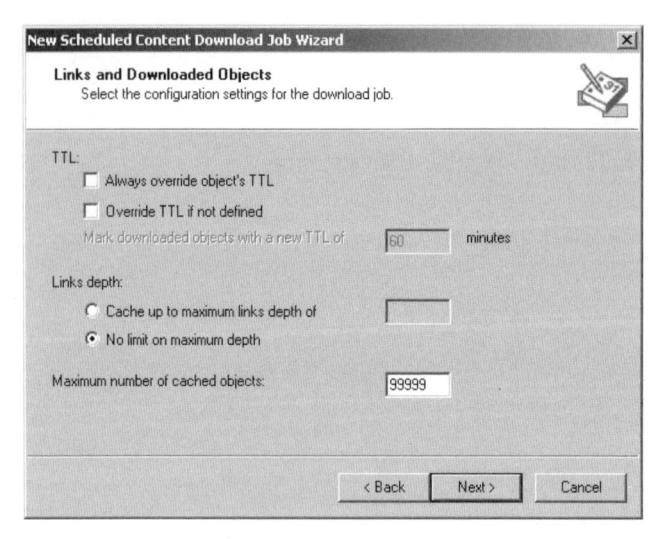

Figure 2-6. *The Links And Downloaded Objects dialog box determines content Time to Live (TTL) and link depth.*

8. On the summary page, click Finish to complete the Scheduled Content Download Job Wizard.

Installing ISA Server Feature Pack 1

Microsoft ISA Server Feature Pack 1 brings additional security features to ISA Server in the form of an OWA publishing wizard, an RPC configuration wizard, an enhanced SMTP filter, a URLScan filter, and an RSA SecurID authentication. These features, along with additional features and documentation, make ISA Server richer and easier to use.

Installing ISA Server Feature Pack 1 requires the same steps whether your ISA Server is installed on the Windows 2000 platform or the Windows Server 2003 platform. Feature Pack 1 files are distributed separately in seven different downloads, as shown below:

- Isafp1.exe—Feature Pack 1 Core Files (must be installed prior to Isafp1sd.exe or Isafp1ur.exe)
- Isafp1_readme.htm—Feature Pack 1 Release Notes
- Isafp1sd.exe—Web filter for RSA SecurID
- SecurID_readme.htm—Feature Pack 1 release notes for RSA SecurID Web filter
- Isafp1ur.exe—URLScan filter download
- Urlscan_readme.htm—Feature Pack 1 release notes for URLScan filter
- Docs.zip—Technical documentation and walkthroughs

Chapter 2   Installing and Configuring Microsoft ISA Server 2000 | 41

Tip   ISA Server Service Pack 1 must be installed before attempting to install ISA Server Feature Pack 1. Also, the Feature Pack will not install on an evaluation copy of ISA Server.

Installing Feature Pack 1 requires the ISA Server services to be restarted; however, downtime is less than one minute. Follow these steps to install ISA Server Feature Pack 1:

1. Download the ISA Server Feature Pack 1 from *http://www.microsoft.com/isaserver/downloads/*.
2. Double-click the file Isafp1.exe to begin the installation.

Caution   Ensure that all MMC applications have been closed before continuing.

3. Click I Agree to accept the EULA.
4. If there are active MMC consoles, the Feature Pack installation will warn you to close the MMC applications before continuing.
5. The ISA Server services are stopped, the Feature Pack files are written to the ISA Server installation directory, and the ISA Server services are restarted.
6. Click OK to complete the installation of ISA Server Feature Pack 1. If you do not want to read the documentation, clear the Read About ISA Server Feature Pack 1 check box before clicking OK.

Note   If you have an array of ISA Servers, Feature Pack 1 must be installed on each array member. A reboot of the ISA Server is not necessary after the installation of Feature Pack 1.

To confirm the installation of ISA Feature Pack 1:

1. Open the ISA Management console.
2. In the left pane, select the Computer node.
3. In the right pane, highlight the ISA server and verify that the Version column displays 3.0.1200.235 SP1 FP1.

Uninstalling ISA Server Feature Pack 1

To uninstall ISA Server Feature Pack 1 using Add/Remove Programs, complete the following steps:

1. Open the Control Panel. Click Add Or Remove Programs.
2. Select Microsoft ISA Server 2000 Updates and then click Change.
3. Select Feature Pack 1 and then click Remove. After the uninstall completes, click OK.

Uninstalling ISA Server

When you must uninstall ISA Server, you have two options: Add/Remove Programs and Rmisa.exe. Add/Remove Programs is a familiar means of uninstalling applications, but the Rmisa.exe tool allows a quick means of removing ISA without being prompted, and it's useful for automating ISA Server removal.

Performing an Uninstall with Add/Remove Programs

To uninstall ISA Server using Add/Remove Programs, complete the following steps:

1. Open the Control Panel. Click Add Or Remove Programs.
2. Select Microsoft Internet Security And Acceleration Server and then click Remove.
3. When prompted to confirm the uninstall of ISA Server, click Yes.
4. Setup searches for installed components and stops relevant services.
5. When prompted to remove logs and backup configuration files, click Yes.
6. The uninstall program removes ISA Server program files and updates the system.
7. Click OK to complete the removal of ISA Server.

Note When removing ISA Server, the uninstall program removes ISA Server Service Pack 1 if it's present on the server.

Performing an Uninstall with Rmisa.exe

To uninstall ISA Server using Rmisa.exe, complete the following steps:

1. Double-click the file Rmisa.exe to begin the removal of ISA Server.

Note The file Rmisa.exe is located under \ISA\i386 directory on the ISA Server CD.

2. When prompted, type **Y** to remove ISA Server.
3. Please be patient while the uninstall occurs. When it's complete, the DOS window closes and ISA Server has been completely removed from the server.

Additional Resources

For more information on topics covered in this chapter, consult the following:

- "Running ISA Server on the Windows Server 2003 Family" at *http://www.microsoft.com/isaserver/setupserver2003.asp*.
- "Best Practices and Troubleshooting for Installing ISA Server" at *http://members.microsoft.com/partner/products/servers/internetsecurityaccelerationserver/BestPracticesMEC.aspx*
- "Designing an ISA Server Solution on a Complex Network" at *http://www.isaserver.org/tutorials/Designing_An_ISA_Server_Solution_on_a_Complex_Network.html*
- You can go to Microsoft Knowledge Base to find the following articles. Their URLs are *http://support.microsoft.com/?kbid=**article number*** (insert the article number at the end of the URL).
  - Article 813774, "Support Webcast: Microsoft Internet Security and Acceleration (ISA) Server: An Overview of Feature Pack 1"
  - Article 319380, "ISA Server 2000 Feature Pack 1 Overview"
  - Article 323387, "HOW TO: Safely Connect Your Company to the Internet in the Windows .NET Server Family"
  - Article 292287, "Error 907 When You Try to Remove or Reinstall ISA Server"
  - Article 313139, "How to Obtain the Latest Internet Security and Acceleration Server 2000 Service Pack"
  - Article 309814, "HOW TO: Configure Firewall and Web Proxy Client Autodiscovery in Windows 2000"
  - Article 296591, "A Description of the Automatic Discovery Feature"
  - Article 284831, "The ISA Server Control Service May Report Event 14158 After You Have Installed ISA Server"
  - Article 288396, "ISA Server Event 14120 Is Logged and Packet Filter Cannot Be Created"
  - Article 279631, "How to Use the SPCheck Tool to Determine the Service Pack Level Components"

Chapter 3
Installing and Configuring Microsoft ISA Server 2000 Clients

Microsoft ISA Server 2000 clients represent different ways the computers in your environment can connect to resources on your ISA Server's external interface. This chapter focuses on installing and configuring each of the three possible ISA Server client types and provides procedures that explain the following subjects:

- Automating the installation of the clients
- Configuring multiple client types on the same workstation
- Identifying the dependencies these clients have on infrastructure services

ISA Server 2000 clients are determined by how the computer requesting external resources connects to and through the ISA Server firewall. Table 3-1 shows the three clients and their capabilities.

Table 3-1. ISA Server 2000 Clients and Their Functionality

	Web Proxy	Firewall	SecureNAT
Supported Protocols	Hypertext Transfer Protocol (HTTP), Hypertext Transfer Protocol Secure (HTTPS), File Transfer Protocol (FTP), and Gopher	Limited by protocol rules	Limited by protocol rules; can't support secondary connections without use of application filters.
Supported Modes	Cache, firewall, integrated	Firewall, integrated	Firewall, integrated
Advantages	Simple, with many options for automating configuration	Provides access to all protocols. Supports authentication.	Easiest configuration in a simple network.
Disadvantages	Limited only to Web protocols	Must install software on client.	Complex networks require additional configuration. Limited protocols and authentication.

Working with the SecureNAT Client

If ease of configuration is your primary goal, SecureNAT clients require only that you configure the gateway on the clients to route to the ISA Server. SecureNAT clients support almost any type of browser or operating system.

Planning for SecureNAT implementations requires you to understand how the default gateways are configured on your clients. If you're using Dynamic Host Configuration Protocol (DHCP), you can automatically configure the default gateway. A SecureNAT client might also be a Web proxy client.

Installation

The installation of the SecureNAT client doesn't require you to run an executable; instead, simply configure the default gateway on the local workstation to point to the ISA Server's internal IP address. See the following steps on how to configure the network adapter properties for both manually and dynamically assigned IP addresses.

To configure the network adapter on a system with a manually configured IP address, complete the following steps:

1. Open Network And Dial-Up Connections (also known simply as Network Connections). The exact steps to open Network Connections will vary according to the client operating system, but the interface generally can be found within the Control Panel.

2. Select the network adapter installed on the workstation, right-click it, and select Properties.

3. Select Internet Protocol (TCP/IP) and click Properties.

4. In the Default Gateway field, type the IP address of the internal network adapter on the ISA server and click OK twice to close all windows.

In addition to configuring the default gateway, the IP address and subnet mask fields should also contain IP addresses. Remember that Steps 1–4 above are for client workstations with a static Internet Protocol (IP) address defined; follow the steps below for DHCP-assigned addresses.

If all the workstations are dynamically assigned IP addresses from a DHCP server, you may configure each workstation as a SecureNAT client by configuring the scope option 003 Router.

To define the router scope option, follow these steps:

1. Open the DHCP console by clicking the Start menu, selecting Programs, Administrative Tools, and then DHCP.

2. In the left pane, click the plus sign (+) next to the DHCP server name object.

3. Click the plus sign (+) next to the appropriate scope and then select Scope Options. If each scope utilizes the same default gateway address, you don't have to add the router option to each scope individually. You can configure

a server option to apply the router option once across all scopes configured on the DHCP server.

Note Configuring server options is the same procedure as configuring Scope Options, except that, in the left pane, you view the Server Options properties instead of the Scope Options properties.

4. Right-click Scope Options and select Configure Options. In the General tab, select the 003 Router check box, which will activate additional fields within the window.
5. In the IP Address field, type the IP address of the ISA server's internal network adapter. As an option, you can type the ISA server's server name and click Resolve to have the IP Address field populated automatically. Click Add to add the IP address. Click OK to close.

Tip If you do provide the server name and click Resolve, ensure that the IP address is set to the ISA server's internal interface before clicking Add.

Simple Network vs. Complex Network

For simple networks (namely, networks in which no routing takes place) simply configure the 003 Router Scope option to point to the ISA Server's internal IP address. If DHCP isn't available, make the change manually. For complex—or routed—networks, make the ISA Server's internal IP address the default gateway for routers connected to one of the ISA Server's network segments. This configuration eliminates the need to change gateway settings on the clients because the routers will automatically forward the clients' traffic.

Configuration

The beauty of SecureNAT clients is that no configuration beyond the default gateway needs to take place on the client. If, however, the IP address of the ISA server's internal interface changes, be sure to update the default gateway and routes.

For SecureNAT clients to access Web resources on the ISA server itself, you must enable the HTTP Redirector.

Configuring the HTTP Redirector Filter

To configure the HTTP redirector filter, complete the following steps:

1. Open the ISA Management console.
2. Expand the Extensions node and then click the Application Filters folder.
3. Select the HTTP Redirector Filter option in the right pane and then double-click it.

4. Select the Options tab.
5. Ensure that Redirect To Local Web Proxy Service is selected, and also the If The Local Service Is Unavailable, Redirect Requests To Requested Web Server option. See Figure 3-1 for an example.

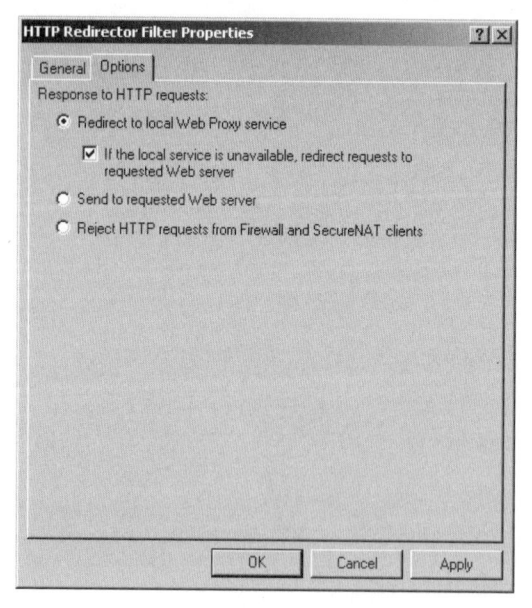

Figure 3-1. *Use the HTTP Redirector Properties dialog box to configure the HTTP redirector filter.*

Working with the Web Proxy Client

The Web proxy client works with any HTTP 1.1 CERN–compatible browser, and allows access to HTTP, HTTPS, FTP, and Gopher. Your clients' browsers must be configured to point to the Web proxy. You can configure this setting in three ways: use an automated configuration script in conjunction with the installation of the firewall client, manually, or through using scripts (such as a logon script). The Web proxy service will work with non-Windows 32-bit clients.

The Web proxy client supports user authentication, which provides the ability to restrict access by a client's NT user account.

Note that only a limited range of protocols is supported using the Web proxy alone; if clients require access to other Winsock applications, install the firewall client.

Installation

To manually configure the Web proxy client, complete the following steps on the client workstation:

1. Open Internet Explorer.
2. Open the Tools menu and then choose Internet Options.
3. Select the Connections tab and then click the LAN Settings button near the bottom of the window.
4. In the Proxy Server group, select Use A Proxy Server For Your LAN, type in the IP address of the internal network adapter on the ISA server, and then type in the port on which the ISA server listens on for outbound requests.
5. Optionally, you can select Bypass Proxy Server For Local Addresses to avoid sending requests for internal resources through the proxy server. Click Advanced and, in the Exceptions box, type all applicable internal domains or IP ranges used on the internal network. Click OK.
6. Click OK twice to return to Internet Explorer.

Configuration

To automatically configure a workstation as a Web proxy client when the firewall client is installed, complete the following steps:

1. Open the ISA Management console and then, in the left pane, select the Client Configuration node. Typically, you'd expand Servers And Arrays and then the server node (your ISA server's name).
2. In the right pane, right-click Web Browser and then click Properties.
3. In the General tab, select the Configure Web Browser During Firewall Client Setup check box so that the browser will be configured during the installation of the firewall client.
4. In the DNS Name field, type the Domain Name System (DNS) name or NetBIOS name of your ISA server. Optionally, you can click Browse, click the appropriate ISA server name, and then click OK.
5. The port field is unavailable because the port can't be changed using this interface.

Tip The default port, 8080, used for outbound requests is configured in the Outgoing Web Requests tab located in your ISA Server properties dialog box. To open this dialog box, right-click the ISA server entry in the ISA Management Console and then choose Properties.

6. If you'd like to configure Autodiscovery information for the Web proxy client, select the Automatically Discover Settings check box.

> **More Info** When you select this option, the Web proxy clients locate the ISA server by using either DNS or DHCP, depending on which service was used to publish the WPAD (Web Proxy Autodiscovery Protocol) entry.

7. Select the Set Web Browser To Use Automatic Configuration Script check box to enable Web proxy clients to take advantage of CARP (Cache Array Routing Protocol).

> **Note** The default Uniform Resource Locator (URL) for the configuration script is set to *http://yourISAservername:portnumber/array.dll?Get.Routing.Script*.

8. All the options on the General page are set in the browser only during a firewall client installation. You can make updates to the setting in the browser for a Web proxy client at any time after the firewall client installation.
9. Select the Direct Access tab.
10. The options in this tab allow for direct access by Web proxy clients. To have Web proxy clients access internal resources directly without communicating with the ISA server, select Bypass Proxy For Local Servers.

> **Note** This setting allows only the client to bypass the Web proxy service running on ISA Server if using short names, not fully qualified domain names (FQDNs) or names that include periods. This is the case even if the resource is a local resource.

11. Select the option Directly Access Computers Specified In The Local Domain Table (LDT) to allow Web proxy clients to access domain names supplied in the LDT directly without going through the Web proxy service.
12. Click Add to supply domain names to be directly accessed by bypassing the Web proxy service. If domains are added, the client workstation must either be configured as a SecureNAT or firewall client because the browser won't use the Web proxy service to access the defined sites.
13. Finally, select the Backup Route tab. This tab tells ISA Server how to handle a client that's requesting Web resources when the Web proxy service is down. To enable the backup route option, select the If ISA Server Is Unavailable, Use This Backup Route To Connect To The Internet check box.

> **Tip** Enabling this option won't work unless the autoconfiguration script in the General tab is configured.

14. Select Direct Access to allow the Web proxy client to bypass ISA Server Web proxy service.

Chapter 3   Installing and Configuring Microsoft ISA Server 2000 Clients | 51

Note   The client must be configured as a SecureNAT or firewall client, or both, or have its own external connection to connect to the Internet when utilizing Direct Access.

15. Select Alternate ISA Server and type the name of an alternate ISA server to allow a Web proxy client connectivity when its primary ISA server's Web proxy service is down.
16. Click OK to close.

Working with the Firewall Client

The firewall client requires that a software package be installed on the clients. However, if you're using Active Directory directory service, you can easily install the software using Group Policy Software Distribution. Minor client education and support will be required.

Only Microsoft Windows 32-bit operating systems are supported (Microsoft Windows 95, Windows 98, Windows Millennium Edition, Windows NT, Windows 2000, Windows XP, Windows Server 2003), which means that any Macintosh, Linux, or legacy Windows computers can't use this client.

Note   In order for a firewall client to access the Web cache, the HTTP redirector filter must be enabled in ISA Server.

The firewall client allows the use of all Winsock protocols, and you can manage it from the ISA Server. You can configure the client from the server, and it will refresh on restart and once every subsequent six-hour period.

Caution   Never install the firewall client on the ISA server. Doing so will cause problems. See Microsoft Knowledge Base article 313430, located at *http://support.microsoft.com/?kbid=313430,* and 304919, located at *http://support.microsoft.com/?kbid=304919.* They explain the reasons why.

Installation

You can install the firewall client in several ways, making it easier for administrators to distribute the software.

UNC-Based Installation

To install the firewall client by Universal Naming Convention (UNC), follow these steps:

1. Connect to the mspclnt share on the ISA server by UNC path or by establishing a mapped network drive to *YourIsaServer*\mspclnt.
2. Double-click Setup.exe to launch the installation.

3. On the Welcome screen, click Next to continue.
4. If you need to change the default location of the firewall client installation, click Change, type the folder name path, and click OK. Click Next to continue the wizard.
5. Click Install to begin the installation.
6. The firewall client files are copied to the destination directory. Click Finish to complete.

IIS Web-Based Installation

To allow the firewall client to be downloaded from the Internet Information Server (IIS) Web server, follow these steps:

1. At the ISA server, launch Windows Explorer and browse to the Microsoft ISA Server program installation directory.

   Tip By default, the directory is located at C:\Program Files\Microsoft ISA Server.

2. Right-click the Clients folder, click Properties, and then select the Web Sharing tab (see Figure 3-2).

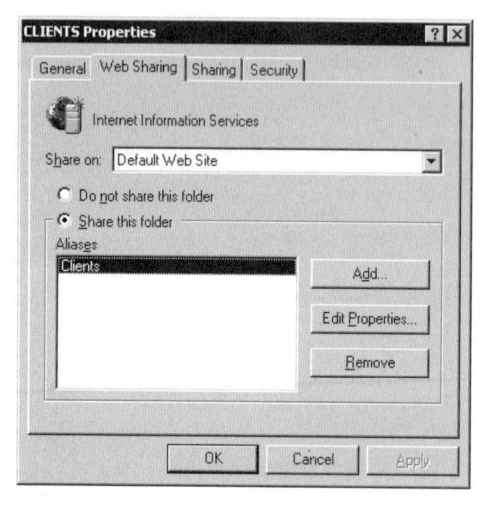

Figure 3-2. *Use the Web Sharing tab to share the ISA Server Clients folder.*

3. Select Share This Folder.
4. The Edit Alias window opens. Type an applicable name in the Alias field and then select the Scripts check box.

   Tip You need only choose Read access for clients to install from this share.

5. Click OK twice to close.
6. Open Internet Services Manager by clicking Start and choosing Programs. Click Administrative Tools and then choose Internet Services Manager.
7. Click the plus sign (+) next to the name of your IIS server, click the plus sign (+) next to Default Web Site, and locate the virtual directory you created in Step 4.
8. At a client requiring the firewall client, click the Start button, choose Programs, and then choose Internet Explorer. Type in the URL **http://*yourIIS-servername*/*aliasname*/webinst** and press Enter.
9. The default Web page for the firewall client installation loads immediately. Click the Firewall Client Software hyperlink to begin the installation.
10. The installation procedures are identical to the steps described earlier in the section of this chapter entitled "UNC-Based Installation."

Group Policy–Based Installation

To install the firewall client using Group Policies in an Active Directory environment, follow these steps:

1. Open the Active Directory Users And Computers console by clicking Start and then choosing Programs. Click Administrative Tools and then choose Active Directory Users And Computers.
2. In the left pane, click the plus sign (+) next to your domain object and then select the organizational unit that contains the users who require the firewall client.
3. Right-click the selected organizational unit and then click Properties.
4. Select the Group Policy tab, click New, type a name for the Group Policy object (GPO), and press Enter.
5. Click Edit to open the Group Policy Object Editor.

Note If an existing GPO will be used, select the GPO highest in the list to edit, as this GPO's settings are applied last and so have the greatest priority for the user.

6. In the left pane, click the plus sign (+) next to User Configuration, click the plus sign (+) next to Software Settings, right-click Software Installation, select New, and then select Package.
7. The Open dialog box launches. Browse the location on the network where the shared firewall client (Mspclnt) is located, select MS_FWC.MSI, and then click Open.

Note When you Assign an application, it installs completely on the user's computer. When you Publish an application, it's simply available to the user and installs only when invoked. Always choose the Assigned option when deploying the firewall client.

8. In the Deploy Software dialog box, click Assigned and then click OK (see Figure 3-3).

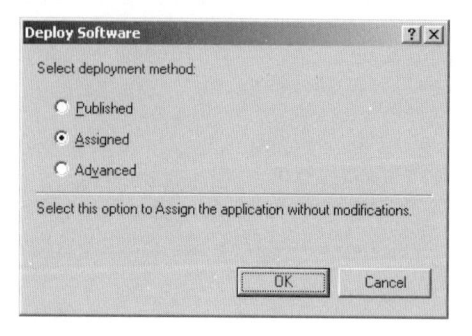

Figure 3-3. *Use the Deploy Software dialog box to assign the firewall client using Group Policies.*

9. In the right pane, the Microsoft Firewall Client package appears.

The process of assigning the firewall client to users by using group policy is complete. Users located in the OU will soon have the firewall client installed.

Silent Installations

You might want to distribute the firewall client using another method, such as a logon script or a batch file. In those cases follow these steps:

1. Confirm that the firewall client installation files are available on your ISA server's mspclnt share (that is, *YourIsaServer*\mspclnt). If it isn't there, create a share by sharing the C:\Program Files\Microsoft ISA Server\CLIENTS on the ISA server.

   Note Users must have administrative rights to install the firewall client reliably, unless you have configured the client operating systems to allow MSI-based installations to run with elevated rights. Microsoft Knowledge Base article 259459, located at *http://support.microsoft.com/?kbid=259459*, describes how to grant that privilege.

2. Create a batch file or run the silent installation by using the following command lines:

   - For automated installations with full screen dialog box views where the reboot isn't forced, run *YourIsaServer*\mspclnt\setup.exe /s /v/qr+.

   - For automated installations with full screen dialog box views where the reboot is forced, run *YourIsaServer*\mspclnt\setup.exe /s /v/qr-.

- For automated installations with basic screen dialog views where the reboot isn't forced, run *YourIsaServer*\mspclnt\setup.exe /s /v/qb+.
- For automated installations with basic screen dialog box views where the reboot is forced, run *YourIsaServer*\mspclnt\setup.exe /s /v/qr-.
- For completely silent, automated installations where the reboot isn't forced and an installation failure will create a dialog box, run *YourIsaServer*\mspclnt\setup.exe /s /v/qn+.
- For completely silent, automated installations, run *YourIsaServer*\ mspclnt\setup.exe /s /v/qn.

Configuration

The firewall client is loaded into the Control Panel. An icon representing the firewall client will automatically be placed in the Task Bar. You can open the firewall configuration properties from either of the following locations:

- **Control Panel** Open the Control Panel by clicking Start, choosing Settings, and then clicking Control Panel.
- **Task Bar** Right-click the firewall client icon in the taskbar menu area and then click Configure.

There are several configurable options for the firewall client, as shown in Figure 3-4.

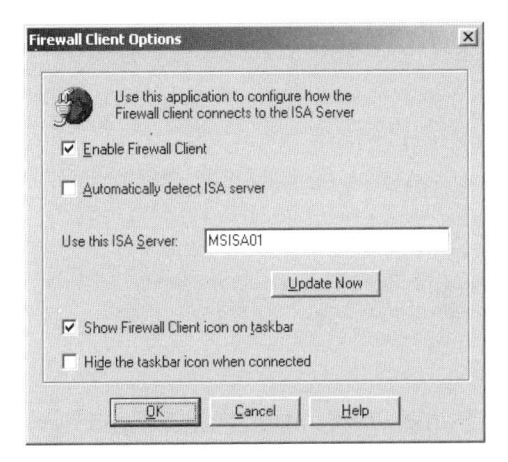

Figure 3-4. *In the Firewall Client Options dialog box, you have several configurable options for the firewall client.*

Table 3-2 explains each of the firewall client configuration options and the effects of selecting each one.

Table 3-2. Firewall Client Configuration

Options	Description
Enable Firewall Client	When checked, this option enables the firewall client; clear the box to prevent the firewall client from running.
Automatically Detect ISA Server	Informs the firewall client to query the DHCP server for the autoconfiguration URL supplied by the 252 option in a DHCP scope.
Use This ISA Server	The field in which you specify the name of your ISA server; this name can be either a FQDN DNS name, a NetBIOS name, or an IP address. Automatically Detect ISA Server Option is selected.
Show Firewall Client Icon On Taskbar	Determines whether the firewall client icon will appear in the desktop's taskbar area.
Hide The Taskbar Icon When Connected	Hides the firewall client icon when the client is successfully connected to the ISA Server firewall service. If a connection isn't being established with the firewall service, a red down arrow will appear.

Firewall Client Configuration

To configure the firewall client, follow these steps:

1. Open the Control Panel by clicking Start, choosing Settings, and then the Control Panel. Then double-click the Firewall Client icon.
2. Ensure that the Enable Firewall Client check box is selected. If it isn't, the firewall client is disabled. Type the name of the ISA server in the Use This ISA Server field and then click Update Now.
3. Choose the options you wish for your environment:
   - If you want the firewall client to autodetect the ISA Server, select the Automatically Detect ISA Server check box.
   - If you want the icon to appear in the taskbar, select the Show Firewall Client Icon On The Taskbar check box. If you don't, select the Hide The Taskbar Icon When Connected check box.
4. Click OK to close.

Firewall Client Configuration Properties in the ISA Management Console

Follow these steps to configure the firewall client properties in the ISA Management console:

1. Open ISA Management and then, in the left pane, select the Client Configuration node. Typically, you'd expand Servers And Arrays and then the server node (the name of your ISA server).
2. In the right pane, right-click Firewall Client and then click Properties.

Chapter 3 Installing and Configuring Microsoft ISA Server 2000 Clients | 57

3. In the General tab, you can configure how firewall clients will connect to the ISA server: by DNS name, by NetBIOS name, or by IP address. You can type the DNS name or NetBIOS name in the field, or click Browse, click the appropriate ISA server name, and then click OK.
4. To enable Autodiscovery, select the Enable ISA Firewall Automatic Discovery In Firewall Client check box.
5. Select the Application Settings tab. This tab shows the application settings that are configured in the server-side copy of the client configuration file. See the ISA Server Help file for more information.
6. Click OK to close.

Configuring a Workstation with All Clients

You can also configure firewall clients and SecureNAT clients as Web proxy clients. When such a client accesses an application that uses HTTP, HTTPS, FTP, or Gopher, the client will have its request routed to the Web proxy service. All other protocol requests are routed through the firewall service.

Client Dependencies on the Infrastructure

Clients are dependent on some network infrastructure configurations. Most important is the DNS configuration.

DNS Requirements and Considerations

Web proxy and SecureNAT clients require that the ISA Server can resolve DNS requests. ISA Server acts as a proxy for name resolution for these clients. SecureNAT and Web proxy resource requests are sent to the local DNS server based on the Transmission Control Protocol/Internet Protocol (TCP/IP) configuration on the client. ISA Server uses the Local Address Table (LAT) and Local Domain Table (LDT) to determine local DNS from remote DNS entries.

If your SecureNAT client does not require DNS to resolve any internal resources, then you can configure the SecureNAT client to use your ISP's DNS server. However, best practices call for all published servers to use an internal DNS server IP address assigned to their internal network adapter for internal name resolution. Also, while it is possible to configure published servers as firewall clients, less administration is required to configure them as SecureNAT clients. SecureNAT clients are not, however, available in cache mode.

Configure a Protocol Rule to Allow DNS Lookups

SecureNAT clients don't allow ISA Server to maintain pronoun-antecedent agreement; therefore, these clients need to be configured to point to a DNS server that can resolve internal and external requests, and the ISA Server has to allow DNS requests to be sent to the Internet.

1. Open the ISA Management console.
2. For Enterprise installations, expand the Enterprise node and choose the appropriate Enterprise Policy. For stand-alone installations, expand the Servers And

Arrays node, expand the appropriate server or array, and then expand Access Policy.

3. Right-click the Protocol Rules folder.
4. Choose New and then choose Rule.
5. Type a protocol rule name and then click Next.
6. Choose Allow and then click Next.
7. From the Apply This Rule To dialog box, choose the Selected Protocols option. The Protocols list appears.
8. Select the DNS Query and DNS Zone Transfer options from the Protocols box and then click Next.
9. Maintain the default of setting the schedule as Always and then choose Next.
10. Review your selections in the Completing The New Protocol Rule page and then click Finish.

DHCP Services

Best practices recommend that you use DHCP to assign client addresses, as it's much easier to administer clients, assigning default gateways, routers, and other scope options from a central location.

Additional Resources

- For more information on installing and configuring DHCP services, see *Microsoft Windows 2000 Administrator's Pocket Consultant* or *Microsoft Windows Server 2003 Administrator's Pocket Consultant*, both published by Microsoft Press and written by William R. Stanek

- Microsoft Knowledge Base includes several articles on topics covered in this chapter. The articles' URLs are *http://support.microsoft.com/?kbid=article number* (insert the article number at the end of the URL).

  - Article 297515, "All Requests from SecureNAT and Firewall Clients Are Denied"
  - Article 304919, "The Internet Security and Acceleration Server 2000 Firewall Client Is Not Supported on Internet Security and Acceleration Server 2000"
  - Article 303379, "Firewall Client Conflict with Third-Party Layered Service Providers Causes Connectivity Problems"
  - Article 312391, "ISA Firewall Client Shows Connection to Server Name Instead of IP Address"

Chapter 4
Configuring ISA Server on Small Business Server Installations

Microsoft Small Business Server 2000 (SBS) is targeted toward small businesses that have fewer than 50 computers. SBS includes several applications that interoperate to provide a robust business platform. Microsoft Windows 2000 Server provides the base on which the rest of the suite runs. Microsoft SQL Server 2000 supplies database functionality, while Microsoft Exchange Server 2000 furnishes messaging. Protecting the entire suite of products is ISA Server 2000, which installs as an array in integrated mode by default.

Originally offered in 1997, SBS started with version 4.0 to coincide with Windows NT 4.0. SBS version 4.5 became available in 1999. SBS 2000 can be either installed on a new server or upgraded from a previous version. Earlier versions of SBS used Windows NT 4.0 and Microsoft Proxy Server 2.0.

Note Upgrading to SBS 2000 can take place only from an SBS 4.5 installation. Microsoft offers a free upgrade to version 4.5 for customers licensed on SBS 4.0 to ease the upgrade to SBS. To order an upgrade, visit the SBS Web site at *http://www.microsoft.com/sbserver/techinfo/deployment/40/upgrade.asp* or call (888) 296-6588.

In this chapter we discuss some limitations and differences you'll notice when running ISA Server on SBS. Then we discuss the Internet Connection Wizard (ICW), configures the ISA Server in SBS. Finally, we end with a discussion of some common troubleshooting tips and techniques.

Limitations and Differences of ISA Server with SBS

Quite simply, the biggest difference in running ISA Server on SBS is that ISA Server must share the computer with all other SBS applications, such as Internet Information Services (IIS), SQL Server, Exchange, Fax Services, and the like. Not only does the SBS machine host all these applications, but also it acts as a

Domain Controller and can host all infrastructure services, like Domain Name System (DNS), Windows Internet Name Service (WINS), Dynamic Host Configuration Protocol (DHCP), and more.

This configuration provides smaller businesses with a very powerful set of well-integrated applications at a very reasonable price. The complexity of the single machine, however, is much greater than if these same systems were distributed across several servers. With greater complexity comes more potential problems, and that's why we devote a section of this chapter to addressing common issues with ISA Server and SBS and provide links to resources that can help you through any issues you might encounter.

Installation

Installing ISA Server on SBS is a bit different from installing ISA Server in other environments. SBS has its own installation wizard that steps through the configuration of ISA Server along with the other included applications, like SQL Server 2000 and Exchange 2000 Server. To install ISA Server when running the Small Business Server 2000 Setup Wizard, follow the steps below:

1. After the SBS Setup process installs Windows 2000 Server, the Component Selection page, as shown in Figure 4-1, lets you choose the components you wish to install. All components—which are really applications, like Microsoft Exchange 2000 Server—are selected by default. Click Next.

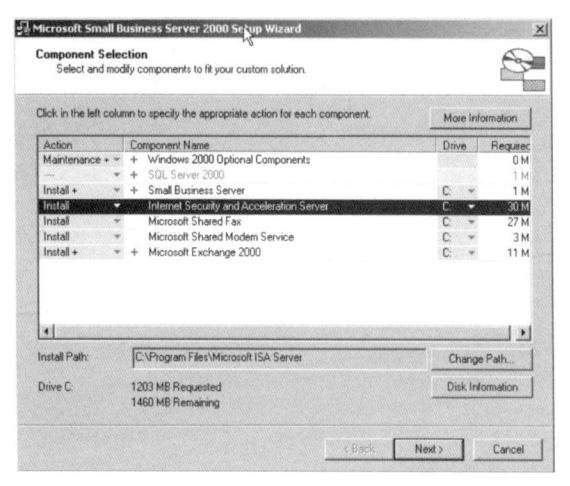

Figure 4-1. *In the Microsoft Small Business Server 2000 Setup Wizard, ISA Server appears in the available list of applications.*

2. The ISA Server Cache Drives page specifies where you should locate the cache and how large it should be, as shown in Figure 4-2. Specify the size of the cache, which is listed in MB.

Chapter 4   Configuring ISA Server on Small Business Server Installations | 61

Tip   Unless you have no other option, don't run the cache on the computer's system drive; this configuration could harm Operating System performance in some cases.

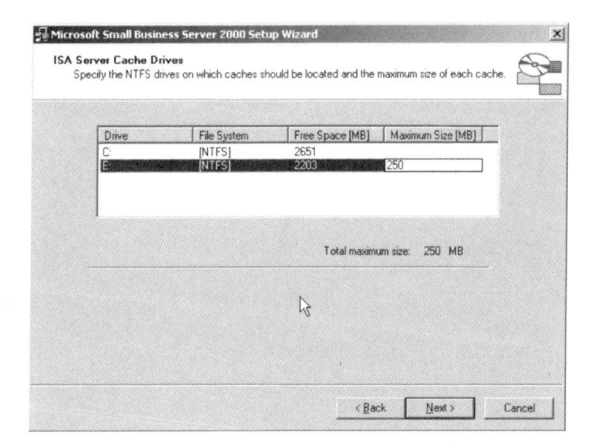

Figure 4-2. *Choose the location and size of the cache.*

3. You can populate what ISA Server defines as internal addresses in the ISA Server Construct Local Address Table page, as shown in Figure 4-3. This screen allows you to choose common internal address ranges (like 10.* and 192.168.*), as well as internal routing table information from particular network adapters. Be sure that if you select a network adapter, you've identified the internal interface. If you choose the external network adapter, Internet traffic will have access to your internal network (which opens a gaping hole in your firewall).

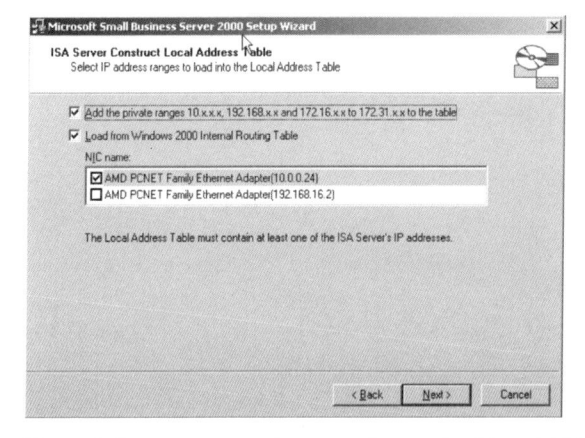

Figure 4-3. *You can easily create the Local Address Table (LAT) from the ISA Server Construct Local Address Table page.*

4. After choosing your addresses, click Next.
5. In the ISA Server Local Address Table Configuration page, as shown in Figure 4-4, customize the Local Address Table (LAT) and then click Next.

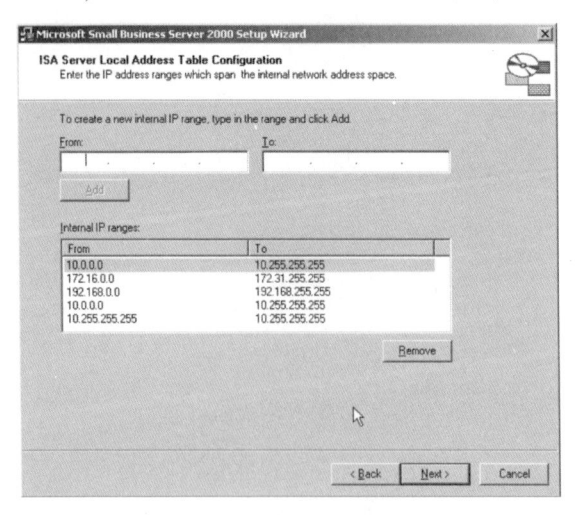

Figure 4-4. *You can create additional LAT entries using the ISA Server Local Address Table Configuration page.*

6. Confirm Data Folders (which aren't relevant to ISA) and then click Next.
7. View the Installation Summary and then click Next.
8. You're prompted to extend the schema (see Figure 4-5). Choose OK.

Figure 4-5. *The message states that the Active Directory service schema will be extended to accommodate new components, such as Exchange 2000 and ISA Server 2000.*

9. The setup wizard installs the Microsoft Shared Fax service and then begins the installation of ISA Server, as shown in Figure 4-6.
10. Choose the defaults until you are prompted to restart your server. Once your server restarts, you can begin configuration.

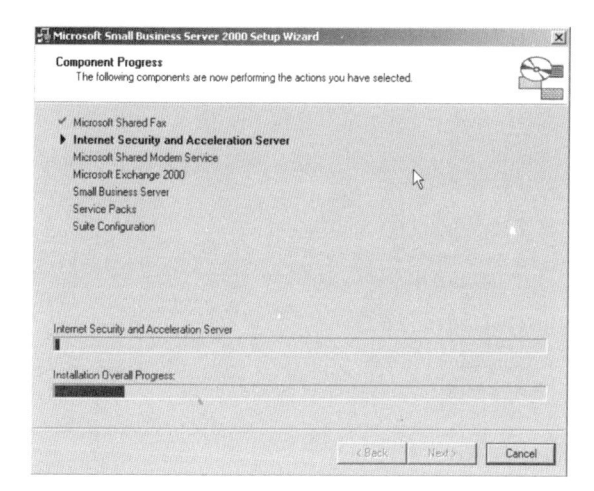

Figure 4-6. *This screen shows the ISA Server installation process.*

Configuration

In most respects, configuring an ISA Server installation is the same in a regular environment as that of SBS. You do the initial setup, however, through the Small Business Server Internet Connection Wizard (ICW) rather than through the Getting Started Wizard. The ICW creates site and content rules, protocol rules, and packet filters in ISA Server that allow clients access to internal resources.

Note SBS is designed for networks with 50 or fewer clients and will reject requests if more than 50 clients attempt to connect simultaneously. This limitation extends to ISA Server.

Small Business Server Internet Connection Wizard

The Internet Connection Wizard (ICW) steps you through defining and creating the LAT, defining connections to the internal and external network, and configuring packet filters.

To configure ISA using the ICW, complete the following steps:

1. After the SBS installation is completed, the SBS To Do List appears. Click Internet Configuration Wizard. The Welcome dialog box appears. Click Next.

2. If you need to open the To Do List after the initial setup process, go to the Start menu, choose Programs, choose Microsoft Small Business Server, and then click Small Business Server Administrator Console. In the console, expand the Small Business Server (Back Office Manager) node and then click To Do List.

3. In the Configure Hardware dialog box, choose the device your system will use to connect to the Internet. You have four options. The first three each

have forms available that can be used to help gather required information. To access the form, choose the appropriate option button and then click the appropriate Form button. For example, Figure 4-8 shows the form for configuring a router.

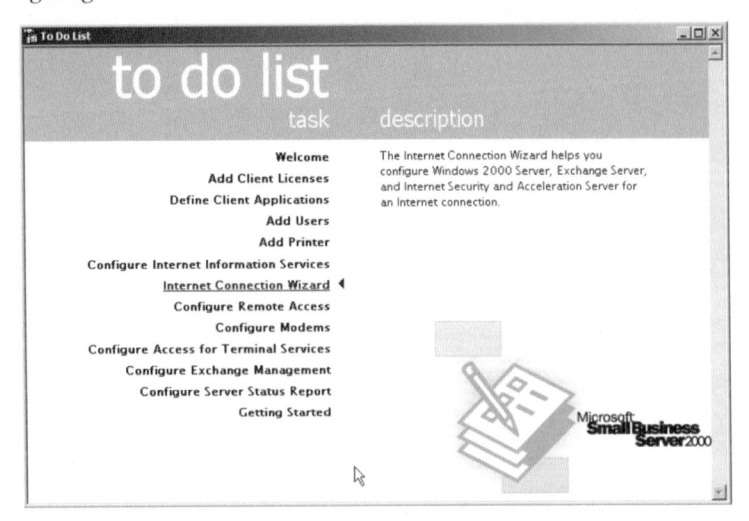

Figure 4-7. *From the To Do List you can start the Internet Connection Wizard.*

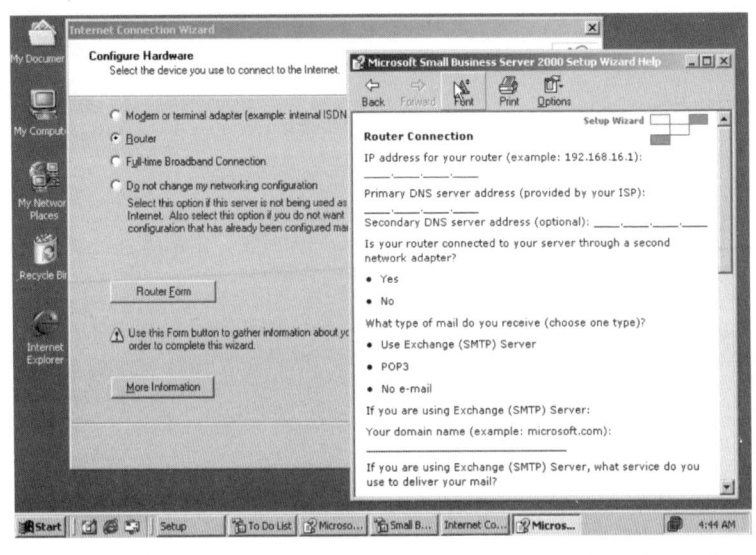

Figure 4-8. *Forms are useful for gathering information about the configuration of a network device.*

Forms are also available for the Modem And Terminal Adapter and Full-Time Broadband Connection device options. Use these forms to gather information needed for the next step:

- **Modem Or Terminal Adapter** Choose this option when you connect to the Internet using a dial-up networking connection using either a modem or Integrated Services Digital Network (ISDN) terminal adapter.
- **Router** Choose this option when your computer is connected to the Internet using a router and your service provider dynamically assigns your IP address. The router can be connected to any type of Internet connection, including Digital Subscriber Line (DSL), cable modem, satellite, or a dedicated circuit.
- **Full-Time Broadband Connection** Choose this option when you have a persistent connection to the Internet connected directly to a dedicated network adapter on your server. This is a common configuration for DSL, cable modem, and satellite connections. Note that the network adapter must have a static Internet Protocol (IP) address. If you choose this option, skip to Step 4.
- **Do Not Change My Networking Configuration** Choose this option when you want to configure connectivity manually. If you choose this option, skip to Step 5.

4. Choose Next to move to the Set Up Modem/Router Connection To ISP page and then fill in the information you gathered using the appropriate form in Step 2.

Tip If you use a broadband connection (such as DSL) that requires Point-to-Point Protocol over Ethernet (PPPoE), you might need to take some additional steps. For more information, see Microsoft Knowledge Base article 296534, "*How to Configure ISA Server to Use a PPPoE Connection*," at *http://support.microsoft.com/?kbid=296534*.

5. In the Configure Network Adapters page, choose the local internal network interface for your SBS ISA server. If you choose the Full-Time Broadband Connection option, you'll also specify the external interface that connects to the Internet for your server. Choose Next and then specify the default gateway and DNS servers for the external network adapter. Click Next to continue.
6. In the Configure Packet Filtering page (see Figure 4-9), specify what network traffic will be allowed to travel into and out of your network. You can choose to enable, disable, or not change the packet filtering settings on the SBS machine. Packet filtering should always be enabled; otherwise, ISA Server offers no protection. If you wish to configure your own packet filters and not have the ICW do all the work, choose Do Not Change Packet Filtering Settings. Click Next to continue.

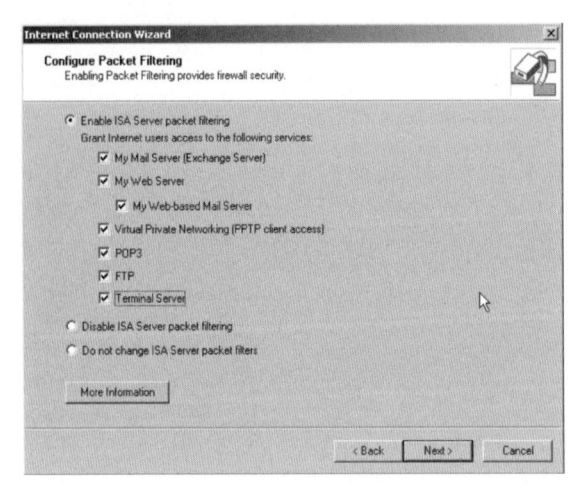

66 | Part I Microsoft ISA Server 2000 Administration Fundamentals

Figure 4-9. *The Configure Packet Filtering dialog allows you to choose the Packet Filters you wish the ICW to enable.*

7. You might receive the following two messages; click OK when prompted.
   - To View Changes, You Must Close The ISA Server Snap-In Or Refresh The Management Console.
   - Existing ISA Filters Will Be Disabled. Click OK To Continue. Click Cancel To Change Your Settings.

   Tip The ICW configures ISA Server 2000 to provide IP packet filtering. The wizard doesn't configure content or protocol filtering on ISA Server. For information on configuring those security settings, refer to ISA Server documentation.

8. The Completing The Small Business Server Internet Connection Wizard page appears, summarizing the settings you configured. Review them carefully, make any corrections, and then click Finish.

9. Finally, as illustrated in Figure 4-10, the Internet Connection Configuration Status dialog box tracks the configuration of ISA Server settings. Once the Internet connection and ISA Server settings are complete, click OK.

Chapter 4   Configuring ISA Server on Small Business Server Installations | 67

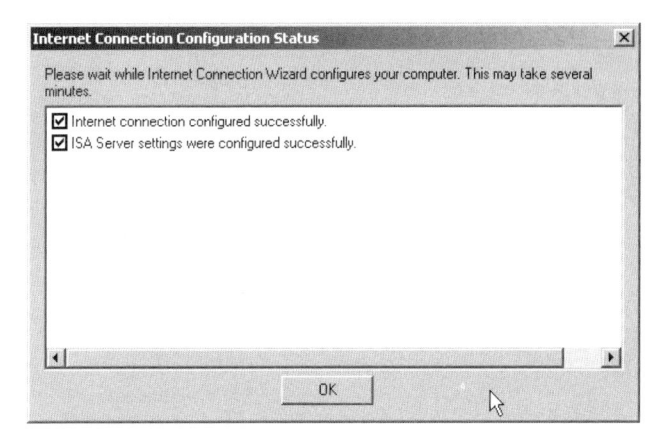

Figure 4-10. *When the ICW is done configuring your options, the Internet Connection Configuration Status dialog box has all boxes selected.*

SBS creates the appropriate Web publishing rules and packet filters to enable the functions that you chose to make available. All automatically configured filters and rules are preceded by the word *BackOffice*. See Figure 4-11 for an example.

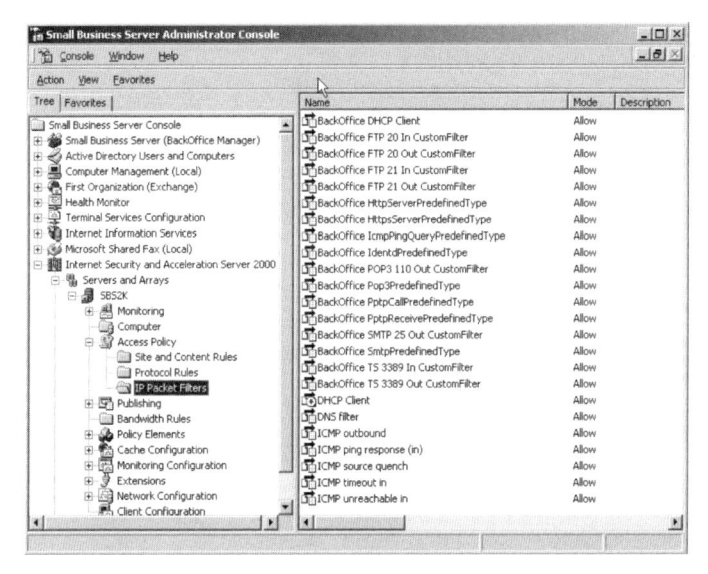

Figure 4-11. *Packet filters created by the ICW are preceded by the word* BackOffice.

Common Procedures and Troubleshooting Steps

Because the SBS configuration concentrates so much power in a single machine, the environment is more complex than if ISA Server were installed on a dedicated server. This section touches on some common issues related to ISA Server running in an SBS environment. By no means is this section comprehensive; there simply isn't room in this volume to address every situation. At the end, therefore, we provide you with links to other helpful sources for troubleshooting ISA Server on SBS.

Internet Connection Wizard Doesn't Start

You'll receive the following error message if ICW isn't installed or if it was removed: "Cannot Find The File 'ICW' (Or One Of Its Components). Make Sure The Path And Filename Are Correct And That The Required Libraries Are Available."

To resolve this issue, run Add/Remove Programs from the Control Panel and then follow these steps:

1. Choose Microsoft Small Business Server 2000 and then click Change/Remove.
2. Accept the default settings until the Component Selection page appears.
3. Expand the Small Business Server node and then expand the Connectivity node.
4. Click Maintenance in the Action column next to Internet Connection Wizard. If the ICW appears to already be installed, click Reinstall.
5. Click Next twice and then choose Finish.

ISA Server Services Won't Start If Network Address Translation (NAT) is Enabled

ISA Server services won't start when a computer with ISA Server installed also has the Network Address Translation (NAT) routing protocol enabled through Routing and Remote Access Service (RRAS). The NAT configuration in RRAS conflicts with ISA Server's NAT service. To correct this problem, disable the NAT configuration in RRAS. You do that by completing the following steps:

1. Open the Routing And Remote Access console. To do this, click Start, choose All Programs, select Administrative Tools and then click Routing And Remote Access.
2. Expand the node that represents your server and then select IP Routing.
3. In the Details Pane, right-click Network Address Translation (NAT) and then click Delete.
4. Click Yes to verify removal of the NAT from the computer.

Use Only the Dial-Up Connection Specified in ISA Server to Connect to the Internet

Use only the dial-up connection defined in ISA Server to ensure that it properly monitors network traffic and can therefore identify potential security risks. The ICW will allow you to easily select the dial-up connection you wish to use to connect to the Internet.

Dynamic DNS Services for Small Businesses

With many small to mid-sized companies, a typical external connection to the Internet relies on a DHCP-assigned IP address rather than a static IP address. A DHCP-assigned IP address complicates publishing servers located behind the ISA server. One common issue is that the IP address will be lost and a different one will be provided in its place. How do you ensure that a hostname (for example, *www.northwindtraders.com*) consistently maps to the DHCP-assigned IP address configured on your ISA server's external network adapter? Fortunately, several services provide dynamic DNS, which ensures the proper fully qualified domain name (FQDN) to IP mapping. These include:

- **TZO**   Service offering available at *www.tzo.com*.
- **DynDNS**   Service offering available at *www.dyndns.org*.

Can't Renew DHCP Assigned IP Address on External ISA Interface

If your external interface is configured to use DHCP, you can renew only the existing IP address. You might receive an error message that states, "The Following Error Occurred When Renewing Adapter MyAdapterName: DHCP Server Unreachable."

You'll need to ensure that ISA SP1 is installed and then obtain a hotfix from Microsoft support. For more detailed information, refer to Microsoft Knowledge Base article 326116, "Cannot Renew DHCP Assigned IP Address on External ISA Interface," at *http://support.microsoft.com/?kbid=326116*.

Disabling ICW for Dial-Up Connections

By default, ISA Server enables active caching, which causes ISA Server to dial at intervals to retrieve Web content. If ISA Server is configured to connect to the Internet service provider (ISP) using a dial-up connection, the modem dials at intervals, even if no user is requesting Web content. To correct this problem, run the ICW and disable active caching. As an alternative, perform the following steps:

1. Open ISA Management and, in the left pane, select the Cache Configuration node. Typically, you'd expand Servers and Arrays and then the server node (the name of your ISA server).
2. Right-click Cache Configuration and then select Properties.
3. Select the Active Caching tab and then clear the Enable Active Caching check box.
4. Click OK to save your changes.

Manually Assigning Fax Server Privileges

Existing users will not automatically receive permissions to use either ISA Server 2000 or the fax server when either of these services aren't installed initially and you later add them. New users who are added to the system after the services are installed receive appropriate permissions. You must manually set permissions for users who were in the system before these services were installed.

Perform the following steps to add existing users to the appropriate Active Directory security group(s):

1. Open either the Small Business Server or BackOffice Personal console.
2. Under Favorites, click Security Groups.
3. In the Security Groups window, locate the appropriate group. (For the fax server use "BackOffice Fax Operators Group." For ISA server use "BackOffice Internet Users Group.")
4. Open Security Group and then select the Members tab.
5. Click Add.
6. Select the users to be added to the service, click Add, and then click OK when all users have been selected.
7. Click Apply and then click OK.

Logging User Activity

ISA Server logs provide a lot of good information, but to make use of them you'll likely need to either build your own database to filter log files or take advantage of third-party applications that provide full-featured reporting. For links to Microsoft partners who provide reporting applications, visit *http://www.microsoft.com/isaserver/partners/reporting.asp*.

Problems with ISA Server and IIS on the Same Computer

When ISA Server and IIS reside on the same computer and you want to use more advanced configurations, you can sometimes have problems. One issue that appears often is that of socket pooling, in which IIS services can listen on all interfaces of a computer. This feature is useful on dedicated IIS boxes, but it can hog a lot of valuable resources if it's running on your SBS machine.

For a detailed explanation of the problem and clear instructions on the solution, visit *http://www.isaserver.org/shinder/*. You'll find an article called "The Misery of IIS 5.0 Socket Pooling."

Removing ISA Server from SBS

To remove ISA Server from SBS, go to the Start menu, choose Settings, and then choose Control Panel. Click the Add/Remove Programs utility, choose Microsoft Internet Security And Acceleration Server, and then click the Remove button. Alternately, you can run the Rmisa.exe utility from a command line; it's located on the second SBS installation disk in CD:\ISA30\ISA\I386.

Additional Resources

For more information on topics covered in this chapter, consult the following:

- Microsoft Knowledge Base article "Internet Connection Wizard Does Not Succeed When the Server Does Not Have an Interface in the LAT" at *http://support.microsoft.com/?kbid=293286*
- The Small Business Server FAQ page provides help with frequently asked questions about all aspects of ISA Server. It is located at *http://www.smallbizserver.net*.
- The primary newsgroup where people pose and answer questions related to ISA Server on SBS every day is located at *news://msnews.microsoft.com/microsoft.public.backoffice.smallbiz2000*.
- You can look at Microsoft's ISA newsgroups at *http://www.microsoft.com/isaserver/community/newsgroups*.

Chapter 5

Migrating from Microsoft Proxy Server 2.0

This chapter will help those who are still administering Microsoft Proxy Server 2.0 and need to perform an upgrade to Microsoft ISA Server 2000. It contains all necessary information for migrating from Proxy Server 2.0 to ISA Server. The information covered in this chapter includes

- Prerequisites for performing the upgrade
- Steps to upgrade a Microsoft NT 4.0 server running Proxy 2.0 Server to the Microsoft Windows 2000 operating system
- Steps to upgrade Proxy Server 2.0 to ISA Server 2000
- Explanations of key differences between the two products

Prerequisites to Upgrading Proxy Server 2.0 to ISA Server

Before upgrading to ISA Server, make certain that your environment supports the upgrade. Following are some basic requirements, helpful information, and mitigating conditions that will affect your upgrade process.

Caution Before you make any changes to your Proxy Server 2.0 environment, always, always, always be sure to back up your configuration. See the procedure listed later in the chapter for step-by-step instructions on how to perform this task.

To upgrade correctly, your proxy server must be running at least Windows 2000 Server with Service Pack 1. See the steps for upgrading to Windows 2000 SP1 later in this chapter. You should also refer to the hardware requirements listed in Chapter 1, "Overview of Microsoft ISA Server 2000 Administration." Finally, ensure that no Internetwork Packet Exchange/Sequenced Packet Exchange (IPX/SPX) traffic needs to pass through the firewall, as ISA Server doesn't support these protocols.

You'll want to know how the old Proxy Server 2.0 terminology translates to ISA Server components. Learning the ISA Server terminology is pretty straightforward. Use Table 5-1 as a reference.

Table 5-1. Comparing ISA Server and Proxy Server 2.0 Terminology

ISA Server Term	Corresponding Proxy Server 2.0 Term
Protocol rules	Winsock permission settings
Web publishing rules	Publishing properties
Site and content rules	Domain filters
Allow or block Internet Protocol (IP) packet filters	Static packet filters
Routing rules	Web proxy routing rules

If you're just migrating to ISA stand-alone servers—that is, servers that don't install into arrays—your new server will inherit almost all the rules and other configurations from the old proxy server systems. If, however, you'll be migrating from Proxy Server arrays, you should remove each of those servers from the Proxy 2.0 arrays. After you create the new ISA Server array, you can then migrate the Proxy 2.0 systems into that array.

To reduce the time and effort it takes to configure your policies in the new environment, be sure to upgrade using an account with Enterprise Admin rights. Although it's possible to upgrade with just Domain Admin or local server Administrators rights, only Enterprise Admins can change the enterprise policy settings in Active Directory directory service for the upgrade and thereby migrate *all* information.

Specifically, users without Enterprise Admin rights can migrate all settings if ISA Server is configured to Use Array Policy Only. If the enterprise policy is set to Use Enterprise Policy Only, then none of the Proxy Server rules can be migrated. If Use Enterprise And Array Policy is configured, only the Proxy Server "Deny" rules will be migrated.

Upgrading the Proxy Server from Windows NT 4 to Windows 2000

If you're administering a Proxy 2.0 Server, there's a good chance your server is still running on Windows NT Server 4.0. Because ISA Server 2000 won't run on the NT Server 4.0 platform, your first step is to upgrade your server operating system to Windows 2000.

To upgrade the operating system to Windows 2000, follow these steps:

- Back up existing configuration of the Proxy Server.
- Remove the Proxy Server software.
- Upgrade the operating system to Windows 2000.

- Install the Proxy Server software.
- Restore the configuration from the backup.

Backing Up the Proxy 2.0 Server

Backing up the proxy server configuration data is an important step prior to uninstalling the Proxy server software because, if any issues arise, you might need to restore your old environment.

To back up your Proxy configuration data, follow these steps:

1. Open the Internet Service Manager.
2. In the left pane, right-click Winsock Proxy or Web Proxy and then click Properties.
3. In the Services tab, click the Server Backup button.
4. Specify a directory to save the backup file and click OK twice to return to the Internet Services Manager.

Note The default location for the server backup is C:\msp\config. The filename will be in the format of MSPYYYYMMDD.mpc.

5. Close the Internet Services Manager.

Uninstalling Proxy Server 2.0

Once you've migrated your server, you can clean up the system by uninstalling Proxy Server 2.0. To do this, follow these steps:

1. Click Uninstall from the Microsoft Proxy Server program menu.
2. Click Yes to begin the removal of Proxy Server 2.0.
3. When prompted to remove the cache content, logs, and configuration backup files generated by Proxy Server, click No.

Tip By clicking No, you're ensuring that all of your Proxy server configuration will be restored after upgrading the operating system to Windows 2000 and performing the restore.

4. Click OK to finish.

Upgrading the Operating System to Windows 2000

The upgrade of the operating system from Windows NT Server 4.0 to Windows 2000 is well-documented and isn't described in detail in this book. For more information on performing an in-place upgrade, see the helpful white papers and other resources at *http://www.microsoft.com/ntserver/*.

Installing the Microsoft Proxy Server 2.0 Update for Windows 2000

Before Microsoft Proxy Server 2.0 will run correctly on the Windows 2000 operating system, you must apply an update to the Windows 2000 server. The update, Msp2wizi.exe, was released in mid-2001.

> **Note** You can download the Proxy Server 2.0 update from *http://www.microsoft.com/isaserver/evaluation/previousversions/dlwindows2000hotfix.asp*.

Follow these steps to apply the update:

1. Double-click Msp2wizi.exe to begin installing the update.
2. Click Yes to agree to the license agreement.
3. Files are copied to your system, and you're prompted to ensure that the Proxy Server 2.0 source files are available before continuing. Click Continue to apply the update.
4. Click Continue to begin the installation of Proxy Server 2.0, and respond to any prompts that appear.

> **Caution** Applying the Proxy Server 2.0 Update for Windows 2000 automatically begins the installation of Proxy Server 2.0. Be sure that the source files are available.

Restoring the Proxy Server 2.0 Configuration

Should you need to recover the old Proxy Server 2.0 environment, you can execute a restore process.

To restore the data, complete the following steps:

1. Open the Proxy Server Management console.
2. Right-click Winsock Proxy and then click Properties.
3. Click Server Restore and then select the backup file to restore.
4. Click OK to finish the restore and then close the console.

Performing an Upgrade to ISA Server 2000

Before upgrading Proxy Server 2.0 to ISA Server, be sure to follow the prerequisite steps listed above, which ensure the environment is prepared for the upgrade. Take these actions to perform the upgrade from Proxy Server 2.0 to ISA Server 2000:

- Back up your Proxy Server to collect all current configuration data as described in the text above.

- Stop all Proxy Server services as described in the following section.
- If the server is a member of an array, remove the server from its array before continuing with the upgrade as described in "Removing a Proxy 2.0 Server from an Array" in this chapter.

Note See Microsoft Knowledge Base article 253131, "How to Install Proxy Server 2.0 on Windows 2000" at *http://support.microsoft.com/?kbid=253131* for more information.

Stopping Proxy 2.0 Server Services

To stop each of the Proxy Server services, you may either use a command line or the Services console.

To stop Proxy Server services from a command line, follow these steps:

1. Open a command prompt.
2. Use the net stop service command to stop individual services:
   - To stop the Proxy Server Administration service, type **net stop mspadmin**.
   - To stop the Proxy Alert Notification service, type **net stop mailalrt**.
   - To stop the Winsock Proxy service, type **net stop wspsrv**.
   - To stop the World Wide Web Publishing service, type **net stop w3svc**.

Tip Stop the Proxy Server Administration service first. By doing so, the Proxy Alert Notification service also stops because of its dependency on the Proxy Server Administration service.

3. Close the command prompt window by typing **exit**.

To stop Proxy Server services from the Services console, follow these steps:

1. Open the Services console. The Services console can be opened from the Administrative Programs group in the Control Panel.
2. Right-click each service named in Step 2 above and then click Stop.
3. Repeat Steps 1 and 2 for each service until all have been stopped.
4. Close the Services console.

Removing a Proxy 2.0 Server from an Array

When you have multiple Proxy 2.0 servers configured in an array, disjoin each member from its array before upgrading to ISA Server 2000.

Note When the Proxy 2.0 server is disjoined from an array, the rules and configuration settings from the array are stored locally on the server.

To disjoin a Proxy server from an array, complete the following steps:
1. Open the Internet Services Manager.
2. Right-click the Proxy Server service icon and then click Properties.
3. Click the Array button.
4. If you launched Internet Services Manager from a different system, select the Proxy Server to remove and then click Remove From Array. If you launched Internet Services Manager from the Proxy Server you are removing from the array, click Leave Array.
5. Click OK.
6. Close the Internet Services Manager.

Installing ISA Server to Upgrade Proxy Server 2.0

For detailed instructions on installing ISA Server 2000, refer to the steps outlined in Chapter 2, "Installing and Configuring ISA Server 2000." This section points out only the unique differences that occur when upgrading from Proxy Server 2.0.

- When the installation begins, the installation program detects that a previous version is installed and asks you to take one of two actions:

  - Click OK to replace the previous upgrade. This option overwrites the existing Proxy Server 2.0 installation with ISA Server.

  - Click Change Folder to install a new version in a different folder (as shown in Figure 5-1). This option allows you to retain the Proxy Server 2.0 while installing the new ISA Server configuration. When presented with the default directory for the ISA source, click OK to accept the default directory or *C:\msp* to replace the Proxy Server 2.0 installation; your path may differ based on where your Proxy Server 2.0 installation is installed.

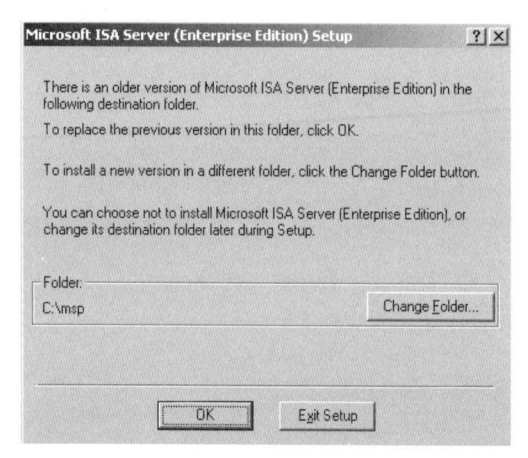

Figure 5-1. *ISA setup prompts you to overwrite a Proxy Server 2.0 installation.*

- The next unique dialog box, which is not seen during a typical ISA Server installation, asks whether you wish to migrate Proxy Server policies and settings to an ISA Server policy as shown in Figure 5-2. Click Yes to accept and continue with the upgrade.

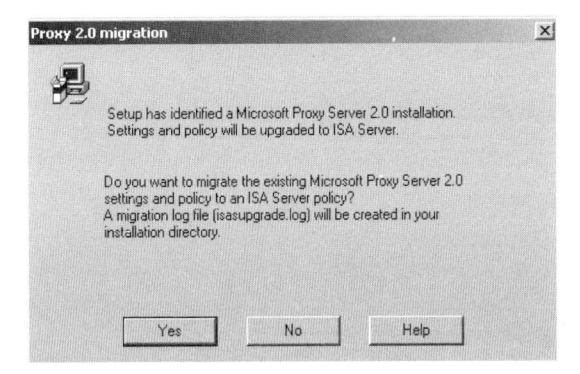

Figure 5-2. *When upgrading from Proxy Server 2.0, you're asked if you wish to migrate settings to an ISA Server policy.*

- Because ISA Server—unlike Proxy Server 2.0—doesn't require that Internet Information Services (IIS) be installed on the ISA server, when the upgrade stops server services, all IIS services stop as well. You'll be prompted to either reconfigure IIS or remove it completely after the upgrade is completed. Figure 5-3 displays this message. Click OK to continue.

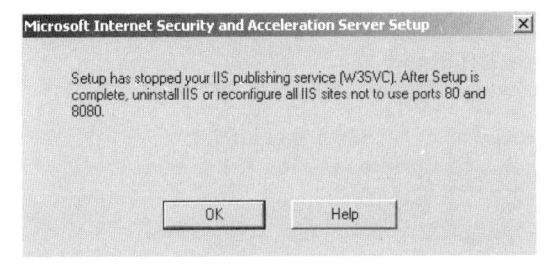

Figure 5-3. *After the upgrade is complete, you're asked if you want to reconfigure IIS or remove it.*

Note The change of ISA Server not requiring IIS is detailed later in the chapter in the section entitled "Reconfigure IIS After Installing ISA Server." Best practices recommend not running IIS on your ISA server.

- The remainder of the upgrade is exactly like performing a clean ISA Server installation, as described in Chapter 2.

Differences Between Proxy Server and ISA Server

After you've completed your upgrade, adjust your installation to accommodate some differences between the old Proxy Server 2.0 environment and your new ISA Server environment.

Configure the Outbound Web Requests Listener

When administering Proxy Server 2.0, the Web proxy listens on port 80 for outbound requests from internal clients. After upgrading to ISA Server, the outbound Web requests listener is changed to default to port 8080. In some environments this change can cause problems. Instead of modifying each client on your network, you have the option to change the Outbound Web Requests Listener back to port 80.

To change the Outbound Web Requests Listener, follow these steps:

1. Open the ISA Management console.
2. In the left pane, right-click the name of your ISA server and then click Properties.
3. Select the Outgoing Web Requests tab.
4. In the TCP Port box, type the new port number and then click OK.
5. When prompted to restart the services, select Save The Changes And Restart The Service(s), and then click OK.

Be Aware of Differences Between the Winsock Client and the ISA Firewall Client

ISA Server 2000 introduces a new Winsock client known as the firewall client. When upgrading Proxy Server 2.0 to ISA Server, you don't have to upgrade your Winsock clients in order for clients to work with ISA Server. The Proxy 2.0 Winsock client is compatible with ISA Server.

> **Note** Best practices recommend upgrading Winsock clients to firewall clients. If you do plan to upgrade to firewall clients, ensure that no 16-bit operating systems in your environment require it, as the firewall client doesn't support 16-bit platforms.

For deployment methods, see Chapter 3, "Installing and Configuring Microsoft ISA Server 2000 Clients."

Configure Published Servers as SecureN Clients for Convenience

Winsock clients were necessary in order to publish an int users when running Proxy 2.0 Server. Using the Winsock ing an INI file—Wspcfg.ini—for every published server on y With ISA Server, the pain of configuring published servers is gone. To co a published server, you may simply make it a SecureNAT client. In a network with a single network segment, this implies that the default gateway IP address on the published server should be set to your ISA Server's internal IP address. Although you can still configure a published server with the firewall client (or a Proxy 2.0 Winsock client), we recommend that you configure each server to be published as a SecureNAT client for greater manageability. Therefore, after performing an upgrade to ISA Server, uninstall the Winsock client and configure each server as a SecureNAT client.

To remove the Proxy 2.0 Winsock client, click Start, select Programs, select Microsoft Proxy Client, and then click Uninstall.

Reconfigure IIS After Installing ISA Server

Proxy Server 2.0 was integrated with IIS and the World Wide Web Publishing service. ISA Server doesn't maintain the dependency on IIS, so, after performing an upgrade, removing IIS helps to eliminate some known issues when ISA Server and IIS coexist on the same server. If you can't separate the two functions, you might reconfigure IIS's default Web site to listen on a unique port other than port 80.

To reconfigure the default Web site port value, follow these steps:

1. Open the Internet Services Manager.
2. In the left pane, click the plus sign (+) to expand the name of your IIS server, expand Web Sites if necessary, right-click Default Web Site, and then click Properties.
3. In the Web Site tab, in the TCP Port field, type a new port number that's unique across all running Web sites on that system, and then click OK.

Tip To determine open ports, you can use a utility known as Netstat. From a command prompt, type **netstat -na** to display all ports currently in use by the computer.

Additional Resources

Consult Microsoft Knowledge Base article KB271471, "Firewall Client-Based Client Computers Are Unable to Access Resources," at *http://support.microsoft.com/?kbid=271471* for more information on this topic.

Chapter 6
Monitoring and Reporting

Effective administration of Microsoft ISA Server requires the ability to monitor activities related to ISA Server services, user sessions, triggered alerts, and events. Reporting allows administrators to make sense of the information that ISA Server captures in order to help audit the computing environment and make appropriate business decisions. In this chapter we examine each of ISA Server's monitoring and reporting capabilities.

Services

Five services, or specialized processes, provide ISA Server functions:

- **Microsoft ISA Server Control** Controls restarting other services when needed—the main service
- **Microsoft Firewall** Acts as a proxy for Winsock applications run by firewall clients
- **Microsoft Web Proxy** Gives any CERN-compatible browser the ability to connect to Internet content
- **Microsoft H.323 Gatekeeper** Enables H.323 clients, like Microsoft NetMeeting, to connect to Internet resources
- **Microsoft Scheduled Cache Content Download** Directly updates the ISA Server cache with Hypertext Transfer Protocol (HTTP) content

We discuss each of these services in more detail below.

Monitoring ISA Server Services

You can monitor ISA Server services through three interfaces:

- ISA Management console
- Services console
- Command line

Service Monitoring in ISA Management Console

The ISA Management console allows administrators to manage all aspects of ISA Server, including monitoring of services.

To check the status of a service, follow these steps:

1. Open the ISA Management console.
2. In the left pane, expand the branch under your ISA server. Click the plus sign (+) to expand Monitoring.
3. Click Services.

From the Services container, you have the ability to view certain properties on three of the ISA services:

- Web Proxy
- Firewall
- Scheduled Content Download

As illustrated in Table 6-1, you can collect a variety of information about each ISA service.

Table 6-1. Column Information Provided for Monitoring Services

Column	Description
Server	Identifies the specified ISA Server.
Service	Identifies three ISA Server services: Web Proxy, Firewall, Scheduled Content Download.
Status	Provides status of service. Status is shown as Running or Stopped.
Number Of Sessions	Identifies current number of sessions in use per service.
Service-Up Time	Identifies length of time service has been in a running state.

To start or stop any one of the three services, right-click the service name and then choose Start or Stop from the shortcut menu.

Services Console

One service clearly absent from the Services container in the ISA Management console is the ISA Server Control service. To manage the ISA Server Control service or the H.323 Gatekeeper service, you must use the Services console found within the Administrative Tools menu. Of course, you may also directly administer the Firewall, Web Proxy, and Scheduled Content Download services from the Services console, as well.

Note Since the ISA Server Control service is the parent service to the Microsoft Firewall service, the Microsoft Web Proxy service, and the Microsoft Scheduled Cache Content Download service, you can quickly bring down an ISA server by simply stopping the ISA Server Control service.

Command-Line Service Management

Besides using the ISA Management console or the Services console, you can also control ISA Server services from the command line. To start or stop a service from the command line, type **net start** *servicename* or **net stop** *servicename*. Table 6-2 identifies the executable name of each ISA Server service.

Table 6-2. ISA Server Services Executable Names

ISA Server Service	Service Executable Name
Microsoft ISA Server Control	Isactrl
Microsoft Firewall	Fwsrv
Microsoft Web proxy	W3proxy
Microsoft H.323 Gatekeeper	Gksvc
Microsoft Scheduled Content Download	W3schdwn

To stop the firewall service, for example, you can type **net stop**.

Sessions

A group of connections to the ISA servers from a particular client is known as a *session*. ISA Server lets you quickly see the users with active sessions and the type of connection or connections that client is making.

Monitoring Sessions

As soon as you make Internet access available to the end users in your organization, you'll find that you need to know which users are connected to ISA Server and whether they're connected as firewall clients, SecureNAT clients, Web proxy clients, or all three.

To view active sessions, complete the following steps:

1. Open the ISA Management console.
2. In the left pane, click the plus sign (+) to expand the Monitoring container.
3. Select Sessions. All active sessions appear in the console's right pane.

The right pane contains six descriptive columns on active sessions. Table 6-3 illustrates the type of information you can gather from the Sessions container.

Table 6-3. Session Information

Title	Description
Server	Identifies the specified ISA Server.
Session Type	Identifies the session type: Web Session or Firewall Session.
User Name	Displays the authenticated user name.
Client Computer	Displays the authenticated computer name.
Client Address	Displays the authenticated computer's Internet Protocol (IP) address.
Activation	Provides the date and time the session was activated.

Determining Session Type

As we saw in Chapter 3, "Installing and Configuring Microsoft ISA Server 2000 Clients," there are three types of ISA Server clients:

- SecureNAT
- Web proxy
- Firewall

Since each of these clients is able to pass Internet requests to ISA Server, as a network administrator, it's beneficial for you to know who's connected and how they're connected.

Session types appear only in the form of a firewall session or Web session. The characteristics of each type of client session depend on authentication.

- An authenticated SecureNAT session is displayed as a firewall session with no user name shown in the User Name column.
- An authenticated SecureNAT session is displayed as a firewall session with only the IP address shown instead of a computer name in the Client Computer column.
- An authenticated firewall session is displayed as a firewall session with the name of the user and computer shown.
- An authenticated Web session is displayed as a Web session with the user name shown and the computer name not shown.

Aborting Sessions

You can abort, or disconnect, a session in various ways. Since the ISA Management console provides two views for administering ISA Server, the way each network administrator performs a daily task might vary. We normally show only the Advanced view, but in this case we first show you how to disconnect or abort a session in Taskpad view, since it has some additional options available.

To disconnect a session, follow these steps:
1. Select the session to disconnect.
2. Click the Disconnect A Session icon (the disconnect occurs immediately without warning).

To abort a session, follow these steps:
1. Select the session to abort.
2. Open the Action menu and then select Abort Session.

When using the Advanced view, you'll find that the Disconnect A Session icon isn't available; instead, you can right-click the session and click the Abort Session option on the shortcut menu.

Aborting an active session becomes more important when you're changing rules and policies. For example, you reconfigure a protocol rule to use Users And Groups for outbound Internet access. During the day you decide to remove access from a group that currently has access. After you remove the group, you notice that users in that group can still access the Internet. If any of those users in the group have an active session on the ISA Server when you make a policy change, the users are allowed to remain on the Internet until they end their sessions. You can abort those users' sessions so that Internet access will immediately be denied to the group.

Events

You accomplish event monitoring in ISA Server through the Event Viewer, a built-in administrative tool. In this section we explore first how to monitor and then analyze events. To open the Event Viewer, select Event Viewer from the Administrative Tools menu.

Monitoring Events

You can start and stop ISA Server services through the ISA Management console, the Services Microsoft Management Console (MMC), or from a command line. Each time a service status changes, an event is created. All ISA Server events are written to the Application log in Event Viewer. As a network administrator, whether you're determining a cause of a problem or merely checking on past server activity, the Event Viewer is your primary resource.

In the section of this chapter entitled "Alerts" we take an in-depth look at the role of alerts in ISA Server. All 45 alerts are preconfigured to write an event to the Windows 2000 application log. Because of the variety of events maintained in Event Viewer, it's nearly impossible to gain knowledge of each type of ISA Server event. For many network administrators, knowing the meaning of every event isn't as important as knowing where to find the information to resolve the event. Microsoft has collected lists of event messages for each of the ISA services and has made those events available in the ISA Server Help. To locate more information on a specific event, open ISA Server Help and type **Event Messages** into the search field. From the ISA help file, you can then find more events in the following categories:

- Alert
- Bandwidth
- Caching
- Common service
- Dial-up connection
- Intrusion detection
- ISA Server control service
- ISA Server firewall service
- ISA Server Web proxy service
- Log
- Packet filter
- Server

Analyzing Events

In the Microsoft Knowledge Base, located at *http://support.microsoft.com/*, you can perform searches against an indexed catalog of support articles related to ISA Server. As most event descriptions seem cryptic, your search results against the Microsoft Knowledge Base will help discover support articles that provide more detailed explanations of the problem, cause, and resolution.

> **Note** A great way to stay informed of events is to implement an event monitoring solution such as Microsoft Operations Manager 2000, which makes available an application pack specifically for ISA Server. For more information on Microsoft Operations Manager, visit *http://www.microsoft.com/mom/*.

Alerts

Alerts give network administrators a way to proactively assess the security of the ISA Server. By default, there are 45 predefined alerts. These alerts offer information on a variety of events such as IP Packet Dropped, POP Intrusions, and Service Shutdown.

Creating an Alert

The most basic step in this process is to create an alert for the first time.

To create a new alert, follow these steps:

1. Open the ISA Management console.
2. In the left pane, click the plus sign (+) to expand Monitoring Configuration.

Chapter 6   Monitoring and Reporting | 89

3. Right-click Alerts, click New, and then click Alert.
4. On the Welcome To The New Alert Wizard page, type a name that represents the type of alert you'll create. Click Next.
5. On the Events And Conditions page, select an event that will trigger the alert from the drop-down list. Click Next.

Note   Some events have additional conditions that you may select. For example, clicking DNS Intrusion from the event list gives you the ability to specify an additional condition, which allows you to specify that an alert be triggered only when a Domain Name System (DNS) intrusion of type Hostname Overflow is met.

6. On the Actions page, select one or more actions you'd like to execute when the alert is triggered. The five actions alerts can trigger are:

   - Sending an e-mail message
   - Running a program
   - Reporting the event to a Windows 2000 event log
   - Stopping selected ISA services
   - Starting selected ISA services

Note   You must select at least one action or the New Alert Wizard won't continue.

The following sections provide instructions for configuring each of the possible actions.

Sending an E-Mail Message

To inform you when an alert takes place on the machine, you might configure an Alert to send an e-mail to the address of your choosing by following these steps:

1. On the Actions page, select the Send An E-Mail Message check box.
2. On the Sending E-Mail Messages page, type the name of a Simple Mail Transfer Protocol (SMTP) server.

Note   The SMTP server could be either one available on your internal network or an external SMTP server that supports relaying.

3. In the From, To, and CC fields, type e-mail addresses of the people you'd like to notify when the alert is triggered. Many administrators send messages to cell phones and pagers that have e-mail addresses. Click Next.
4. On the Completing The New Alert Wizard page, click Finish.

> **Note** Configuring an Alert action to send an e-mail message allows the ISA Server administrator to be notified of intrusions even when away from the office.

Running a Program

You can configure an alert to start and run a program of your choosing by completing the following steps:

1. On the Actions page, select the Run A Program check box.
2. On the Running A Program page, type the directory path to the specific program intended to be executed. Select whether the program will be executed as a Local System Account or as a defined user name. If you select User Name, you can either type the name or browse to find the name in the selected directory database. To complete this stage of the wizard, you'll also be required to type in the password for the user name and then confirm the password. Click Next to continue.
3. On the Completing The New Alert Wizard page, click Finish.

Reporting the Event to a Windows 2000 Event Log

To keep all reporting consistent for your machine, you might want ISA Server to log its alerts into a centralized tracking location: the Windows 2000 Event Log.

To configure the Windows 2000 Event Log to capture alerts, follow these steps:

1. On the Actions page, select the Report The Event To A Windows 2000 Event Log check box. Click Next.
2. On the Completing The New Alert Wizard page, click Finish.

Stopping Selected ISA Server Services

You might need to start or stop an ISA Server service to allow changes to take place or to back up your system. To do that, follow these steps:

1. On the Actions page, select the Stop Selected ISA Server Services check box.
2. On the Stopping Services page, you can stop the following ISA services:
   - Firewall
   - Schedule Content Download
   - Web Proxy

   You can check the ISA services individually or choose the Select All or Clear All boxes. Click Next to continue.
3. On the Completing the New Alert Wizard page, click Finish.

Starting Selected ISA Server Services

Starting ISA Server services follows almost the same steps as stopping services. To start ISA Server services, follow these steps:

1. On the Actions page, select the Start Selected ISA Server Services check box.

2. On the Starting Service page, the options available are the same as choosing Stop Selected ISA Services. After making a selection, click Next to continue.
3. On the Completing The New Alert Wizard page, click Finish.

Note If you select multiple actions, the wizard loads pages for the actions in the order in which they're listed.

Configuring an Alert

After you've walked through the wizard to create a new alert, you can configure additional alert properties. By right-clicking any alert in the right-hand pane and then selecting Properties, you'll see the three tabs described in Table 6-4.

Table 6-4. Alert Configuration Options

Tab Name	Tab Description
General	Provides name, description, and a check box to enable or disable the alert.
Events	Provides the event and description of the event used in triggering the alert. Displays additional conditions if applicable. Contains the specific settings for defining how many times the event should occur before triggering the alert, along with how to handle recurring actions.
Actions	Provides check boxes for the five actions that can be used in notification when an alert is triggered.

Note You can right-click any alert regardless of whether your view is set to Taskpad or Advanced.

In the General tab you can enable or disable the alert. Microsoft has added a special icon—which looks like a red circle—to easily distinguish when an alert is disabled. By default, the following six alerts are disabled:

- Cached Object Discarded
- Event Log Failure
- IP Packet Dropped
- IP Protocol Violation
- Network Configuration Changed
- Server Publishing Is Not Applicable

Note In addition to enabling or disabling an alert through the General tab, the Action menu provides this capability along with the Enable/Disable icon on the menu bar.

The Events tab is important because it contains properties you can't configure using the Creating A New Alert wizard. From the Events tab, you can configure the items below:

- Number Of Occurrences Before The Alert Is Issued
- Number Of Events Per Second Before The Alert Is Issued
- Recurring Actions Are Performed
  - Immediately
  - After Manual Reset Of Alert
  - If Time Since Last Execution Is More Than *a certain number* Minutes

In the Actions tab you can modify the five types of actions that are executed when an alert is triggered. By default, all predefined alerts are configured to Report To The Windows 2000 Event Log.

Viewing Alerts

After you create a new alert, the next step is to verify that the alert is working properly. Expand the Monitoring Configuration node in the ISA Server Management console to create new and configure predefined alerts.

To view when an alert has been triggered, complete the following steps:

1. Open the ISA Management console.
2. In the left pane, click the plus sign (+) to expand Monitoring and then select Alerts.

Note The Monitoring container is for viewing alerts that have been triggered, whereas the Monitoring Configuration container is where you create and configure the alerts.

In the right pane you'll find a list of all alerts that have been triggered by some action that has occurred either on or against the ISA Server. The alerts themselves don't provide any significant information except for the alert type. In the right pane, whether in Taskpad or Advanced view, it's not possible to check the alert's properties to determine the exact root cause. The information you require to determine how to assess the situation is provided in the ISA Server Help files under the topic of Alert Event Messages. If the information provided by the alert doesn't assist in determining the exact cause, because all *predefined* alerts write to the Windows 2000 Event log, you can open up Event Viewer, locate the specific Event ID and description, and use Microsoft's Knowledge Base to find more information.

Resetting Alerts

After locating and investigating the root cause of alerts that have been triggered, your next step is to reset the alert so that ISA will continue to monitor against the event.

To reset an alert, follow these steps:

1. Open the ISA Management console.
2. In the left pane, click the plus sign (+) to expand Monitoring, and then select Alerts.
3. In the right pane, when using Taskpad view, a Reset Alert icon will be present.
4. To reset an alert when using Advanced view, right-click the specified alert and select Reset. ISA Server won't prompt for confirmation, and the alert will be reset immediately. You may also use the Action menu to reset a specified alert.

Note You can't reset an alert by right-clicking the alert in Taskpad view. You must be in Advanced viewing mode to perform the operation.

Reporting with ISA Server

One of the most common requests made to firewall administrators is to deliver reports: reports of Web usage by employees, of traffic through the firewall, and so on. ISA Server can provide an almost unlimited amount of information about ISA Server activity if you interrogate its logs. In this section we examine how to set up and access preconfigured ISA Server reports.

Tip If you choose to log to a database (as described later in this chapter), you can easily create custom reports using Access, Crystal Reports, or other tools.

Generating Reports

To ensure that you can generate reports, you'll need to configure the properties for your ISA Server's report jobs. Next, you'll create a job, review the types of reports, and verify that your report is created.

Reporting Job Properties

The first step in generating reports is to ensure that both reporting and log summaries are enabled. Both should be enabled by default. To view the properties of the reports, follow these steps:

1. Open the ISA Management console.
2. In the left pane, click the plus sign (+) to expand Monitoring Configuration.
3. Right-click Report Jobs and then click Properties.
4. You'll see two tabs, General and Log Summaries, which are explained in Table 6-5.

Table 6-5. Configurable Report Properties

Report Properties	Tab Selections
General tab	Ensure that the Enable Reports check box is selected. The Report Location defaults to ISAReports, a folder created inside the default ISA installation path (C:\Program Files\Microsoft ISA Server). You can leave the default folder or specify a folder on any other disk.
Log Summaries tab	Ensure that the Enable Daily And Monthly Summaries check box is selected. The Location Of Saved Summaries defaults to ISASummaries, a folder created inside the default ISA Server installation path noted above. As with ISAReports, you can leave the default folder or specify any folder on disk. In Number Of Summaries Saved, the default number of Daily Summaries is 35 and Monthly Summaries is 13. You can adjust the number of summaries (maximum is 999).

Creating a Report

Once you ensure that reporting and log summaries are enabled, you can create a report by completing the following steps:

1. Open the ISA Management console.
2. In the left pane, click the plus sign (+) to expand Monitoring Configuration.
3. Right-click Report Jobs, click New, and then click Report Job.
4. In the General tab, type a name and description of the report to be created. In this tab you can easily disable the report job by clearing the Enable check box.
5. In the Period tab, define the period of log activity that will be included in the report. The selections are daily, weekly, monthly, yearly, and custom. When specifying custom, you must type a start date and a stop date.
6. In the Schedule tab, specify when ISA Server should create the report job: either immediately or at a defined time that you set. You also configure the recurrence pattern by selecting Generate Once, Generate Every Day, Generate On The Following Days, or Generate Monthly. The recurrence pattern configures the report generator to create a new report based upon the reporting period specified.
7. In the Credentials tab, you must specify a user name, password, and the domain name of an account that has permissions to create the report.

Note If the ISA Server is part of an ISA Server array, the account you specify must have permissions on all members of the ISA Server array or the report will fail.

Report Types

There are five different categories of reports, each of which provides in-depth information on various aspects of ISA Server. Table 6-6 defines the five unique report categories located under the Reports container.

Table 6-6. Built-In Report Categories and Descriptions

Report Category	Description
Summary	Includes statistics of ISA Server usage including protocols, top users, and top Web sites. Generated from data collected in the firewall service and Web proxy service logs.
Web Usage	Includes statistics on top Web users, Web browsers, operating systems, and protocols. Generated from data collected in the Web proxy service logs.
Application Usage	Includes statistics from top application users, top applications, and top destinations. Generated from data collected in the firewall service logs.
Traffic & Utilization	Includes statistics on traffic, connections, daily traffic, and errors. Generated from data collected in the firewall service and Web proxy service logs.
Security	Includes statistics on authorization failures and dropped packets. Generated from data collected in the firewall service, Web proxy service, and packet filters logs.

Viewing Reports

Once the reports have been created and configured, the final step is to verify that ISA Server successfully created the report. To view a report created by the report generator, follow these steps:

1. Open the ISA Management console.
2. In the left pane, click the plus sign (+) to expand Monitoring, and then click Reports.

Note The right-hand pane displays all the available report jobs stored on the ISA Server. You cannot open and view the report file at the Reports container.

3. To open a report, expand Reports and click one of the five report type containers. For example, click Summary and in the right pane, double-click the report file. The report is launched in Internet Explorer or your configured browser as a Web page (.htm) file type.

Saving Reports

Reports can be saved as either a Web page (.htm) or Microsoft Excel Workbook (.xls) file type (as long as Excel is installed on the server).

To save a report as a Web page (.htm) file, follow these steps:

1. Open the ISA Management console.
2. In the left pane, click the plus sign (+) to expand Monitoring, click the plus sign (+) to expand Reports, and then select one of the five report type containers.
3. In the right-hand pane, right-click a report file and click Save As.
4. In the Save As dialog box, provide a name for the report and ensure that the Save As Type list displays Web Page (.htm).

To save a report as an Excel (.xls) file type, follow these steps:

1. Open the ISA Management console.
2. In the left pane, click the plus sign (+) to expand Monitoring and then click Reports.
3. In the right-hand pane, right-click a report job and select Save As.
4. In the Save As dialog box, provide a name for the report and ensure that the Save As Type displays Microsoft Excel Workbook (.xls).

Logging Transactions in ISA Server

ISA Server creates logs to gather all activity that takes place with the firewall service, the Web proxy service, and packet filters. These logs are the source of the reports generated in the previous section, and you can use them for further analysis and troubleshooting.

ISA Log Components

ISA creates logs for three different ISA services: Packet Filters, ISA Server Firewall Service, and ISA Server Web Proxy service.

You can recognize each of the three types of logs by their individual naming structure, as shown in Table 6-7.

Table 6-7. ISA Server Log Types

Log Component	File Format Type—Log Name
Packet Filters	W3C Extended–IPPEXTDyyyymmdd.log ISA Server file–IPPDyyyymmdd.log
ISA Server Firewall Service	W3C Extended–FWSEXTDyyyymmdd.log ISA Server file–FWSDyyyymmdd.log
ISA Server Web Proxy Service	W3C Extended–WEBEXTDyyyymmdd.log ISA Server file–WEBDyyyymmdd.log

The Ds in the log file names in Table 6-7 represents daily logs. Logs can also be created weekly (W), monthly (M), and yearly (Y). For example, if you were to view a log file stored in the C:\Program Files\Microsoft ISA Server\ISALogs\ folder with the name of WEBEXTM20030101.log, you can determine the exact type of the log file, as follows:

- WEB represents the ISA Server Web proxy service.
- EXT represents the log file format of W3C Extended.
- M represents a monthly log file.
- 20030101 represents the date the log file was created—January 1, 2003.

Configuring Logs

Logging is enabled and executed daily for each of the three components by default. To configure the logs, follow these steps:

1. Open the ISA Management console.

2. In the left pane, click the plus sign (+) to expand Monitoring Configuration and then select Logs.

3. The right pane displays the three components used for logging transactions:
    - Packet Filters
    - ISA Server Firewall Service
    - ISA Server Web Proxy Service

4. In the right pane, right-click a component and then click Properties. Two tabs are available.

    - The log tab provides a check box to enable or disable logging for the service. By default, the logging of the service is enabled. The Log tab also provides the option to log straight to a file (the default option) or to an ODBC database.

    - The Fields tab allows you to define the individual attributes of information that you'd like to be contained in the logs. The logging of individual fields is handled differently depending on the log file format used. The supported ISA Server log formats are shown in Table 6-8.

Table 6-8. ISA Server Log File Formats

Log File Format	Log Format Description	Field Handling
W3C Extended Log File Format	Tab-delimited—records time in GMT rather than local time.	Only selected fields are logged; unselected fields aren't logged.
ISA Server File Format	Comma-delimited—records time in local time.	All fields are logged regardless; unselected fields are logged as dashes.

Logging to a File

When logging to a file, you can configure a range of different parameters. For example, you can specify the log file format and how often logs are created—daily, weekly, monthly, or yearly.

For additional properties in the Log tab, click Options. ISA allows you to define the following settings:

- The location of the logs
- The compression of logs
- The ability to limit the number of logs to a specified number you set

By default, logs are stored in the ISALogs folder, which is created in the ISA Server installation folder. If you installed ISA Server with the default settings, the log file location would be C:\Program Files\Microsoft ISA Server\ISALogs\. Compression is enabled, and logs are limited to seven instances to conserve disk space.

Whether you choose to view the properties of the Packet Filters, ISA Server Firewall Service, or ISA Server Web Proxy Service, the configurable settings are similar.

Logging to a Database

Logging to a database adds an extra flexibility, especially for administrators managing ISA Server in a large enterprise environment. If you centrally store all the log file data from one or more ISA Servers into a single database—such as Microsoft SQL Server or Microsoft Access—you've greatly improved your ability to quickly query information you need to discover.

Configuring an ODBC database for logging involves several steps:

- Executing SQL scripts to configure the database.
- Defining an ODBC System data source name (DSN).
- Selecting Database as the log storage format.
- Providing an ODBC DSN, table name, and user account in the log component properties.

Executing SQL Scripts

Located on the ISA Server CD-ROM in the \ISA folder are three SQL scripts you can use to create the necessary database tables for sending ISA logs to an ODBC database. The SQL scripts are shown in Table 6-9.

Table 6-9. SQL Server Scripts for Creating Log Tables

SQL Filename	SQL File Description
Pf.sql	Defines the packet filter log table known as PacketFilterLog.
Fwsrv.sql	Defines the Firewall service log table known as FirewallLog.
W3proxy.sql	Defines the Web proxy service log table known as WebProxyLog.

To create the new database table in SQL Server 2000 for one of the three log components, complete the following steps:

1. Open the Query Analyzer from the Microsoft SQL Server program group, and connect to your SQL Server.

Caution For performance reasons, Microsoft recommends not placing SQL Server on the same server as ISA Server. SQL Server should be loaded on a separate server on the network.

2. From the Query menu, click Change Database. Select the database you will use to store the logs in, and click OK.
3. From the File menu, click Open. Select the SQL query file from the ISA Server installation CD, and click Open.
4. From the Query menu, click Execute to create the database table. After executing the query, you should receive a message saying The Command(s) Completed Successfully.

Defining an ODBC System DSN

The second step in logging to an ODBC database is to create a System DSN on the ISA Server. To do that, follow these steps:

1. Open the Data Sources (ODBC) console from the Administrative Tools program group.
2. Select the System DSN tab and then click Add.
3. Select a driver for the data source you'll be using. For example, you may choose either Microsoft Access Driver or SQL Server. Click Finish.
4. Complete the necessary information required to complete the Create New Data Source Wizard.

Configuring ISA to Log to an ODBC Database

In the next step, configure ISA Server to log to the database you designated in the steps above by following these steps:

1. Open the ISA Management console.
2. In the left pane, click the plus sign (+) to expand Monitoring Configuration and then select Logs.
3. In the right pane, right-click one of the three log components and select Properties.
4. In the Log tab, select Database.
5. Type the ODBC data source name and the table name. Click Set Account to provide the user name and password of an account that has the appropriate permissions.
6. Click OK.

> **Caution** You'll receive an error if your services can't log to the database. Check your account's access permissions to the SQL Server or other ODBC database. See Microsoft Knowledge Base article 300215, "ISA Services Do Not Start if They Are Unable to Log to the Database," at *http://support.microsoft.com/?kbid=300215* for more information.

After configuration is complete, the built-in reporting performed by ISA Server won't generate any data. When logging to an ODBC database, you'll have to manually create any reports you wish to use.

Additional Resources

Many companies provide robust and useful reporting solutions that work with ISA Server. Follow the links below to see various tools that will help expand ISA Server's reporting functionality.

- *http://www.microsoft.com/isaserver/partners/reporting.asp*
- *http://www.isaserver.org/software/ISA/Reporting/*

You may also want to consult the following articles, which can be found on Microsoft Knowledge Base; the articles' URLs are *http://support.microsoft.com/?kbid=article number* (insert the article number at the end of the URL).

- Article 258237, "All Logs in ISA Server Use GMT (UTC) Times"
- Article 278462, "How to Generate ISA Monthly Reports"
- Article 818032, "'The <Logname> Log or Alert Has Not Started...' Error Message When You Start ISA Server 2000 Performance Counter Logs"
- Article 293310, "No E-Mail Message Is Received After You Configure Monitoring Alerts to Send an E-Mail Message"
- Article 818036, "'The Remote Procedure Call Failed' Error Message Occurs When You Stop the Firewall Service"

Part II
Microsoft ISA Server 2000 Policy Management and Publishing Services

Part II deals with Microsoft ISA Server's policy and publishing capabilities. Chapter 7 covers the different policy elements and their purposes and explains how they're used in inbound and outbound access policies. Chapter 8 focuses on defining an access policy through the establishment of various rules: specifically, site and content rules and protocol rules, along with IP Packet filters and outbound authentication. Chapter 9 turns to inbound access through both server and Web publishing rules. Chapter 10 covers the most common types of published servers and the best way to make them accessible to external clients.

Chapter 7
Configuring ISA Policy Elements

ISA Server policy elements are an important component of defining an effective outbound access policy for your internal clients. Policy elements alone don't allow or deny users' access to Internet resources, but they do function as the building blocks of ISA Server rules. In this chapter we define all seven of the policy elements, describe best practices for their use, and explain how to implement them in your environment.

There are seven ISA Server policy elements:

- Schedules
- Destination sets
- Client address sets
- Protocol definitions
- Content groups
- Dial-up entries
- Bandwidth priorities

Policy Elements Explained

Policy elements alone don't make an access policy. Site and content rules and protocol rules employ policy elements to further control when, what, and how users connect to Internet resources.

Understanding what function policy elements perform within an access policy is the first step toward knowing how best to use them. Table 7-1 explains each of the seven policy elements and defines the access policy rules with which they are associated.

Table 7-1. Policy Element Definitions

Policy Element	Description	Associated Rules
Schedules	Define the time of day and day of the week when Internet access is allowed or denied.	Site and content rules, protocol rules, and bandwidth rules
Destination sets	Specify a range of computers through the use of host names, Internet Protocol (IP) addresses, domain names, or paths and file names.	Site and content rules, bandwidth rules, Web publishing rules, and routing rules
Client address sets	Define connections based on a single client IP address or range of addresses.	Site and content rules, protocol rules, bandwidth rules, server publishing rules, and Web publishing rules
Protocol definitions	Specify connections based on application layer protocols, which are defined by port number, transport protocol, direction of the request, and remote procedure call (RPC) interfaces.	Protocol rules
Content groups	Define content of Web sites based on file extensions or Multipurpose Internet Mail Extensions (MIME) types.	Site and content rules and bandwidth rules
Dial-up entries	Identify a connection created in the Network And Dial-Up Connections interface of the ISA server.	Routing rules and firewall chaining
Bandwidth priorities	Define priority levels between 1 and 200 for inbound and outbound access; the higher number provides higher priority.	Bandwidth rules

Serving Multiple Purposes

ISA Server enables the administrator to control both outbound and inbound access policies. The use and meaning of policy elements changes based on the type of policy in which they're used. For example, when using a client address set in an outbound access policy, the clients represent internal workstations. When used in an inbound access policy (Publishing), client address sets represent external workstations accessing resources on your network from the Internet. To create the most effective policies, become familiar with the uses for each policy element and learn how best to utilize its capabilities.

Enterprise Policies and Policy Elements

When using Array or Enterprise policies, you can configure only certain policies at the Enterprise level. If you try to administer these policy elements at the server level, you receive a warning, as shown in Figure 7-1.

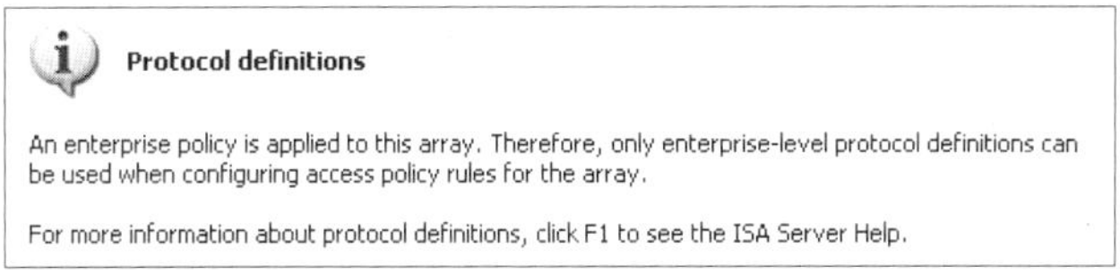

> **(i) Protocol definitions**
>
> An enterprise policy is applied to this array. Therefore, only enterprise-level protocol definitions can be used when configuring access policy rules for the array.
>
> For more information about protocol definitions, click F1 to see the ISA Server Help.

Figure 7-1. *If you're using an Enterprise policy, when you attempt to modify policy elements at the server, you see this warning.*

Array-level rules can use both Enterprise-level and Array-level policy elements; however, stand-alone installations can define and use only Array-level policy elements. Policy elements that can be defined at the Enterprise level include:

- Schedules
- Destination sets
- Client address sets
- Protocol definitions
- Content groups

Schedules

Use schedules to define the periods throughout the day or night when access to the Internet is allowed or denied. By default, ISA Server ships with two predefined schedules:

- **Weekends** Allow access all day Saturday and Sunday (midnight Saturday morning through midnight Sunday evening).
- **Work Hours** Allow access from 9 A.M. to 5 P.M., Monday through Friday.

Creating New Schedules

Creating new schedules allows you to precisely control when users can connect to Internet resources. To create a new schedule, follow these steps:

1. Open the ISA Management Console.
2. Click the plus sign (+) next to Policy Elements to expand the node. Right-click the Schedules object, select New, and then select Schedule.
3. Type a name for the schedule and, if you prefer, provide a description.

4. By default a schedule allows access 7 days a week, 24 hours a day. Click and drag the selected periods of the day(s) you wish to exclude, and then select the Inactive option to set your new schedule.

> **Note** Schedules are defined on an hourly basis. You can't set schedules for anything shorter than one hour.

5. Click OK to complete the creation of your new schedule.

Deleting Schedules

With the proper planning, deleting schedules should be a rare occurrence, but often management might hand you new restrictions to force you to either delete or modify existing schedules.

To delete an existing schedule, complete the following steps:

1. Select the Schedules node in the left pane of the ISA Management console.

2. In the right pane, select the appropriate schedule, and then click Delete.

> **Note** In taskpad view, you can highlight the appropriate schedule and then click the Delete A Schedule icon.

3. In the Confirm Delete dialog box, ensure that the check box Verify That No Rules Use This Element is selected, and then click Yes.

> **Caution** If an existing rule uses the policy element, ISA Server can't delete the object and so displays an error. You can click Details to determine which rule is using the policy element you're trying to delete. Click Continue to close the ISA Error window.

Adjusting Existing Schedules

You can easily adjust schedules within the ISA Management console by following these steps:

1. Select Schedules in the left pane of the ISA Management console.
2. In the right pane, double-click the appropriate schedule.
3. In the General tab, you can alter the name and description.
4. In the Schedule tab, you can choose to define new periods of activity or inactivity.
5. Click OK to complete your modifications.

Destination Sets

Destination sets generally define the location of content that clients wish to access. This policy element can indicate destinations inside your network or external destinations for Internet content. For your outbound policy, destination sets define computers outside your internal network. These computers are referenced by IP addresses (either an individual address or a range) or by Domain Name System (DNS) names (fully qualified domain names, like *.northwindtraders.com).

For inbound access policies (or publishing rules), destination sets indicate local network resources that will be accessed from clients on the Internet. Table 7-2 illustrates the options that are available when you're creating a destination set and explains how best to configure each field when using a destination set for either outbound or inbound access control.

Table 7-2. Destination Set Properties and Explanations

Field Settings	Outbound Access Explanation	Inbound Access Explanation
Destination	Defines the host name or domain located outside your internal network.	Used when publishing internal resources; defines the host name or domain in your internal network.
IP Addresses	Define the IP or range of IP addresses located outside your internal network.	Used when publishing internal resources; define the IP address or range of IP addresses located in your internal network.
Path	Defines the files on the external host. The path is applicable only when using Hypertext Transfer Protocol (HTTP).	Defines the file access to the host located in your internal network.

Note Be sure to verify that you're using the right destination sets for internal and outbound rules.

Creating New Destination Sets

Create a new destination set to specify destinations to which you wish to permit or deny access. To create a destination set, follow these steps:

1. Open the ISA Management console.
2. Click the plus sign (+) next to Policy Elements to expand the node, right-click Destination Sets, select New, and then select Set.
3. Type a name for the destination set and type a description if you desire.
4. Click Add.

5. On the Add/Edit Destination page, your choices are to add a destination based on a fully qualified domain name (FQDN) or IP addresses. Wildcards are acceptable for the FQDN destinations. You may also use a single IP address by typing it in the From field only. For more details on how to configure the settings on this page, refer to Table 7-2.
6. In the Path field, you can further define what directories or files are available for the computers identified by domain name or IP addresses.
7. Click OK when you've provided the necessary information.
8. To configure additional computers within the same destination set, repeat Steps 4-7 as necessary.
9. Click OK to finish.

Deleting Destination Sets

You might need to delete a destination set because it's no longer used. Follow these steps to delete a destination set.

1. Select Destination Sets in the left pane of the ISA Management console.
2. In the right pane, right-click the appropriate destination set and then click Delete.

Note In taskpad view, you can highlight the appropriate destination set and click the Delete A Destination Set icon.

3. In the Confirm Delete dialog box, ensure that the check box Verify That No Rules Use This Element is selected, and then click Yes.

Caution If a rule is using the policy element, ISA Server displays an error because it can't delete the object. You can click Details to determine which rule is using the policy element you're trying to delete. Click Continue to close the ISA Error window.

Configuring Destination Sets

Once you've defined a destination set, you might need to alter it to include or remove certain destinations. To modify a destination set, follow these steps:

1. Select Destination Sets in the left pane of the ISA Management console.
2. In the right pane, double-click the appropriate destination set.
3. In the General tab, you can alter the name and description.
4. In the Destinations tab, you can add, edit, and remove individual destinations. When editing a destination, reconfigure the appropriate fields based on the information provided in Table 7-2.
5. Click OK.

Client Address Sets

Client address sets use ranges of IP addresses to designate groups of computers. You'll use client address sets in both outbound and inbound access policies. The purpose of the client address set is illustrated in Table 7-3.

Table 7-3. Uses of the Client Address Set

Client Address Set Role	Explanation
Outbound Access Policy	Defines the computers located within your internal network and is used for controlling access to Internet resources
Publishing: Inbound Access	Defines the computers located outside your internal network and is used for controlling which computers can access published resources

Creating Client Address Sets

You'll need to define a group of computers by IP address. Be certain to gather the IP addresses for the clients you wish to define before beginning.

To create a client address set, follow these steps:

1. Open the ISA Management console.
2. Click the plus sign (+) next to Policy Elements to expand the node, right-click Client Address Sets, select New, and then click Set.
3. Type a name for the client address set and optionally type a description.
4. Click Add.
5. On the Add/Edit IP Addresses page, type a starting and ending IP address in the From and To fields, and then click OK.
6. Repeat Steps 4 and 5 as necessary to add IP address ranges to the client address set.
7. Click OK to finish.

Deleting Client Address Sets

You might need to delete a client address set because its IP addresses are no longer valid or needed. To delete an existing destination set, complete the following steps:

1. Select Client Address Sets in the left pane of the ISA Management console.
2. In the right pane, right-click the appropriate client address set and then click Delete.

Note In taskpad view, you can highlight the appropriate client address set and click the Delete A Client Set icon.

3. On the Confirm Delete page, leave the check box Verify That No Rules Use This Element selected and click Yes.

> **Caution** If a rule is using the policy element, ISA Server displays an error because it can't delete the object. You can click Details to determine which of the rules is using the policy element you're trying to delete. Click Continue to close the ISA Error window.

Configuring Client Address Sets

Once you've created a client address set, you might need to change, add, or remove IP addresses for the specified clients. To modify a client address set, follow these steps:

1. Select Client Address Sets in the left pane of the ISA Management console.
2. In the right pane, double-click the appropriate client address set.
3. In the General tab, you may alter the name and description if you choose.
4. In the Addresses tab, highlight the range of IP addresses you wish to modify, click Edit, and then type the new IP addresses in the From and To fields. You can also highlight a range of IP addresses and click Remove. Finally, you can add a new range of IP addresses by clicking Add.
5. Click OK to finish.

User Manager

When viewing client address sets in taskpad view, you have the option to open the User Manager console to administer both local and domain users and groups. User Manager allows you to configure which of the users or groups your outbound access policy will control. Actually selecting a user or group for access control is performed when creating a rule, which we discuss further in Chapter 8, "Configuring ISA Access Policy."

Protocol Definitions

ISA Servers delivers 87 predefined protocol definitions allowing different application communications. SecureNAT clients rely exclusively on the protocol definitions for access to applications and outbound communications. ISA Server application filters create 13 of the 87 protocol definitions. Application filters will create protocol definitions automatically, but you can also create them manually as needed. If you disable an application filter that a protocol definition relies upon, you'll disable the use of that particular protocol definition. In order to create a protocol definition, an understanding of the necessary information is required, as shown in Table 7-4.

Table 7-4. Protocol Definitions

Definition Field	Explanation
Port Number	Represents a port number between 1 and 65,535 that's used for the initial connection.
Protocol Type	Represents Transmission Control Protocol (TCP) or User Datagram Protocol (UDP).
Direction	Specifies how the communication is initiated between two parties. Selections include Send only, Receive only, Send Receive, Receive Send (for UDP protocol) or Inbound, Outbound (for TCP protocol).
Secondary Connection(s)	Certain protocols require additional connections to be established in order to fulfill communication requests. Selections include port numbers, protocol, and direction of the additional connections.

Creating Protocol Definitions

Before creating a protocol definition, you need to have the information about the protocol, as described in Table 7-4. To create a protocol definition, follow these steps:

1. Open the ISA Management console.
2. Click the plus sign (+) next to Policy Elements to expand the node, right-click Protocol Definitions, select New, and then click Definition.
3. Type a name for the protocol definition and then click Next.
4. Type the Port Number used by the definition, select the Protocol Type (TCP or UDP), select the Direction, and then select Next.
5. On the Secondary Connections page, if the definition requires secondary connections, select Yes, click New, and provide the Port Range, Protocol Type, and Direction. Click OK.
6. Click Next to continue.
7. Review the configuration and click Finish to complete.

Deleting Protocol Definitions

You can't delete the preconfigured protocol definitions that ship out of the box with ISA Server. It's possible, on the other hand, to delete custom-built protocol definitions.

To delete a custom protocol definition, complete the following steps:

1. Select Protocol Definitions in the left pane of the ISA Management console.
2. In the right pane, right-click the appropriate protocol definition and then click Delete.

> **Note** In taskpad view, you can highlight the appropriate protocol definition and then click the Delete A Protocol Definition icon.

3. On the Confirm Delete dialog, leave the check box Verify That No Rules Use This Element selected and then click Yes.

> **Caution** If a rule is using the policy element, ISA Server displays an error because it can't delete the object. You can click Details to determine which rule is using the policy element you're trying to delete. Click Continue to close the ISA Error window.

Configuring Protocol Definitions

You can modify only custom-built definitions. You can't edit any of the predefined protocol definitions.

To modify a protocol definition, follow these steps:

1. Select Protocol Definitions in the left pane of the ISA Management console.
2. In the right pane, double-click the appropriate protocol definition.
3. In the General tab, you can alter the name and description.
4. In the Parameters tab, you can modify the port number, protocol type, direction, and secondary connections as necessary.
5. Click OK to complete the modifications.

> **Note** You can't modify preconfigured protocol definitions. The only property that you can change on an existing protocol definition is the description. All other properties are unavailable, and appear dimmed.

Content Groups

Content groups allow the filtering of specific content that travels as an HTTP request or File Transfer Protocol (FTP) request tunneled within HTTP. The content consists of MIME types and file extensions.

There are eleven predefined content groups, as shown in Figure 7-2.

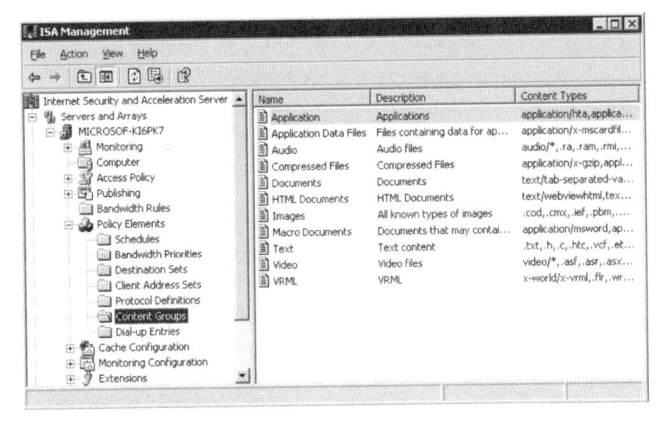

Figure 7-2. *ISA Server ships with eleven predefined content groups that cover a variety of common MIME types and file extensions.*

Creating Content Groups

Creating content groups gives you control of the various content types found in HTTP and FTP pages. Content groups aren't applied to Hypertext Transfer Protocol Secure (HTTPS) requests made by the internal clients.

To create a content group, follow these steps:

1. Open the ISA Management console.
2. Click the plus sign (+) next to Policy Elements to expand the node, right-click Content Groups, select New, and then click Content Group.
3. Type a name and, optionally, a description.
4. In the Available Types drop-down list box, specify each MIME type or file type to be included in the content group, and click Add to add it to the Selected Types list.
5. Repeat Step 3 as necessary to include additional content types.
6. Click OK.

Deleting Content Groups

Deleting a content group is a straightforward task; however, be cautious and confirm that the content group isn't being used by a current rule on the ISA server.

To delete a content group, complete the following steps:

1. Select Content Groups in the left pane of the ISA Management console.
2. In the right pane, right-click the appropriate content group and then select Delete.
3. On the Confirm Delete page, leave the check box Verify That No Rules Use This Element selected and then click Yes.

> **Caution** If an existing rule uses the policy element, ISA Server can't delete the object and so displays an error. You can click Details to determine which rule is using the policy element you're trying to delete. Click Continue to close the ISA Error window.

Configuring Content Groups

Once you've created content groups, you might need to make changes to add, redefine, or otherwise alter the composition of a group. To modify a content group, follow these steps:

1. Select Content Groups in the left pane of the ISA Management console.
2. In the right pane, double-click the appropriate content group.
3. In the General tab, you can alter the Name and Description.
4. In the Content Types tab, you can add file types or remove types by highlighting the file type and clicking Remove.
5. Click OK.

Dial-Up Entries

An ISA server doesn't require a persistent external connection to the Internet. ISA Server supports dial-on demand modem connections as an external interface. Dial-up entries are created to map a dial-on demand connection to the existing network dial-up connection created on the Windows 2000 Server or the Windows Server 2003 system.

> **More Info** For more information on creating network dial-up connections in Windows 2000 or Windows Server 2003, see *Microsoft Windows 2000 Administrator's Pocket Consultant* or *Microsoft Windows Server 2003 Administrator's Pocket Consultant*, both published by Microsoft Press and written by William R. Stanek.

Configuring a Network Dial-Up Connection on Windows 2000 Server

Before you can create a dial-up entry in ISA Server, you must already have or you must create a dial-up entry in the Network And Dial-Up Connections folder of the individual ISA server.

To see existing dial-up entries, follow these steps:

1. Click the Start button, select Settings, and then choose Control Panel.
2. Double-click the Network And Dial-up Connections icon.
3. Check to see if any dial-up entries exist.

If no dial-up entries exist, create one using these steps:

1. Double-click the Make New Connection icon. If necessary, provide your location information when prompted.
2. The Network Connection Wizard appears. Click Next.
3. Select the Dial-Up To The Internet option from the Network Connection Type page and then click Next. The Internet Connection Wizard appears.
4. Select the I Want To Set Up My Internet Connection Manually option, and then choose Next.
5. Choose the I Connect Through A Phone Line And A Modem option.

Note If your modem isn't configured, you'll need to set it up by using the Install New Modem wizard.

6. Enter the telephone number of the connection to which you're dialing and then click Next.
7. Enter the account and password necessary to authenticate to the dial-up service and then click Next.
8. Type a descriptive name in the Connection Name field and then click Next.
9. Choose No when prompted to set up an Internet mail account and then click Next.
10. Click Finish. Your server immediately tries to connect to the Internet. Ensure that the connection is successful.

Configuring a Network Dial-Up Connection on Windows Server 2003

Before you can create a dial-up entry in ISA Server, you must already have or you must create a dial-up entry in the Network And Dial-Up Connections folder of the individual ISA server. To see existing dial-up entries, follow these steps:

1. Click the Start button, select Control panel, highlight Network connections, and then select New Connection Wizard.
2. If no dial-up entries already exist, select New Connection Wizard. The New Connection Wizard appears. Click Next.
3. Select the Connect To The Internet option from the Network Connection Type page and then click Next.
4. Select Connect Using A Dial-Up Modem and then click Next.
5. Fill in the ISP Name field on the Connection Name page, and then click Next.
6. Enter the telephone number of the connection to which you're dialing, and then click Next.
7. On the Connection Availability page, select Anyone's Use, and then click Next.

8. On the Internet Account Information page, enter the account and password necessary to authenticate to the dial-up service, and then click Next.

9. Click Finish. Your server immediately tries to connect to the Internet. Ensure that the connection is successful.

Creating Dial-Up Entries

You must create a dial-up entry to map to an existing network dial-up connection that has been configured on the ISA server. To create a dial-up entry, follow these steps:

1. Open the ISA Management console.
2. Click the plus sign (+) next to Policy Elements to expand the node, right-click Dial-Up Entries, select New, and then click Dial-Up Entry.
3. Type a name and, optionally, a description.
4. Under Network Dial-up Connection, click Select to choose a configured network dial-up connection. After selecting a connection, click OK.

Caution For ISA arrays, the dial-up entries must be the same for each array member and the name of each network dial-up connection used by the dial-up entry must be identical to each array member. If you haven't configured a network dial-up connection before attempting to create a dial-up entry, you'll be presented with an error, "Only Network Dial-Up Connections That Exist On All Array Members Can Be Used. No Such Network Dial-Up Connections Exist."

5. Under Network Dial-Up Account, click Set Account. Either type the user name or click Browse to select the user account from the local server or domain. Type the password and confirm it, and then click OK.
6. Click OK to finish.

Deleting Dial-Up Entries

You might need to delete a dial-up entry when a network dial-up connection is no longer needed. To delete a dial-up entry, complete the following steps:

1. Select Dial-Up Entries in the left pane of the ISA Management console.
2. In taskpad view, in the right pane, select the appropriate dial-up entry and click Delete A Dial-Up Entry.

Note In Advanced view, you can't right-click the dial-up entry and click Delete. The Delete option isn't available.

3. Click Yes to confirm the deletion of the dial-up entry.

Note If you try to delete the dial-up entry set as the active entry, ISA won't allow you to delete the entry.

Configuring Dial-Up Entries

Modifications to a dial-up entry will be required if a new network dial-up connection has been created on the ISA server, and the new connection must be used for ISA to establish dial-on-demand access. To modify a dial-up entry, follow these steps:

1. Select Dial-Up Entries in the left pane of the ISA Management console.
2. In the right pane, double-click the appropriate dial-up entry.
3. In the General tab, you can alter the name and description.
4. In the Dial-Up Entry tab, you can alter the network dial-up connection used by the entry, along with the network dial-up account.
5. In the Bandwidth tab, you can select the Enable Bandwidth Control check box to manage the effective bandwidth for this connection. Type the effective bandwidth in kilobits per second.

Note The value you type for effective bandwidth should match the speed of the modem installed in the ISA server.

6. Click OK to complete the modifications.

Bandwidth Priorities

To paraphrase George Orwell, we all know that some users are more equal than others. When you have certain users or machines that need to have higher priority to Internet access, you'll want to use bandwidth priorities to configure the importance of a particular machine for either inbound or outbound bandwidth. Inbound bandwidth consists of requests from machines outside the network for content inside. Outbound bandwidth consists of requests from clients inside the network for Internet content.

Bandwidth priority ranges from 1 to 200. Any assigned bandwidth, by default, will have priority over any client that doesn't have any bandwidth assigned.

Creating Bandwidth Priority Entries

You can create bandwidth priorities to assign different levels of priority to select workstations for Internet access. Based on your access policy, one or more bandwidth priorities might be necessary.

To create a bandwidth priority entry, follow these steps:

1. Open the ISA Management console.
2. Click the plus sign (+) next to Policy Elements to expand the node, right-click Bandwidth Priorities, select New, and then click Bandwidth Priority.
3. Type a name and, optionally, a description.

4. Type a value between 1 and 200 for Outbound bandwidth.
5. Type a value between 1 and 200 for Inbound bandwidth.
6. Click OK to finish.

Deleting Bandwidth Priority Entries

Deleting a bandwidth priority might be necessary when changes have been made to your company's access policy. To delete a bandwidth priority entry, complete the following steps:

1. Select Bandwidth Priorities in the left pane of the ISA Management console.
2. In the right pane, right-click the appropriate bandwidth priority and then click Delete.
3. Click Yes to confirm the deletion of the bandwidth priority.

Configuring Bandwidth Priorities

You can adjust the outbound and inbound access priorities between values of 1 and 200, with the higher value taking priority. Over time, you might need to adjust the values.

To modify a bandwidth priority entry, follow these steps:

1. Select Bandwidth Priorities in the left pane of the ISA Management console.
2. In the right pane, double-click the appropriate bandwidth priority.
3. In the General tab, you can alter the name and description.
4. In the Bandwidth tab, you can alter the values for Outbound and Inbound bandwidth accordingly.
5. Click OK.

Additional Resources

The following resources provide additional information you may find helpful:

- Read about policy elements in the ISA Server 2000 Help Documentation.
- For scripting information, read more about the FPCPolicyElements Object in the MSDN library online at *http://msdn.microsoft.com/library*.
- Look for preconfigured destination sets at *http://www.isatools.org* and at *http://www.toolzz.com/ISAToolzz.htm*.
- There is helpful information in Microsoft Knowledge Base article 315667, "HOW TO: Configure an Enterprise Policy in ISA Server," at *http://support.microsoft.com/ ?kbid315667*.
- You can also check Microsoft Knowledge Base article 300492, "HOW TO: Prevent Users from Accessing Unauthorized Web Sites in ISA Server," at *http://support.microsoft.com/?kbid=300492*.

Chapter 8
Configuring ISA Access Policy

Microsoft ISA Server 2000 allows you to securely connect your company's network to the Internet by regulating the protocols, Internet sites, and content that your internal computers can access. Access policies apply to requests received from Web proxy, firewall, and SecureNAT clients.

An access policy consists of primary and ancillary components: primary components are required for an outgoing request to succeed; ancillary components influence the request for external content in some way. Primary components are protocol rules, site and content rules, IP packet filters, and policy elements. Ancillary components are routing rules, bandwidth rules, authentication, and outgoing Web requests.

Processing Outgoing Requests

For an outgoing request to succeed, your protocol rules and site and content rules must explicitly allow it and there must not be any rules that deny access to any part of the request. Deny rules take precedence over any configured allow rules in every circumstance except for Hypertext Transfer Protocol (HTTP) requests, where anonymous access is processed before a deny rule. Any outgoing request received by ISA Server is processed by the components in the order listed in Table 8-1.

Table 8-1. Order of Evaluation for Outgoing Requests

Order	Rule Evaluated	Request Allowed	Request Blocked
1	Protocol rules	Allow rule exists.	An allow rule doesn't exist, or there's an explicit deny rule.
2	Site and content rules	Allow rule exists.	An allow rule doesn't exist, or there's an explicit deny rule.
3	IP packet filters	Packet filters don't specifically block the request.	Packet filters are configured to block the request.

(continued)

Table 8-1. Order of Evaluation for Outgoing Requests *(continued)*

Order	Rule Evaluated	Request Allowed	Request Blocked
4	Routing rules (Web proxy client), or firewall chaining (firewall or SecureNAT clients)	Route request to Internet if available, or upstream server.	Route unavailable.

At any point during the processing of the request, ISA Server components can deny the request.

> **Note** The minimum requirements to enable access to a site require you to have an allow site and content rule in addition to a protocol rule that allows access. If you have a deny rule and an allow rule for the same site, the deny rule always takes precedence. Beyond deny rules overriding allow rules, no other ordering of site and content rules takes place.

Primary Access Policy Components

Primary components include protocol rules, site and content rules, IP packet filters, and policy elements. Protocol rules determine the protocols allowed in and out of your network, and site and content rules determine the destinations from which your clients can access content. Without defined and configured primary access policy components, your internal clients won't be able to access the Internet.

> **Note** As you learned in Chapter 7, "Configuring ISA Policy Elements," policy elements are the building blocks of protocol and site and content rules. We'll assume that you understand these policy elements in this chapter and already have configured them. If you haven't, please revisit Chapter 7.

Site and Content Rules

Site and content rules permit you to either allow or deny access to a site based on certain policy elements, which include destinations, schedules, client address sets, and content groups. In this section you'll learn how to create, delete, and configure site and content rules. Enterprise installations of ISA Server will change the way in which site and content rules operate, so you'll also see how this environment changes your requirements.

Creating a Site and Content Rule

At least one site and content rule is necessary to control access to particular sites. To create a site and content rule, follow these steps:

1. Open the ISA Management console.
2. If an Enterprise policy has been created, expand the Enterprise node, expand the Policies node, and then expand the Enterprise Policy node. Right-click Site And Content Rules, highlight New, and then select Rule.

Note If the ISA server is a stand-alone server, expand your ISA server node, and then expand Access Policy. Right-click Site And Content Rules, highlight New, and then select Rule. If the option to create a new site and content Rule isn't available at the server level, an enterprise policy is present and you need to create the site and content rule under the Enterprise node as described in Step 2.

3. Type a name to be given to the rule and then click Next.
4. On the Rule Action page, select the type of action this rule should perform—Allow or Deny—and then click Next.

Note If Deny is selected, you may redirect all denied requests to an internal Web site by selecting the If HTTP Request, Redirect Request To This Site check box and then typing the Uniform Resource Locator (URL) path for the site.

5. On the Rule Configuration page, configure how to control access based on destination, schedule, or type of client as shown in Table 8-2. Click Next to continue.

Table 8-2. Rule Configuration Page Properties

Rule Type	Policy Elements Used
Allow/Deny Access Based On Destination	You'll restrict access based on a computer name, a single IP address, or a range of IP addresses, which are known as destination sets and can also include a path. See "Configuring Destination Sets" in the ISA Server 2000 Help documentation for more information. Complete Step 6 and then skip to Step 9.
Allow/Deny Access Only At Certain Times	You'll allow or restrict access based on a schedule. Complete Step 7 and then skip to Step 9.
Allow Some/Deny Selected Clients Access To All External Sites	You'll allow or restrict access based on a client address set. Complete Step 8 and continue to Step 9.
Custom	You'll combine the elements used above with one another. Follow Steps 6–9 below.

6. On the Destination Sets page, select the destination set to apply to this rule, as shown in Table 8-3, and then click Next.

Table 8-3. Controlling Access Based on Destination Sets

Destination Type	Explanation
All Destinations	Applies to all destinations
All Internal Destinations	Applies to all destinations defined in the Local Address Table (LAT) or Local Domain Table (LDT)
All External Destinations	Applies to all destinations not defined in the LAT or LDT
Specified Destination Set	Applies to a custom destination set that you'll choose from a drop-down list
All Destinations Except Selected Set	Applies to all destinations excluding a custom destination set you choose from a drop-down list

7. If you choose a schedule option, choose a schedule from those available on the server.

Note You create and configure schedules in the Policy Elements node at either the Enterprise level (for Enterprise installations) or the Servers And Arrays level. See Chapter 7 for more information.

8. The Client Type address sets require you to specify the IP address of given computers to restrict access based on IP address or to specify certain groups and users. Maintain the default Any Request selection unless you have a well-documented reason for so doing.

Note If you chose Custom, you'll see each of these steps.

9. Review the rule configuration and click Finish.

Deleting a Site and Content Rule

Should you need to remove a site and content rule, complete the following steps:

1. In the left pane, select the Site And Content Rules node.
2. In the right pane, right-click the rule and then select Delete. When prompted, click Yes to confirm the deletion.

Note In taskpad view, you can also delete a rule by selecting the rule and clicking the Delete A Site And Content Rule icon.

Configuring a Site and Content Rule

When your environment or requirements change, you might need to alter an existing site and content rule. To do this, complete the following steps:

1. In the left pane, select the Site And Content Rules node.
2. In the right pane, double-click the rule.
3. Each of the property pages that were configured when a protocol rule was created is available to be modified.
4. Click OK when you've made the necessary modifications of the tabs explained in Table 8-4.

Table 8-4. Configuring a Site and Content Rule

Property Tab	Purpose
General	By default this rule is active and applies to all clients. Ensure that the rule is enabled.
Destinations	Choose your destination set from this tab.
Schedule	Choose your schedule from the drop-down menu.
Action	This tab allows you to specify whether you'll allow or deny the use of this machine based on testing.
Applies To	You specify the client address set, users, or groups to which the request should apply.
HTTP Content	You can use the HTTP Content tab to restrict Internet usage to content groups.

Enabling and Disabling a Site and Content Rule

At times you might need to enable or disable a site and content rule. For example, it might be needed only during certain times of the year, such as when year-end budgets are created, and your accounting department needs to have access to certain external sites.

To enable or disable a site and content rule, complete the following steps:

1. In the left pane, select the Site And Content Rules node.
2. Double-click the site and content rule, and in the General tab, select or clear the Enable check box.
3. A red down arrow icon appears for the disabled rule.

Protocol Rules

Protocol rules permit you to either allow or deny access to a site based on certain policy elements, which include destinations, schedules, client address sets, and content groups. In this section you'll learn how to create, delete, and configure protocol rules.

Creating a Protocol Rule

You'll need to create a protocol rule to control access for given protocols. To create a protocol rule, follow these steps:

1. Open the ISA Management console.
2. If an Enterprise policy has been created, expand the Enterprise node, expand the Policies node, and then expand your Enterprise policy. Right-click Protocol Rules, highlight New, and then select Rule.

> **Note** If the ISA server is a stand-alone server, expand your ISA server, and then expand Access Policy. Right-click Protocol Rules, highlight New, and then select Rule. If the option to create a new protocol rule isn't available at the server level, an enterprise policy is present and you need to create the protocol rule under the Enterprise node as shown in Step 2.

3. Type a name to be given to the rule and then click Next.
4. On the Rule Action page, select whether this rule should allow or deny client requests and then click Next.
5. On the Protocols page, select the types of protocols to which this rule applies (see Table 8-5 for more information), and then click Next.

Table 8-5. Protocols Available in Protocol Rules

Option	Explanation
All IP Traffic	This option applies to all Transmission Control Protocol/Internet Protocol (TCP/IP)-based traffic.
Selected Protocols	This option applies the rule to certain protocols from a list that will appear. Check the box next to the protocol to enable it.
All IP Traffic Except Selected	This option applies the rule to all, except certain protocols listed in a box that will appear. Check the box next to the protocol to enable it.

6. On the Schedule page, select a schedule and then click Next.
7. On the Client Type page, select the types of clients this rule applies to by selecting either Any Request, Specific Computers, or Specific Users And Groups, and then click Next.
8. Review the rule configuration and then click Finish to complete.

Deleting a Protocol Rule

You might need to remove a protocol rule when you no longer need it. To delete a protocol rule, complete the following steps:

1. In the left pane, select the Protocol Rules node.
2. In the right pane, right-click the protocol rule and then select Delete. When prompted, click Yes to confirm the deletion.

Note In taskpad view, you can also delete a protocol rule by selecting the Delete A Protocol Rule icon.

Configuring a Protocol Rule

When your environment or requirements change, you might need to alter an existing protocol rule.

To configure a protocol rule, follow these steps:

1. In the left pane, select the Protocol Rules node.
2. In the right pane, double-click the protocol rule.
3. The protocol rule Properties dialog box has five tabs, as described in Table 8-6.
4. Edit the properties of the protocol rule, and click OK when you've made the necessary modifications.

Table 8-6. Configurable Properties for Protocol Rules

Property Tab	Purpose
General	Allows you to enable or disable the rule and alter the rule's name.
Action	You can choose whether the rule will Allow or Deny requests.
Protocol	You'll specify the protocols to which the rule will apply.
Schedule	You'll choose either from a preexisting schedule or define a new one to specify at what times the rule will apply.
Applies To	You'll choose the clients specified by IP address, users, or groups.

To enable or disable a protocol rule, follow these steps:

1. In the left pane, select the Protocol Rules node.
2. Double-click the protocol rule, and in the General tab, select or clear the Enable check box.

Note A red down arrow icon appears for the disabled rule.

IP Packet Filters

IP packet filters regulate the deliveries of "packets"—or packages of information—to clients on your network. You have two options: either Allow Filters, which provide exceptions to the general rule to not allow anything, or Block Filters, which further restrict the ports onto which computers try to access information. In this section you'll learn how to create, delete, and configure IP packet filters. Figure 8-1 illustrates the IP packet filters defined out of the box.

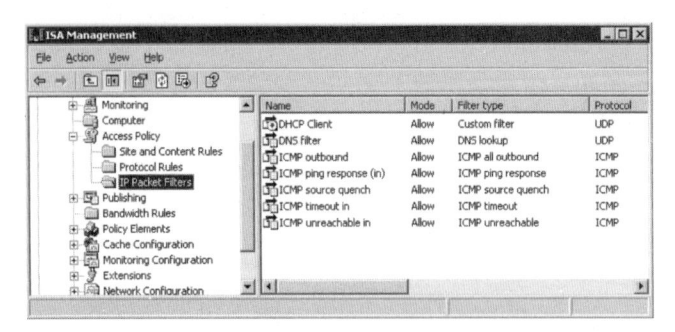

Figure 8-1. *ISA Server ships with predefined packet filters.*

Creating an IP Packet Filter

You might need to create customized packet filters to supplement the preexisting packet filters included with ISA Server.

To create a packet filter, complete the following steps:

1. Open the ISA Management console.

2. In the left pane, expand your ISA Server and then expand Access Policy. Then right-click IP Packet Filters, highlight New, and then select Filter.

3. Type a name to be given to the IP Packet Filter and then click Next.

4. If your have an array of servers, you'll see the Servers page. Set whether the filter should be used by all ISA Server Computers In The Array or select the Only This Server option button and select the ISA server. Click Next to continue.

5. On the Filter Mode page, select whether this packet filter will allow or block packet transmission, and then click Next.

6. On the Filter Type page, if you're creating a predefined filter based on one of ISA Server's 16 protocols, select the Predefined option button and select the protocol. If not, choose Custom. Click Next to continue.

7. If you chose Custom in Step 6, you'll see the Filter Settings page. You'll need to know the information shown in Table 8-7 to continue. Click Next when you've entered the appropriate information.

Table 8-7. Filter Settings

Setting	Available Options	Explanation
IP Protocol	Predefined protocols Any, ICMP, TCP, or UDP	Shows low-level protocols.
Direction	Both, Inbound, or Outbound	Determines the direction that allows access.
Local Port	All Ports, Fixed Ports, or Dynamic	Determines the port on which the filters will apply.
Remote Port	All Ports or Fixed Ports	Determines the ports on the client computers to which the rule applies.
Type	All Types or Fixed Type	Allows you to specify all types defined in Request for Comments (RFC) 1700 or identify a specific type.
Code	All Codes or Fixed Code	Allows you to specify all codes defined in RFC 1700 or identify a specific type.

Note The Type and Code fields are apparent only when ICMP is chosen as the IP Protocol.

8. On the Local Computer page, specify the IP address to which the packet filter applies. Click Next.

9. On the Remote Computers page, select the remote computers to which the packet filter applies. Select either All Remote Computers or Only This Remote Computer. If specifying Only This Remote Computer, type the IP address of the specific remote computer. Click Next to continue.

10. Review the IP packet filter configuration and click Finish to complete.

Deleting an IP Packet Filter

You might need to delete a customized packet filter if it's no longer needed. Remember that you won't be able to delete packet filters included with ISA Server.

To delete an IP Packet Filter, complete the following steps:

1. In the left pane, select the IP Packet Filters node.

2. In the right pane, right-click the IP packet filter and then select Delete. When prompted, click Yes to confirm the deletion.

Note In taskpad view, you can also delete an IP Packet Filter by clicking the Delete A Packet Filter icon.

Configuring an IP Packet Filter

You might need to change the configuration for a customized package filter when your needs or your environment, or both, change.

To modify an IP packet filter, complete the following steps:

1. In the left pane, select the IP Packet Filters node.
2. In the right pane, double-click the IP packet filter.
3. Each of the property pages that were configured when a packet filter was created is available to be modified. These pages are described in Table 8-8.
4. Click OK when you've made the necessary modifications.

Table 8-8. Configure IP Packet Filter Options

Property Tab	Purpose
General	Change the name of the Packet Filter here and select the Enable This Filter check box to enable it.
Filter Type	Change the type of filter by choosing from a predefined filter or by configuring a custom filter.
Local Computer	Define the computers (by IP address) to which the packet filter should apply.
Remote Computer	Designate the remote computers to which the IP packet filter will apply.

Follow these steps to enable or disable an IP Packet Filter:

1. In the left pane, select the IP Packet Filters node.
2. In the right pane, double-click the filter. In the General tab, clear the Enable This Filter check box and click OK.

Note A red down arrow icon appears for the disabled rule.

Ancillary Access Policy Components

Ancillary components include routing rules, bandwidth rules, authentication, outgoing Web requests, and ISA Server extensions. Routing rules determine whether clients will retrieve external objects directly from the destination, from an upstream server, or from an alternate site. Bandwidth rules determine the priority for specified clients. Authentication determines how rules are applied to certain types of clients.

Bandwidth Rules

Bandwidth rules determine what connections have precedence over others. They are used to regulate the flow of information through your organization's network connections. This is an important part of an Access Policy, as it determines how fast information will flow for certain clients. In this section you'll learn how to create, delete and modify a bandwidth rule.

Creating a Bandwidth Rule

You'll need to create a bandwidth rule in addition to the Default Rule provided with ISA Server to enable priority for any of your clients.

To create a bandwidth rule, follow these steps:

1. Open the ISA Management console.
2. In the left pane, right-click Bandwidth Rules, highlight New, and then select Rule.
3. Type a name to be given to the rule and then click Next.
4. On the Protocols page, select the protocols to which this rule should apply, and then click Next.
5. On the Schedule page, in the Use This Schedule list, select a schedule to apply, and then click Next.

Note The scope and description fields will always be dimmed. Scope shows whether the schedule is applied at the array or enterprise level. Description displays the description provided on the Schedule policy element.

6. On the Client Type page, select how you want to process client requests by selecting either Any Request, Specific Computers, or Specific Users And Groups, and then click Next.
7. On the Destination Sets page, select the destinations for this rule, and then click Next. See Table 8-3 above for an explanation of the different destination set options.
8. On the Content Groups page, specify the type of content to apply to this rule by choosing either the All Content Groups option or by specifying Selected Content Groups. You can choose the Show Only Selected Content Groups option to filter only the content groups that have check boxes selected. To continue, click Next.
9. On the Bandwidth Priority page, choose the bandwidth priority to assign to this rule. The rule will use default scheduling priority automatically. To change, select Custom; in the Name field, select a custom bandwidth priority. The description, outbound bandwidth, and inbound bandwidth fields will display the values of the selected custom bandwidth priority. Click Next to continue.
10. Review the rule configuration and click Finish to complete the process.

Deleting a Bandwidth Rule

You can't delete the default rule. ISA Server will assign every request the priority assigned to the default rule, unless custom bandwidth rules have been created that match the client's request; therefore, you can delete only the custom bandwidth rules.

To delete a custom bandwidth rule, complete the following steps:

1. In the left pane, select the Bandwidth Rules node.
2. In the right pane, right-click the custom bandwidth rule and then select Delete. When prompted, click Yes to confirm the deletion.

Modifying a Bandwidth Rule

You can only modify, disable, and delete custom bandwidth rules. You can't configure the default bandwidth rule, and so the property pages for the default Rule are dimmed.

To modify a custom bandwidth rule, follow these steps:

1. In the left pane, select the Bandwidth Rules node.
2. In the right pane, double-click the custom bandwidth rule.
3. Each of the property pages that were configured when a bandwidth rule was created is available to be modified as shown in Table 8-9.
4. Click OK when you've made the necessary modification.

Table 8-9. Property Settings for Bandwidth Rules

Property Tab	Purpose
General	Illustrates bandwidth rule name and description.
Protocol	Choose the protocols to which the rule will apply.
Destinations	You'll choose the destination sets to which the bandwidth rule will apply. See Table 8-3 above for more information.
Schedule	You'll either choose from a preexisting schedule or define a new one to specify at what times the rule will apply.
Applies To	You specify the client address set, users, or groups to which the request should apply.
HTTP Content	You can use the HTTP Content tab to restrict Internet usage to content groups.
Bandwidth	You choose either the default priority specified by the operating system or set a customized priority. The lower the number, the higher the priority (for example, 1 has the highest priority).

To enable or disable a bandwidth rule, follow these steps:

1. In the left pane, select the Bandwidth Rules node.
2. In the right pane, right-click the custom Bandwidth Rule and then select Disable.

Note A red down arrow icon appears for the disabled rule. You can also disable a rule by double-clicking the custom rule, and, in the General tab, clearing the Enable check box.

Modifying Bandwidth Rule Processing Order

Bandwidth rules are applied from top to bottom. When a client request is received, the rules are processed top to bottom until there's a match. If multiple rules match the request, only the highest matching rule will apply.

To modify the processing order, complete the following steps:

1. In the left pane, select the Bandwidth Rules node.
2. In the right pane, right-click the bandwidth rule you'd like to move, and then select Move Up or Move Down, depending on the current order of the custom rule.
3. You must have two or more custom bandwidth rules to change the order.

Routing Rules

Routing rules determine whether a Web request (for HTTP content) is retrieved from the destination requested, routed to an upstream server, or redirected to another site. These rules apply only to Web proxy client requests and are often used to manage requests for particular sites. For example, you might want to redirect all requests for a particular site to your corporate Internet Use Policy page, or you might want to ensure that every time users visit your policies page, they retrieve the page directly from the Web server rather than the cache to ensure that the most current information is available.

Note Routing rules apply only to Web proxy rules. Routing for firewall and SecureNAT clients takes place in the Network Configuration Properties dialog box. See the section of this chapter entitled "Firewall Chaining."

ISA Server ships with a default routing rule, which specifies that all content should be retrieved from the cache. This rule is processed last, so any custom rules you create have precedence over the default.

Creating a Routing Rule

You'll need to create a custom routing rule to allow control over how Web requests are directed. To create a routing rule, follow these steps:

1. Open the ISA Management console.
2. In the left pane, expand your ISA server and then expand the Network Configuration node. Then right-click Routing, highlight New, and then select Rule.
3. Type a name to be given to be given to the routing rule and then click Next.
4. On the Destination Sets page, select the destinations this rule will apply to and then click Next. See Table 8-3 above for an explanation of the different destination set options.

5. On the Request Action page, select the method and action that should occur when client requests are received. The options are:

   - **Retrieve Them Directly From Specified Destination** This option directs the request to the specified Web site every time.
   - **Route To A Specified Upstream Server** This option allows you to send requests to another ISA server.
   - **Redirect To** This option allows you to redirect the request to a specific computer by providing its name, which should be expressed as its fully qualified domain name (FQDN), its port, and the Secure Sockets Layer (SSL) port.

   Click Next after you make your selection.

   Note If the ISA server uses a modem as its external interface, select the Use Dial-up Entry check box. A dial-up entry must have been previously defined. You can create a dial-up entry by expanding the Policy Elements node.

6. If you selected Route To A Specified Upstream Server in Step 5, the Primary Routing page appears. Type the name of the upstream server in the Server Or Array field. You may click Browse to select the server. The Port and SSL Port fields default to port 8080 and 8443, respectively. Type the new ports if necessary. You may send authentication from the ISA Server by selecting the Use This Account check box. Click Set Account to specify the account credentials and click OK. In the Authentication field, select Basic or Integrated Windows. See Table 8-10 for more information about authentication.

Table 8-10. Authentication Types

Authentication Method	Explanation
Basic	Basic authentication is the default for Web requests, but it's also the least secure, as it sends the password without encryption.
Integrated Windows	Integrated Windows authentication is more secure because the username and password cannot be intercepted. Use this option whenever possible.

7. If you selected Route To A Specified Upstream Server in Step 5, the Backup Routing page appears. This page lets you specify a server that will receive requests when the server or array specified in the Primary Routing page is not available. The options closely resemble those listed in Step 5. Select Ignore Requests, Retrieve Requests Directly From Specified Destination, or Route Requests To An Upstream Server. If required, select Use Dial-Up Entry.

8. On the Cache Retrieval Configuration page, select how the rule should search the cache and route the requests for invalid objects. Choose from these three options:

- A Valid Version Of The Object; If None Exists, Retrieve The Request Using The Specified Requested Action
- Any Version Of The Object; If None Exists, Retrieve The Request Using The Specified Request Action
- Any Version Of The Requested Object. Never Route The Request.

Click Next to continue.

If you selected A Valid Version Of The Object or Any Version Of The Object on the Cache Retrieval Configuration page, you'll see the Cache Content Configuration page. Select whether the client request should be cached from the following options:

- All Content, Including Dynamic Content, Will Be Cached
- If Source And Request Headers Indicate To Cache, Then The Content Will Be Cached
- No Content Will Ever Be Cached

9. Click Next to continue.

Note By default, ISA Server caches the content only if the content's source and request headers indicate that it should be cached.

10. Review the Routing Rule configuration and then click Finish to complete.

Deleting a Routing Rule

If you no longer need to use a routing rule, you may delete it by following these steps.

1. Open the ISA Management console.
2. In the left pane, expand your ISA server, expand the Network Configuration node, and then select Routing.
3. Right-click the routing rule in the right pane and then select Delete from the context menu. Click Yes to confirm deletion when prompted.

Configuring a Routing Rule

When you've created a routing rule, you might need to change it based on changes in your requirements or the environment. See Table 8-11 for more information about available configuration options.

Table 8-11. Routing Rule Configuration Properties

Option	Description
General	Allows you to enter a description. You may also enable a routing rule by selecting the Enable check box.
Destinations	Allows you to choose the destination sets to which this rule applies. See Table 8-3 above for more information.
Action	Allows you to configure how ISA Server will process Web proxy requests.

(continued)

Table 8-11. Routing Rule Configuration Properties *(continued)*

Option	Description
Cache	Allows you to configure how Web proxy requests will interact with the cache.
Bridging	Bridging applies primarily to routing inbound requests to internal Web sources. See Chapter 9, "Publishing Fundamentals," for more information.

After you finish changing the settings, click OK to close the dialog box and then restart the ISA Services to ensure that the changes take effect.

To enable or disable a routing rule, follow these steps:

1. In the left pane, select the Routing node.
2. In the right pane, right-click the custom routing rule and then select Disable.

> **Note** A red down arrow icon appears for the disabled rule. You can also disable a rule by double-clicking the custom rule, and, in the General tab, clearing the Enable check box.

Firewall Chaining

You use firewall chaining to determine how requests from firewall and SecureNAT clients are routed.

To configure firewall chaining, follow these steps:

1. Open the ISA Management console.
2. In the left pane, expand your ISA server, right-click Network Configuration, and then select Properties.
3. In the Firewall Chaining tab, you can configure how requests from firewall and SecureNAT clients are routed.

> **Note** The default option is to use the primary connection.

4. If the ISA server uses a modem, select the Use Dial-Up Entry check box, which informs ISA Server to use the current dial-up entry policy element.
5. Select the Chain To This Computer option button to route firewall and SecureNAT client requests to an upstream server. Type the name of the server or click Browse to select the upstream server.
6. Select the Use This Account check box to let ISA Server pass the credentials provided here to the upstream server. Click Set Account, type a name in the User field, or click Browse to select a local or domain account. Type a password, confirm the password, and click OK.

> **Note** Dial-up entry check boxes will be dimmed unless a dial-up entry exists on the local ISA server.

7. If the ISA server uses a modem, select the Use Dial-Up Entry check box, which informs ISA Server to use the current dial-up entry policy element.
8. Click OK to complete the firewall chaining configuration.

Outgoing Web Requests

By default, ISA Server creates an outgoing listener that listens on all internal IP addresses and enforces Basic and Integrated authentication. Although this default setting provides the necessary rights to allow outgoing requests from the ISA Server clients, there might be times when a listener will need to be defined on a specific IP or will need to use a unique authentication method to process certain requests. Figure 8-2 shows the default settings of the Outgoing Web Requests tab for a server in an array.

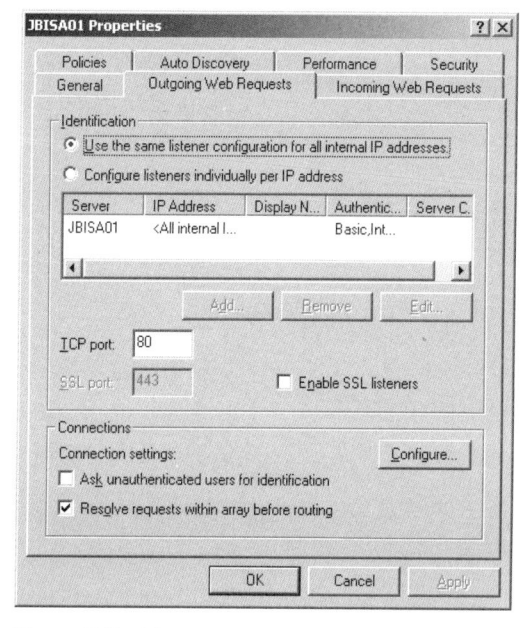

Figure 8-2. *The server properties dialog box allows you to configure settings for outgoing Web requests.*

Creating an Outgoing Listener

You'll need to create an outgoing listener if you want requests for a certain port to be processed in a certain manner.

To create an outgoing listener in the Outgoing Web Requests tab, follow these steps:

1. Open the ISA Management console.

2. In the left pane, right-click your ISA server node and then select Properties.
3. Select the Outgoing Web Requests tab.
4. Select Configure Listeners Individually Per IP Address and then click Add.
5. The Add/Edit Listener page is displayed, a shown in Figure 8-3. On the Add/Edit Listeners page, in the Server field, select the ISA server.
   - In the IP Address field, select the internal IP address to be associated with this listener.
   - You may type a name in the Display Name field.

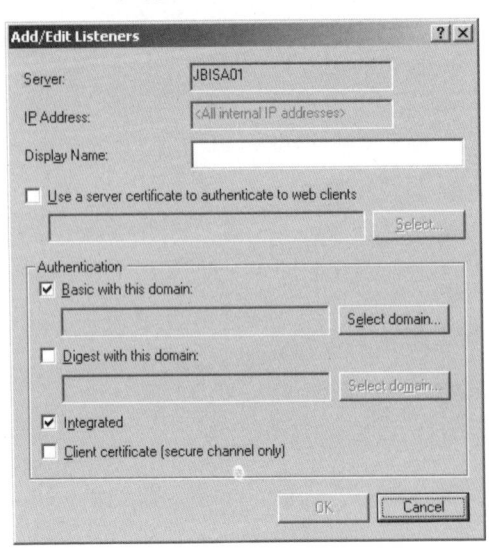

Figure 8-3. *Use the Add/Edit Listener page to configure the properties of an outgoing listener.*

6. Before completing the new listener, you must select the type of authentication to be enforced when this listener receives requests. Table 8-12 explains the options and the reasons to choose each one.

Table 8-12. Authentication Options for a Listener

Setting	Explanation
Use a Server Certificate To Authenticate To Web Clients	Allows you to use a server certificate set up on the server to authenticate requests.
Basic With This Domain	Uses basic authentication for the domain. This passes clear text passwords and is the least secure method.
Digest With This Domain	Digest authentication uses hashing to protect the password and can only be used in Microsoft Windows 2000 or above domains.

Table 8-12. Authentication Options for a Listener

Setting	Explanation
Integrated	Integrated authentication avoids sending the password at all.
Client Certificate (Secure Channel Only)	The client and the server exchange certificate information to authenticate.

7. Click OK to close the Add/Edit Listeners dialog box. Click OK again to close the server properties dialog box.

Configuring and Deleting an Outgoing Listener

Over time, the current Outgoing Web Request listener(s) might need to be modified because of an IP address change or deleted because of policy changes.

To delete an Outgoing Web Request listener, complete the following steps:

1. Open the ISA Management console.
2. In the left pane, right-click your ISA server node and then select Properties.
3. Select the Outgoing Web Requests tab.
4. Select the listener to be removed and click Remove.
5. Click OK.

To configure an Outgoing Web Request listener, complete the following steps:

1. Open the ISA Management console.
2. In the left pane, right-click your ISA server node and then select Properties.
3. Select the Outgoing Web Requests tab.
4. Select the listener to be modified and click Edit.
5. Configure the settings as necessary by following the steps in the section of this chapter entitled "Creating an Outgoing Listener."
6. Click OK to close the Add/Edit Listeners dialog box. Click OK again to close the server properties dialog box.

Configuring Outgoing Authentication

To ensure that logging takes place for Web requests, you'll need to enforce authentication for outgoing Web requests. This setting ensures that the Web proxy authenticates the user requesting Web content.

To enforce authentication for outgoing requests, complete the following steps:

1. Open the ISA Management console.
2. In the left pane, right-click your ISA server node and then select Properties.
3. Select the Outgoing Web Requests tab.
4. Select the Ask Unauthenticated Users For Identification check box.

5. Click OK. If prompted, choose whether to immediately restart the services and click OK.

Resolving Requests Within an Array

This option is available only when your ISA server is configured as an array member. To resolve outgoing requests within an array before routing, complete the following steps:

1. Open the ISA Management console.
2. In the left pane, right-click your ISA server node and then select Properties.
3. Select the Outgoing Web Requests tab.
4. Select the Resolve Requests Within Array Before Routing check box.

Caution The Resolve Requests Within Array Before Routing check box isn't apparent when your ISA server is configured in stand-alone mode.

5. Click OK. If prompted, choose whether to immediately restart the services and click OK.

Altering the Outgoing Web Requests Port Values

ISA Server's default port for Outgoing Web Requests is port 8080. If you worked with Microsoft Proxy Server 2.0 at all, then you know this is a significant change, as Proxy Server 2.0 used port 80. If you're a Proxy administrator deploying ISA server, you'll need to either modify all Web proxy clients to now use port 8080 or change the ISA server's default port to reflect the current port used in Proxy Server 2.0.

To change the TCP Port, follow these steps:

1. Open the ISA Management console.
2. In the left pane, right-click your ISA server node and then select Properties.
3. Select the Outgoing Web Requests tab.
4. In the TCP Port field, type the port number to be used for Web proxy clients for all outgoing requests.

Note The default value is port 8080. This is a significant change from Proxy 2.0, where the default port for outgoing connections was TCP port 80.

5. Click OK. If prompted, choose whether to immediately restart the services and click OK.

The port number for outgoing requests can also be seen in the Web Browser properties located under the Client Configuration node.

Caution You can't modify the outgoing port value from the Web Browser properties page. You can make the change only from the Outgoing Web Requests tab.

To change the SSL port, follow these steps:

1. Open the ISA Management console.
2. In the left pane, right-click your ISA server node and then select Properties.
3. Select the Outgoing Web Requests tab.
4. To alter the default outgoing SSL port, you must first select the Enable SSL Listeners check box to allow the SSL port field to be modified.
5. After enabling SSL listeners, an ISA message box appears, as shown in Figure 8-4.

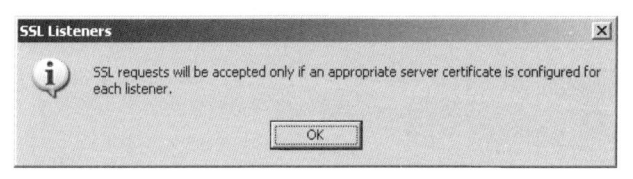

Figure 8-4. *Enabling the use of SSL listeners generates this message.*

6. Click OK. If prompted, choose whether to immediately restart the services and click OK.

Modifying Outgoing Web Requests Connection Settings

ISA Server allows an unlimited number of outgoing connections to be made by default. For controlling the resources consumed by the ISA server, one option might be to define a number of allowed outgoing connections and a time-out value assigned to each session.

To modify the number of connection and time-out values, complete the following steps:

1. Open the ISA Management console.
2. In the left pane, right-click your ISA server node and then select Properties.
3. Select the Outgoing Web Requests tab.
4. Click the Configure button.
5. On the Connection Settings page, you can choose the number of concurrent outgoing connections. By default, unlimited connections are allowed. To set a maximum value, select Maximum and type a number.
6. To specify a connection time-out value, type a number reflected in seconds. The default value is 120 seconds.
7. Click OK to close the Connection Settings page.
8. Click OK to complete. If prompted, choose whether to immediately restart the services and click OK.

Optimizing Server Performance

ISA Server can tune itself based on the number of expected users to be passing requests through its services. This allows businesses from small to enterprise-level companies to accurately reflect the amount of connections and set the performance level accordingly.

To set the performance level of the server, complete the following steps:

1. Open the ISA Management console.
2. In the left pane, right-click your ISA server node and then select Properties.
3. Select the Performance tab.
4. Drag the pointer to reflect an accurate count of the number of users per day. The default is Fewer Than 1000. Other choices include Fewer Than 100 and More Than 1000. ISA Server will adjust its performance based on your selection.

Note There's no benefit to setting the performance level to More Than 1000 if the ISA server will manage fewer sessions per day. Try to provide accurate information for this setting.

5. Click OK.

ISA Server Extensions

Application and Web filters protect client requests from firewall and Web proxy clients. You can install both application and Web filters on ISA by using the filters developed by the vendors. You can't create new filters from the ISA Management console, nor can you delete any of the predefined application filters that ship with ISA Server. However, you can modify any of the predefined application filters.

Application Filters

Application filters reside at the application layer and can examine the data stream of each packet to provide increased firewall security. Application filters rely on the ISA firewall service for processing, and application filters are available only when ISA Server is installed in firewall or integrated mode. Application filters aren't available in cache mode. Table 8-13 describes each of the predefined application filters and how their major influence (outbound or inbound) affects client requests.

Table 8-13. Application Filters Explained

Application Filter	Influence	Purpose
DNS Intrusion Detection Filter	Incoming access requests	Intercepts and analyzes Domain Name System (DNS) traffic destined for the internal network
FTP Access Filter	Outgoing access requests	Enables File Transfer Protocol (FTP) protocols (client and server)
H.323 Filter	Incoming access requests	Provides access for H.323 clients (like NetMeeting)
HTTP Redirector Filter	Outgoing access requests	Redirects requests from SecureNAT and firewall clients to the Web proxy service
POP Intrusion Detection Filter	Incoming access requests	Checks for Post Office Protocol (POP) buffer overflow attacks
RPC Filter	Incoming access requests	Enables publishing of remote procedure call (RPC) servers
SMTP Filter	Incoming access requests	Filters Simple Mail Transfer Protocol (SMTP) traffic
Socks V4 Filter	Outgoing access requests	Enables SOCKS4 communication
Streaming Media Filter	Outgoing access requests	Enables streaming protocols

Enabling/Disabling an Application Filter

By default, all application filters are enabled except for the SMTP filter. You might find it necessary to enable or disable an application filter because of changes in your requirements or your environment.

To disable or enable an application filter, complete the following steps:

1. In the left pane, expand the Extensions node and then select Application Filters.
2. In the right pane, right-click the Application filter and then click Disable.

Note A red down arrow icon appears for the disabled rule. You can also disable a rule by double-clicking the application filter, and, in the General tab, clearing the Enable This Filter check box.

FTP Access Filter

The FTP access filter allows SecureNAT clients access to FTP services by managing the secondary connections required by the FTP protocol dynamically. The FTP Access filter allows internal clients to access external FTP servers and also allows external clients access to internal FTP servers. The use of the FTP Access filter is preferred over creating a protocol definition because the FTP access filter will dynamically open specific ports to be used by the secondary connections, whereas a protocol definition would open a range of ports.

The FTP Access filter installs the following protocol definitions:

- FTP Download Only
- FTP
- FTP Server

The FTP Access filter has no configurable property pages. To enable or disable the filter, follow the steps in the section of this chapter entitled "Enabling/Disabling an Application Filter."

HTTP Redirector Filter

The HTTP Redirector filter gives firewall clients and SecureNAT clients the ability to send HTTP requests through the ISA server Web proxy service, enabling these clients to have their requests cached based on the ISA server's cache configuration.

When using the HTTP Redirector filter, you must configure authentication. When firewall clients and SecureNAT clients are configured to authenticate before sending HTTP requests through the HTTP Redirector to the Web proxy service, all authentication information is lost. For a firewall client and SecureNAT client to access HTTP content, the ISA server must have a configured site and content rule and protocol rule that allows anonymous access.

To configure the HTTP Redirector filter, follow these steps:

1. Open the ISA Management console.
2. In the left pane, expand the Extensions node and then select Application Filters.
3. In the right pane, double-click the HTTP Redirector filter.
4. In the General tab, you can choose to enable or disable this filter.
5. Select the Options tab to determine how the HTTP Redirector should respond to HTTP requests from a SecureNAT client or firewall client. Table 8-14 explains each option.

Table 8-14. Understanding the HTTP Redirector Options

HTTP Redirector Options	Explanation
Redirect To Local Web Proxy Service	This option allows all HTTP requests from firewall client and SecureNAT clients to be passed to the ISA server Web proxy service. This allows these clients to take advantage of the Web cache.
If The Local Service Is Unavailable, Redirect Requests To Requested Web Server	This option allows firewall and SecureNAT client requests to be sent directly to the Internet when the Web proxy service isn't functioning. The sites accessed in this manner won't be cached.
Send To Requested Web Server	This option forces firewall clients and SecureNAT clients to access an Internet server directly for any HTTP requests. The Web proxy service will never process any HTTP requests from these clients.

Table 8-14. Understanding the HTTP Redirector Options

HTTP Redirector Options	Explanation
Reject HTTP Requests From Firewall And SecureNAT Clients	This option forces a firewall client and SecureNAT client to also be configured as a Web proxy client in order to access HTTP content.

6. Click OK to close.

SOCKS V4 Filter

The SOCKS version 4 application filter allows SOCKS application requests to be processed by the ISA server firewall service to determine whether the application can be allowed to communicate with the Internet. By default, all SOCKS application requests coming in to the ISA server are communicated over port 1080.

To configure the SOCKS V4 filter, follow these steps:

1. Open the ISA Management console.
2. In the left pane, expand the Extensions node and then select Application Filters.
3. In the right pane, double-click SOCKS V4 Filter.
4. In the General tab, you can choose to enable or disable this filter.
5. Select the Options tab to type a new port number to be used by SOCKS V4 applications.
6. Click OK to close.

Streaming Media Filter

ISA Server's inclusion of the streaming media filter allows firewall and SecureNAT clients to access streaming media content from the following media protocols:

- **Microsoft Windows Media (MMS)** Allows Windows Media Player client access and server publishing
- **Progressive Networks protocol (PNM)** Allows RealPlayer client access and server publishing
- **Real Time Streaming Protocol (RTSP)** Allows RealPlayer G2 and QuickTime 4 client access and server publishing

The streaming media filter installs the following protocol definitions:

- MMS—Windows Media
- MMS—Windows Media Server
- PNM—RealNetworks Protocol (Client)
- PNM—RealNetworks Protocol (Server)
- RTSP
- RTSP Server

If you disable the streaming media filter, you make clients unable to use the protocols.

With the streaming media filter comes the ability to share media events for multiple users through one single stream connection, known as live stream splitting. Live stream splitting significantly reduces the amount of bandwidth consumed when employing this service. See Table 8-15 for further explanation of live stream splitting.

To configure the Streaming Media filter, follow these steps:

1. Open the ISA Management console.
2. In the left pane, expand the Extensions node and then select Application Filters.
3. In the right pane, double-click the Streaming Media filter.
4. In the General tab, you can choose to enable or disable this filter.
5. Select the Live Stream Splitting tab to determine the live stream splitting mode and the administration account, as described in Table 8-15.

Table 8-15. Configuring Live Stream Splitting

Live Stream Splitting Options	Explanation
Disable WMT Live Stream Splitting	Choose this option if you don't want to use live stream splitting.
Split Live Streams Using a Local WMT Server	Choose this option if you want to use live stream splitting and you have a single ISA server. With this option, Windows Media Server must be installed on the ISA server.
Split Live Streams Using the Following WMT Server Pool	Choose this option if you want to use live stream splitting and you have an array of ISA servers or multiple Windows Media Servers on the internal network.
WMT Server Administrator Account	Provide an Administrator account and password defined on the Windows Media Server when using a WMT (Windows Media Technologies) server pool.

6. Click OK to close.

Web Filters

Web filters rely on ISA Server's Web proxy service for examining HTTP content communication between the internal network and the Internet. Web filters are installed through vendor programs, as there are no Web filters installed out of the box with ISA Server.

Note ISA Server Feature Pack 1 installs the Link Translator filter, which will be discussed in Chapter 9.

Additional Resources

You can find additional information and resources about common scenarios and troubleshooting specific issues below:

- Shinder, Tom, "Common Issues with ISA Server: Access Policy Issues," (September 2001). *http://www.isaserver.org/articles/Common_Issues_with_ ISA_Server_Access_Policy_Issues.html*
- Shinder, Tom and Debra Littlejohn Shinder. *Configuring ISA Server 2000: Building Firewalls for Windows 2000*. Rockland, MA: Syngress Publishing, Inc., 2001.
- Access Policy topics in the ISA Server 2000 Help documentation.
- There is helpful information in Microsoft Knowledge Base article 313338, "Denied Web Proxy User Appears as 'Anonymous' in the Logs."
- There is helpful information in Microsoft Knowledge Base article 313431, " 'Access Denied' Error Message When You Try to Delete a Site and Content Rule in ISA Server 2000."

Chapter 9
Publishing Fundamentals

Publishing, a key component of Microsoft ISA Server, allows users outside your network to access protected servers—such as those hosting Microsoft Exchange and Microsoft SQL Server—located on your internal network. When we use the term *publishing* with ISA Server, it refers to controlling inbound access. There are many ways to publish internal servers using ISA Server, which mainly consist of creating either publishing rules or Internet Protocol (IP) packet filters.

In this chapter we'll explain when to use publishing rules versus packet filters and focus on the following fundamental aspects of publishing:

- Web publishing
- Server publishing
- Packet filters and routing
- Application filters

Installation Modes

The type of publishing you can provide depends upon the mode you chose when you installed your ISA server. Web publishing is available only when your ISA Server is configured in caching or integrated mode. Server publishing and IP packet filters are available only when you install your ISA server in firewall or integrated modes. Secure Sockets Layer (SSL) Certificates provide authentication for Web publishing, while application filters provide additional security for the firewall service.

Note Microsoft's release of ISA Server Feature Pack 1 in January 2003 provided some additional wizards that make configuring inbound access to Web and mail servers much simpler for the administrator. This chapter and Chapter 10, "Common ISA Server 2000 Server and Web Publishing Scenarios," assume that Feature Pack 1 has been installed on your ISA server (see Chapter 2, "Installing and Configuring Microsoft ISA Server 2000," for the steps required). Additional notes will point out Feature Pack 1 enhancements.

Processing Incoming Requests

Any external client that requests content from within your organization must pass through several checks before ISA Server allows it access. For an incoming request to succeed, you must enable packet filters, configure them for access, set up a publishing rule of some sort, and then configure routing rules. Table 9-1 shows, in the order each rule is evaluated, how ISA Server controls incoming requests.

Table 9-1. Order of Evaluation for Incoming Requests

Order	Rule Evaluated	Request Allowed	Request Blocked
1	IP packet filters	Packet filters are configured to allow the request.	Packet filters are configured to block the request.
2	Publishing rules	A publishing rule exists, which explicitly allows access to internal content.	A publishing rule is configured to block the request, or no rule but the default exists, which discards the request.
3	Routing rules (Web proxy client), or firewall chaining (firewall or SecureNAT clients)	Route request to internal Web server or upstream server	Route unavailable, or destination set not configured.

ISA Server components can deny the request at any point in the processing of the request.

Web Publishing

Web publishing protects your Web servers while making their content available to external clients. Although you could use packet filters to poke holes in your firewall and route Web requests to internal Web servers, Web publishing allows you to provide Web content to clients on the Internet by having the ISA server stand in for the Web server. The dynamic access that Web publishing rules allow provides much more protection than IP Packet Filters' statically opened ports.

Note If you wish to publish content on the ISA server itself, you'll have to configure packet filters. This scenario opens your environment up to more risks, but it's sometimes unavoidable. For example, Microsoft Small Business Server (SBS) installations always host both the ISA and Internet Information Services (IIS) server on the same machine and will configure IP Packet filters for inbound Internet content (ports 80 and 443).

Prerequisites

In order to publish a Web server, you'll first need to configure the following items:

- Ensure that the appropriate Domain Name System (DNS) entries exist so that the name of the Web site you're hosting (for example, *http://www.northwind.com*) will resolve to the IP address of your ISA Server's external interface, rather than to the Web server actually hosting the site.
- Create a destination set to identify the *external* fully qualified domain name (FQDN) of your Web server. For information on how to create a destination set, see Chapter 7, "Configuring ISA Policy Elements."
- Set up a listener in the Incoming Web Requests tab of your ISA server's properties, as described in the following section, "Incoming Web Requests."
- If you wish to restrict access to your site to certain clients, configure a client address set as described in Chapter 7.
- If you wish to restrict access to your site to certain users and groups, enable authentication on your ISA server's external interface, as described in the section of this chapter entitled "Configuring Incoming Authentication."

Incoming Web Requests

By default, ISA Server doesn't have a defined incoming listener. An incoming listener allows an ISA server to stand in for requests sent by external users intended to reach an internal server. In order to publish an internal server, you'll need to create an incoming listener to determine how the ISA server will route an incoming Web request. You have the option to configure a single listener for all IP addresses or a listener for each IP address on the ISA server. Each listener's configured IP address and port corresponds to a published server or group of servers. ISA Server routes incoming requests to servers designated by the listener. Figure 9-1 shows the default settings of the Incoming Web Requests tab.

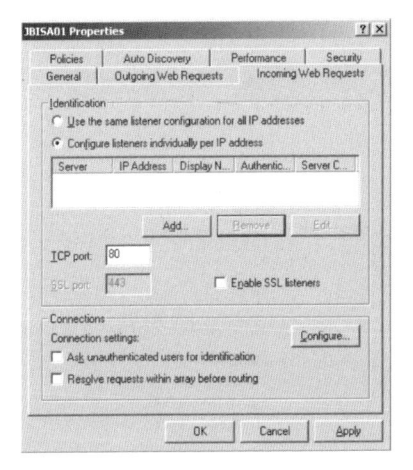

Figure 9-1. *These are the default settings for the Incoming Web Requests tab.*

Creating an Incoming Listener

If you want requests for a certain port to be processed in a certain manner, you'll need to create an incoming listener.

To create an incoming listener, follow these steps:

1. Open the ISA Management console.
2. In the left pane, right-click your ISA server node and select Properties.
3. Select the Incoming Web Requests tab.
4. Select Configure Listeners Individually Per IP Address and then click Add.
5. On the Add/Edit Listeners dialog box, select the ISA server in the Server field. The Add/Edit Listener dialog box is displayed in Figure 9-2.

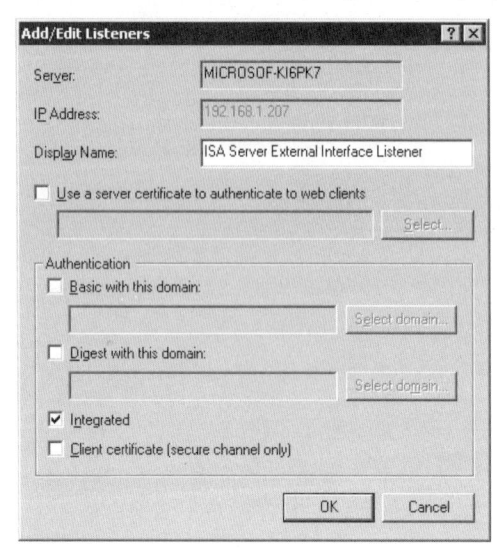

Figure 9-2. *You use the Add/Edit Listener page to configure the properties of an incoming listener.*

6. In the IP Address field, select the external IP address to be associated with this listener.
7. You may type a name in the Display name field. Before completing the new listener, you must select the type of authentication to be enforced when this listener receives requests. Table 9-2 lists the options and explains the reasons for choosing each one.

Table 9-2. Authentication Options for a Listener

Option	Setting	Explanation
Server certificate	Use A Server Certificate To Authenticate To Web Clients	Allows you to use a server certificate set up on the server to authenticate requests.
Basic	Basic With This Domain	Uses basic authentication for the domain. This passes clear text passwords and is the least secure method.
Digest	Digest With This Domain	Digest authentication uses hashing to protect the password and can only be used with accounts in an Active Directory domain.
Integrated	Integrated	Integrated authentication avoids sending the password at all.
Client certificate	Client Certificate (Secure Channel Only)	The client and the server exchange certificate information to authenticate.

8. Click OK to finish creating an incoming listener.

Configuring and Deleting an Incoming Listener

Over time, you might need to modify the current Incoming Web Request listener(s) because of an IP address change or to delete it because of policy changes.

To delete an Incoming Web Request listener, follow these steps:

1. Open the ISA Management console.
2. In the left pane, right-click your ISA server node and then select Properties.
3. Select the Incoming Web Requests tab.
4. Select the listener to be removed and click Remove.
5. Click OK. If prompted, choose whether to immediately restart the services and then click OK.

To configure an Incoming Web Request listener, follow these steps:

1. Open the ISA Management console.
2. In the left pane, right-click your ISA server node and then select Properties.
3. Select the Incoming Web Requests tab.
4. Select the listener to be modified and click Edit.
5. Configure the settings as necessary by following the steps in the section of this chapter entitled "Creating An Incoming Listener".
6. Click OK to return to the server properties dialog box.
7. Click OK again. If prompted, choose whether to immediately restart the services and then click OK.

Configuring Incoming Authentication

To enforce the authentication of all incoming Web requests so that all incoming traffic is captured within the ISA Server logs, you should configure ISA Server to ask unauthenticated users for authentication by completing the following steps:

1. Open the ISA Management console.
2. In the left pane, right-click your ISA server node and then select Properties.
3. Select the Incoming Web Requests tab.
4. Select the Ask Unauthenticated Users For Identification check box.
5. Click OK. If prompted, choose whether to immediately restart the services and then click OK.

Resolving Requests Within an Array

This option is available only when your ISA server is configured as an array member. To resolve incoming requests within an array before routing, complete the following steps:

1. Open the ISA Management console.
2. In the left pane, right-click your ISA server node and then select Properties.
3. Select the Incoming Web Requests tab.
4. Select the Resolve Requests Within Array Before Routing check box.

> **Caution** This check box isn't apparent when your ISA server is configured in stand-alone mode.

5. Click OK. If prompted, choose whether to immediately restart the services and then click OK.

Altering the Incoming Web Requests Port Values

Once you create an incoming listener, you can alter the ports that HTTP and HTTPS requests use by following these steps:

1. Open the ISA Management console.
2. In the left pane, right-click your ISA server node and then select Properties.
3. Select the Incoming Web Requests tab.
4. In the TCP Port field, type the port number to be used for incoming Web requests.

> **Note** The default value is port 80.

5. Click OK. If prompted, choose whether to immediately restart the services and then click OK.

To change the HTTPS port, follow these steps:

1. Open the ISA Management console.
2. In the left pane, right-click your ISA server node and then select Properties.
3. Select the Incoming Web Requests tab.
4. To alter the HTTPS port, you must first select the Enable SSL Listeners check box to allow the SSL Port field to be modified.
5. After enabling SSL listeners, an ISA message box appears, as shown in figure 9-3.

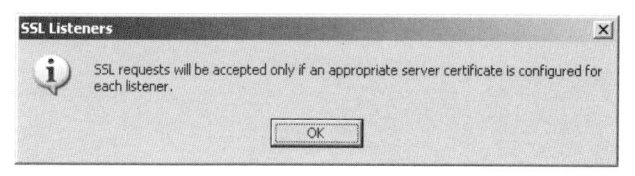

Figure 9-3. *Enabling the use of SSL Listeners generates this message.*

6. Click OK.
7. In the SSL Port field, type the port number to be used for incoming encrypted Web requests.

Note The default value is port 443.

8. Click OK. If prompted, choose whether to immediately restart the services and then click OK.

Modifying Incoming Web Requests Connection Settings

By default, ISA Server allows you to make an unlimited number of incoming connections. You can help secure your environment by restricting the number of connections made through your ISA server. To modify the number of connection and timeout values, complete the following steps:

1. Open the ISA Management console.
2. In the left pane, right-click your ISA server node and then select Properties.
3. Select the Incoming Web Requests tab.
4. Click the Configure button.
5. On the Connection Settings dialog box, you can choose the number of concurrent outgoing connections. By default, unlimited connections are allowed. To set a maximum value, choose Maximum and type a number.
6. To specify a connection timeout value, type a number reflected in seconds. The default value is 120 seconds.
7. Click OK to close the Connection Settings dialog box.
8. Click OK. If prompted, choose whether to immediately restart the services and then click OK.

Creating a Web Publishing Rule

Once you ensure that the prerequisites are in place, you'll need to create a Web publishing rule, which makes your internal Web server available to external clients. To create a Web publishing rule, follow these steps:

1. Open the ISA Management console.
2. In the left pane, expand your ISA server node, and then expand the Publishing node. Right-click Web Publishing Rules, highlight New, and then select Rule.

> **Note** If you've installed ISA Server Feature Pack 1, you'll also see an option to Publish Outlook Web Server, which is discussed in Chapter 10.

3. Type a name to be given to the rule and then click Next.
4. On the Destination Sets page, select the destinations to apply to this rule as explained in Table 9-3, and then click Next.

Table 9-3. Controlling Access Based on Destination Sets

Destination Type	Explanation
All Destinations	Applies to all destinations
All Internal Destinations	Applies to all destinations defined in the Local Address Table (LAT) or Local Domain Table (LDT)
All External Destinations	Applies to all destinations not defined in the LAT or LDT
Specified Destination Set	Applies to a custom destination set that you'll choose from a list
All Destinations Except Selected Set	Applies to all destinations excluding a custom destination set you choose from a list

5. On the Client Type page, select the types of client requests that will be applied to this rule and then click Next. The options include:
   - **Any Request** Applies to any request from any client.

> **Note** If you configured ISA Server to always authenticate users on the Incoming Web Requests tab of the ISA Server properties, this rule will apply only to authenticated users.

   - **Specific Computers (Client Address Sets)** The wizard will prompt you to add a client set. Select the appropriate client set and click Add. Alternatively, click New to create a new client set, click OK twice, and then click Next to go to Step 6.
   - **Specific Users And Groups** The wizard will prompt you to add users or groups. Click Add, type the name of the user or group, click OK, and then click Next to go to Step 6.

6. On the Rule Action page, select the type of action this rule should perform, as shown in Table 9-4.

Table 9-4. Rule Action Page Properties

Rule Response	Explanation
Discard The Request	This option requires the rule to reject any request that meets the configured conditions.
Redirect The Request To This Internal Web Server	You can either type the name of the internal Web server or click Browse and select the server from the domain.
Send The Original Host Header To The Publishing Server Instead Of The Actual One	This option sends the host header to the ISA server that's publishing the Web site rather than to the Web server to which you've redirected requests.
Connect To This Port When Bridging Request As HTTP	Enter in the port number that you'll use internally to redirect Hypertext Transfer Protocol (HTTP) requests. Usually this port is 80.
Connect To This Port When Bridging Request As SSL	Enter in the port number that you'll use internally to redirect Hypertext Transfer Protocol Secure (HTTPS) requests. Usually this port is 443.
Connect To This Port When Bridging Request As FTP	Enter in the port number that you'll use internally to redirect File Transfer Protocol (FTP) requests. Usually this port is 21.

7. Click Next to continue.
8. Review the rule configuration and click Finish.

Deleting a Web Publishing Rule

You might need to remove a Web publishing rule when you no longer need it. To delete a Web publishing rule, complete the following steps:

1. In the left pane, select the Web Publishing Rules node.
2. In the right pane, right-click the Web publishing rule and then click Delete. When prompted, click Yes to confirm the deletion.

Note In taskpad view, you can also delete a Web publishing rule by clicking the Delete A Web Publishing Rule icon.

Configuring a Web Publishing Rule

When your environment or requirements change, you might need to configure an existing Web publishing rule by completing the following steps:

1. In the left pane, select the Web Publishing Rules node.
2. In the right pane, double-click the Web publishing rule.

3. You can modify each of the property pages you configured when creating a Web publishing rule. You can also specify how to bridge different types of requests.

Note If ISA Server Feature Pack 1 is installed, an additional property page labeled Link Translation will be available. Link Translation options are discussed in the section of this chapter entitled "Using Link Translation."

4. Click OK when you've made the necessary modifications of the tabs explained in Table 9-5.

Table 9-5. Configuring a Web Publishing Rule

Property Tab	Purpose
General	By default, this rule is active and applies to all clients. Ensure that the rule is enabled.
Destinations	Choose your destination set from this tab.
Action	Specify how the request should be directed (discarded or redirected). See Table 9-4 for more information.
Bridging	Specify how incoming HTTP and SSL requests should be redirected to the internal server (as HTTP, SSL, or FTP requests). See the section of this chapter entitled "Accessing Secured Sites" for more information.
Applies To	Specify the client address set, users, or groups to which the request should apply.
Link Translation	Allows you to enforce the ISA Server to translate responses received back from the internal published server when responding to an external client's request. See the section of this chapter entitled "Using Link Translation" for more details.

Enabling/Disabling a Web Publishing Rule

At times you might need to enable or disable a Web publishing rule. To enable or disable a Web publishing rule, complete the following steps:

1. In the left pane, select the Web Publishing Rules node.
2. In the right pane, double-click the Web publishing rule. In the General tab, clear the Enable check box.

Note A red down arrow icon will appear for the disabled rule.

Adjusting the Rule Processing Order

The order of Web publishing rules is processed from top to bottom. When a request is received, the first rule is processed for a match; if the match is successful, the rule's actions are followed. If there isn't a match, each remaining rule is processed in the order identified in the ISA Management console until there is a match. If ISA Server processes all predefined Web publishing rules and finds no match, ISA Server processes the default rule and discards the request.

To modify the processing order, complete the following steps:

1. In the left pane, select the Web Publishing Rules node.
2. In the right pane, right-click the Web publishing rule you'd like to move and then select Move Up or Move Down.

Note You can't modify the processing order of rules when the ISA Management console is set to taskpad view.

Accessing Secured Sites

Your ISA Server can provide access to secure sites inside your network through either Web publishing or server publishing. Web publishing requires that you export the Web server's certificate and configure that certificate on the ISA server. Because you might not want to export the Web server's certificate (or, in the case of IIS 3.0, you don't have the option of exporting a certificate), you can also use server publishing in which the ISA Server negotiates an encrypted tunnel between the external clients and the Web server itself.

Note In this section we describe the basic requirements to enable SSL bridging and SSL tunneling. See Chapter 10 for step-by-step instructions on how to export a certificate from a Web server and configure it on your ISA server and how to publish a secure Web site using server publishing.

Web Publishing and SSL Bridging

Web publishing allows ISA Server to act as a translator for external clients to obtain information from a secure Web site behind your ISA server. When a client initiates an SSL connection (using HTTPS), ISA can perform one of two sequences of actions:

- The ISA server will negotiate the secure channel with the client and then decrypt the SSL request. The ISA server then encrypts the request again, sending it on to the Web server, which returns encrypted content to the ISA server. The ISA server, finally, returns the content to the client across the secure channel.
- The ISA server can also negotiate a secure channel with the client, decrypt the SSL request, and then send it on to the Web server as an HTTP request. The Web server returns the content using unencrypted HTTP. The ISA server responds to the client using the secure channel. This relieves the burden of encryption from the Web server while encrypting communications across the external network.

Server Publishing and SSL Tunneling

Whereas SSL tunneling acts as a translator for secure requests, SSL bridging acts as a broker. When a client establishes an SSL connection, the ISA server forwards the request without decrypting it. This encrypted transmission improves the privacy of the communications by limiting even the ISA server's access to unencrypted data.

> **Note** If your IIS server is running on your ISA server, you'll have problems publishing your Web server. To avoid these problems, disable socket pooling as described in the Microsoft Knowledge Base article 238131, "How to Disable Socket Pooling," at *http://support.microsoft.com*.

Web Filters for Inbound Access

By default, no Web filters are installed with ISA Server until you install ISA Server Feature Pack 1. The installation of Feature Pack 1 adds a Web filter known as the Link Translator, which uses dictionary entries to translate absolute links on your internal, published servers for external users.

Using Link Translation

Link translation enables ISA Server to translate responses received from the internal published server (by replacing the internal Web server's name and port with the external name and port being accessed by the client) when responding to an external client's request.

> **Note** For more information on link translation, see "About Link Translation" and "How Link Translation Works" in ISA Server help. Remember that you must install ISA Server Feature Pack 1 to access this functionality.

In order to use link translation on your ISA server, follow these few steps, which we'll list, and then discuss in more detail:

- Enable the Link Translator Web filter.
- Enable Link Translation on a specific Web publishing rule.
- Configure caching for link translation.
- Configure the link translation dictionary.

Enabling the Link Translator Filter To enable the Link Translator Filter, follow these steps:

1. Open the ISA Management console.
2. In the left pane, expand the Extensions node and then click Web Filters.
3. In the right pane, right-click the Link Translator Filter and then select Enable.

Note You can also enable or disable the filter by viewing the properties, and in the General tab, selecting or clearing the Enable This Filter check box.

4. When prompted, you can choose to save the changes, but don't restart the services or save the changes and restart the services. Select the appropriate option button based on the needs of applying the change, and then click OK.

Enabling Link Translation on a Web Publishing Rule To configure link translation for a particular Web publishing rule, follow these steps:

1. Open the ISA Management console.
2. In the left pane, expand your ISA server node, expand the Publishing node, and select Web Publishing Rules.
3. In the right pane, double-click the Web publishing rule in which to enable link translation.
4. Select the Link Translation tab.
5. To enable link translation, select the Perform Link Translation check box as shown in Figure 9-4, and then click OK.

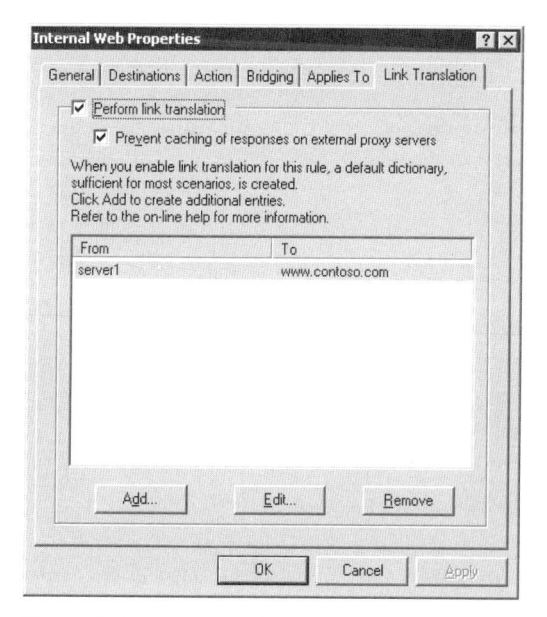

Figure 9-4. *Use the Link Translation tab to enabling link translation on a Web publishing rule.*

Note If the Link Translator Web filter is disabled, you can't select the Perform Link Translation option. To enable the Web filter, select the Web Filters node in the ISA Management MMC, right-click the Link Translator Filter, and select Enable.

Configuring Caching for Link Translation The caching of translated links to an upstream proxy sever can impose a security risk, and as such, is prevented by default. You can change this setting, however.

Note For more information, see "Caching With Link Translation" in the ISA Server Help file.

To enable the caching of translated links, follow these steps:

1. Open the ISA Management console.
2. In the left pane, expand your ISA server node, expand the Publishing node, and select Web Publishing Rules.
3. In the right pane, double-click the Web publishing rule in which to enable link translation.
4. Select the Link Translation tab.
5. Clear the Prevent Caching of Responses On External Proxy Servers check box and then click OK.

Configuring the Link Translation Dictionary When link translation is enabled, a default link translation dictionary is established. The dictionary contains references to the following items:

- All references to the internal Web server referenced in the Action tab of the Web publishing rule's properties.
- When you've configured ports other than 80 for HTTP and 443 for SSL requests in the Incoming Web Requests listener in the properties page of your array or server, the link translation dictionary uses the nondefault ports when replacing links. If you stuck with the defaults, the link translator uses these default settings.
- If the client requests HTTPS, ISA Server ensures that traffic from the published IIS server uses HTTPS.

To add an entry to the link translation dictionary, follow these steps:

1. Open the ISA Management console.
2. In the left pane, expand your ISA server node, expand the Publishing node, and select Web Publishing Rules.
3. In the right pane, double-click the Web publishing rule in which to enable link translation.
4. Select the Link Translation tab.
5. Click the Add button.

6. On the Add/Edit Dictionary Item page, as shown in Figure 9-5, in the top field type the name of the internal server reference and in the bottom field type the FQDN or name of the host header that the Web publishing rule uses, and then click OK.

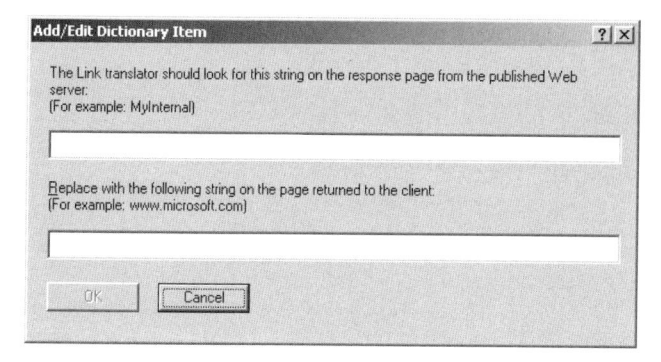

Figure 9-5. *The Add/Edit Dictionary Item page is where you define new dictionary entries.*

7. Click OK to complete.

Server Publishing

Whereas Web publishing is used solely for Web servers, you may use server publishing to make all types of services on the internal network available to external users. Server publishing uses protocol definitions to map a protocol on a defined external IP to the published server's internal IP. Server publishing is similar to Web publishing in that either type of rule is more secure than establishing packet filters; where publishing rules dynamically open and close on the ISA server's external interface, packet filters are static and always open.

Limitations

Server publishing does have its share of limitations. Observe the following guidelines in order to publish services successfully on your internal network.

- Publish a particular service only once per IP address.
- Redirect the published port on the external interface to the same port on the internal server.
- Remember that the ISA Server NAT protocol doesn't allow you to bind an external IP address to an internal IP address.

Prerequisites

In order to publish an internal server with server publishing, you'll first need to verify that your environment has the following prerequisites in place:

- Ensure that the appropriate DNS entries exist so that the name of the Web site you're hosting (for example, *http://www.northwind.com*) will resolve with the IP address of your ISA Server's external interface, rather than for the Web server actually hosting the site.
- Create a protocol definition for the protocol to be published on the internal server. For information on how to create a protocol rule, see Chapter 7.

> **Note** This might not always be necessary, as ISA Server provides many predefined protocol definitions that might suit your publishing needs.

- Set up a listener in the Incoming Web Requests tab of your ISA server's properties as described in the "Incoming Web Requests" section of this chapter.
- If you wish to restrict access to your site to certain clients, configure a client address set as described in Chapter 7.
- Configure the internal server to be published as an ISA client. The preferred and optimal setup is to configure the internal server as a SecureNAT client; however, you often might need to configure the server as a firewall client. See Chapter 3, "Installing and Configuring Microsoft ISA Server 2000 Clients," for details on configuring an ISA client.

Creating a Server Publishing Rule

A server publishing rule allows you to publish internal services (that is, Simple Mail Transfer Protocol [SMTP], Post Office Protocol 3 [POP3], Terminal Services) to external clients.

To create a server publishing rule, follow these steps:

1. Open the ISA Management console.
2. In the left pane, expand your ISA server node, expand the Publishing node, right-click Server Publishing Rules, highlight New, and then select Rule.

> **Note** When you right-click Server Publishing Rules, you'll also see an option to select Secure Mail Server. The Mail Server Security wizard allows secure publishing of an internal mail server, and is described in the Chapter 10 section entitled "Running the Secure Mail Publishing Wizard."

3. Type a name to be given to the rule and then click Next.
4. On the Address Mapping page, specify the external and internal IP addresses you'll associate with this rule. In the IP Address Of Internal Server field, type the IP address of the internal server to be published. If you don't know the IP address, click Find to browse your network to find the server. In the

External IP Address On ISA Server field, type the IP address assigned to the external interface of the ISA server to be associated with the rule. Optionally, you can click Browse, select the IP address, and then click OK. Click Next to continue.

Caution The server publishing rule won't continue beyond this point if no range of external IP addresses is configured on the external interface.

5. On the Protocol Settings page, select the protocol definition to apply to the initial inbound connections and then click Next.

Note If you require a custom protocol that isn't provided with the built-in set of protocol definitions, you must create a protocol definition before creating a server publishing rule. See Chapter 7 for more information.

6. On the Client Type page, select the types of client requests that will be applied to this rule, and then click Next. The options include:
   - **Any Request**
   - **Specific Computers (Client Address Sets)** The wizard will prompt you to add a client address set. Select the appropriate client address set, click Add or New to create a new client address set, click OK, and then click Next to go to Step 7.
7. Review the rule configuration and click Finish.

Deleting a Server Publishing Rule

You might need to remove a server publishing rule when you no longer need it. To delete a server publishing rule, complete the following steps:

1. In the left pane, select the Server Publishing Rules node.
2. In the right pane, right-click the server publishing rule and then click Delete. When prompted, click Yes to confirm the deletion.

Note In taskpad view, you can also delete a server publishing rule by clicking the Delete A Server Publishing Rule icon.

Configuring a Server Publishing Rule

When your environment or requirements change, you might need to alter an existing Web publishing rule. To configure a Server publishing rule, complete the following steps:

1. In the left pane, select the Server Publishing Rules node.
2. In the right pane, double-click the server publishing rule.

3. Each of the property pages that you configured when creating a server publishing rule are available for modification.
4. Click OK when you've made the necessary modifications of the tabs explained in Table 9-6.

Table 9-6. Configuring a Server Publishing Rule

Property Tab	Purpose
General	By default, this rule is active and applies to all clients. The rule is enabled when Enable is selected.
Action	You can choose to alter the internal and external IP address mappings or change the mapped server protocol from this tab.
Applies To	You specify the client address set(s) to which the request should apply.

Enabling/Disabling a Server Publishing Rule

At times you might need to enable or disable a server publishing rule. To enable or disable a server publishing rule, complete the following steps:

1. In the left pane, select the Server Publishing Rules node.
2. In the right pane, double-click the server publishing rule. In the General tab, clear the Enable check box.

Note A red down arrow icon appears for the disabled rule.

Routing and IP Packet Filters

Packet filtering enables ISA server to determine what packets to allow into the network based on information contained in TCP and IP headers. Unless you enable packet filtering, ISA Server's ports are all listening for incoming requests—not a safe state for a firewall. Static and dynamic packet filtering provide access only to clients that request information on certain ports. Static packet filtering requires that a port be opened and kept open for all inbound traffic. Dynamic packet filtering—also known as *stateful packet filtering*—allows ports to be opened only when needed.

Following are some scenarios that would require you to use packet filters. We'll discuss how to configure the most common of these scenarios in Chapter 10.

- When services or applications on the ISA server must listen to Internet requests—Microsoft SBS is a good example of this scenario.
- When you must publish servers in a perimeter (or DMZ) network.
- When your internal network must allow access to protocols other than TCP or User Datagram Protocol (UDP).

Enabling Packet Filtering

Although you should always enable packet filtering to ensure optimum security, you should use packet filtering as a means of allowing access only when Web or server publishing rules won't work. Always prefer dynamic over static packet filtering for the securest environment. You can enable packet filtering by following the steps below:

1. Open the ISA Management console.
2. In the left pane, expand your ISA Server, expand Access Policy, right-click IP Packet Filters, and then select Properties.
3. In the General tab, select the Enable Packet Filtering check box.

Note If there's a configured Enterprise policy that enforces the use of packet filtering, you can't disable IP packet filtering at the array level, as shown in Figure 9-6.

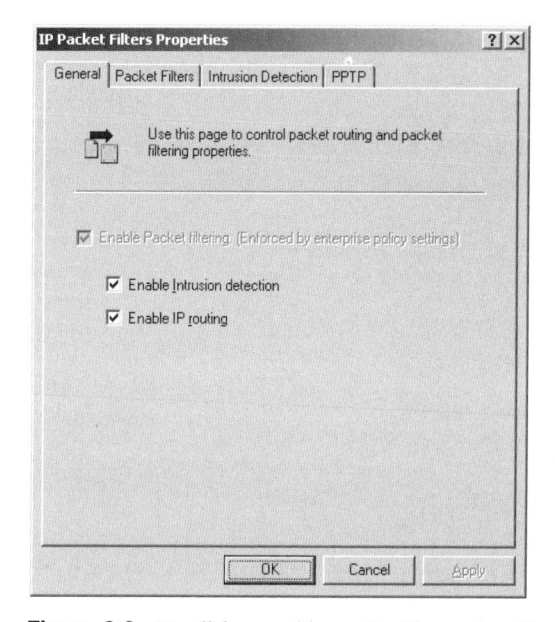

Figure 9-6. *You'll be unable to disable packet filtering if an Enterprise policy enabled it.*

Enabling IP Routing

IP routing is like a conduit that simply moves traffic from one area to another; in this case IP routing moves traffic from the Internet through the firewall to your internal network. Without packet filtering, IP routing provides no protection whatsoever, routing any and all requests. It does, however, help to improve ISA Server's performance and functionality (see Microsoft Knowledge Base article 279347, "Enable IP Routing on ISA Server to Increase Performance," at *http://support.microsoft.com,* for one example).

To enable IP routing, follow these steps:

1. Open the ISA Management console.
2. In the left pane, expand your ISA Server, expand Access Policy, right-click IP Packet Filters, and then select Properties.
3. In the General tab, select the Enable IP Routing check box.

> **Note** If you enable IP Routing through Routing and Remote Access Service on the ISA server, the IP routing function within ISA Server will also be enabled, even though the check box might not be selected.

Application Filters for Inbound Access

As covered in Chapter 8, certain predefined application filters are used with outbound access control and others are used with inbound access control. ISA Server uses the following application filters for inbound access:

- DNS Intrusion Detection Filter
- H.323 Filter
- POP Intrusion Detection Filter
- RPC Filter
- SMTP Filter

We'll examine each of these filters to explain how they affect incoming requests.

DNS Intrusion Detection Filter

The DNS Intrusion Detection filter is enabled by default to monitor certain types of DNS service attacks: DNS host name overflow, DNS length overflow, and DNS zone transfers from privileged ports and high ports.

To configure the DNS Intrusion Detection filter, follow these steps:

1. Open the ISA Management console.
2. In the left pane, expand the Extensions node and then select Application Filters.
3. In the right pane, double-click the DNS Intrusion Detection Filter.

4. In the General tab you can choose to enable or disable this filter.
5. Select the Attacks tab to determine which types of incoming traffic should be filtered. As a best practice, choose all options, and then click OK to close the DNS Intrusion Detection Filter Properties dialog box. For an explanation of each attack, you may either click the question-mark in the upper right corner, then select the attack, or use the Tab key to highlight the attack, and then press the F1 key.
6. Click OK to close.

H.323 Filter

The H.323 application filter allows conferencing applications like NetMeeting to be used with ISA Server. The H.323 filter is enabled by default.

Note The H.323 application filter and the H.323 Gatekeeper configuration are described in more detail in Chapter 13, "Working With Enterprise Technologies and ISA Server 2000."

To configure the H.323 filter, follow these steps:

1. Open the ISA Management console.
2. In the left pane, expand the Extensions node and then select Application Filters.
3. In the right pane, double-click the H.323 Filter.
4. In the General tab you can choose to enable or disable this filter.
5. In the Call Control tab there's a variety of options that define how the H.323 protocol is used for incoming/outgoing calls, audio and video support, and application sharing. Table 9-7 explains each of these options.

Table 9-7. Configuring H.323 Call Control Options

Call Control	Options	Explanation
Gatekeeper Location	Use This Gatekeeper	Specify the H.323 gatekeeper server that ISA will use.
Call Direction	Allow Incoming Calls	Provides external H.323 clients with access into the local network.
	Allow Outgoing Calls	Allows internal H.323 clients out of the local network.
	Use DNS Gatekeeper Lookup And LRQs For Alias Resolution	An option available when you choose Allow Outgoing Calls, this setting restricts H.323 DNS lookups from taking place; instead, DNS will use only type A endpoint, proxy SRV, and proxy TXT queries.

(continued)

Table 9-7. Configuring H.323 Call Control Options *(continued)*

Call Control	Options	Explanation
Media Control	Allow Audio	Enables H.323 audio through the ISA server.
	Allow Video	Enables H.323 video through the ISA server.
	Allow T120 and Application Sharing	Enables H.323 application sharing and remote control through the ISA server.

6. Click OK to close.

POP Intrusion Detection Filter

The POP Intrusion Detection filter is enabled by default to monitor for POP3 buffer overflow attacks.

The POP Intrusion Detection filter has no configurable property pages. To enable or disable the filter, follow the steps entitled "Enabling/Disabling an Application Filter" in Chapter 8, "Configuring ISA Access Policy."

RPC Filter

The RPC filter allows you to publish Remote Procedure Call (RPC) services for all internal servers that require this service for communication.

The RPC filter has no configurable property pages. To enable or disable the filter, follow the steps in Chapter 8 entitled "Enabling/Disabling an Application Filter."

SMTP Filter

The SMTP filter, when used in conjunction with the Message Screener, allows your ISA Server to filter incoming messages received on port 25 and apply rules based on the various property pages. The SMTP filter is disabled by default.

To configure the SMTP filter, follow these steps:

1. Open the ISA Management console.
2. In the left pane, expand the Extensions node and select Application Filters.
3. In the right pane, double-click the SMTP filter.
4. In the General tab you can choose to enable or disable this filter.
5. In the Keywords tab you can specify the action that should be taken when a keyword is found in an incoming message. Table 9-8 explains each of the options.

Table 9-8. Configuring SMTP Filter Keyword Options

Keyword Options	Explanation
Enable Keyword Rule	Enables/disables the keyword rule
Keyword	The name of the keyword the SMTP filter will process

Table 9-8. Configuring SMTP Filter Keyword Options

Keyword Options	Explanation
Apply Action If Keyword Found In	Choose to apply the action if keyword is found in message header or body, message header only, or message body only by selecting the appropriate option button
Action	Choose to delete message, hold message, or forward message

   Click OK to close the Mail Keyword Rule page.
6. In the Users/Domains tab, you can configure users' e-mail addresses and domains that should be rejected when an incoming message is received. In the Sender's Name field, type the e-mail address of the person whose mail should be rejected and click Add. In the Domain Name field, type the domain names that should be rejected and click Add.
7. In the Attachments tab you can filter attachments based on the file extension. The Message Screener is responsible for the performing the actions. Click Add to add a mail attachment rule. Table 9-9 explains each of the options.

Table 9-9. Configuring SMTP Filter Attachment Options

Attachment Options	Explanation
Enable Attachment Rule	Enables/disables the attachment rule
Apply Action to Messages Containing Attachments With One Of These Properties	Choose how to filter the attachment: by name, by extension, or by size limit
Action	Choose to delete message, hold message, or forward message

8. Click OK to close the Mail Attachment Rule page.
9. In the SMTP Commands tab, you can choose to edit any of the 16 predefined SMTP commands or you can create new ones. To create a new command, click Add. On the SMTP Command Rule page, type the command name and maximum length in bytes and click OK.
10. Click OK to close.

Additional Resources

- Microsoft Knowledge Base article 307784, "Server Publishing Rules Intermittently Fail."
- Microsoft Knowledge Base article 313350, "Problems When You Use a Server Publishing Rule that Uses a Protocol Definition."

- Microsoft Knowledge Base article 271272, "How Internet Security and Acceleration Server Handles the Caching of Responses to Requests Received By Web Publishing."
- Microsoft Knowledge Base article 296674, "The SecureNAT Clients Cannot Access the Internal Resources That Are Published by Means of ISA Server."

Chapter 10

Common Web and Server Publishing Scenarios

Since the release of Microsoft ISA Server 2000, the most common questions asked have to do with publishing: how to publish Outlook Web Access (OWA) on the ISA server, how to publish a Terminal Server on an internal network, and so on. In this chapter we'll look at these and a variety of other ISA Server publishing scenarios that use both Web and server publishing rules.

- Publishing a Web server
- Publishing a secured Web site using certificates
- Publishing a File Transfer Protocol (FTP) server
- Publishing a Microsoft Exchange Server service, such as OWA, Simple Mail Transfer Protocol (SMTP), Post Office Protocol 3 (POP3), Internet Message Access Protocol 4 (IMAP4), remote procedure call (RPC)
- Publishing a SQL server
- Publishing a terminal server
- Publishing a Citrix server
- Publishing a Domain Name System (DNS) server

Common Prerequisites

Before you begin publishing, ensure that you cover these general prerequisite steps before moving into any specific scenarios.

- Ensure that the Local Address Table (LAT) is configured correctly
- Verify DNS name resolution
- Confirm your ISA server has routes to all internal networks
- Disable socket pooling

Configuring the LAT

The LAT designates all Internet Protocol (IP) addresses and address ranges that are considered internal to your network. To configure the LAT, follow the steps provided in Chapter 2, "Installing and Configuring Microsoft ISA Server 2000."

Configuring DNS Resolution

At a minimum, your published servers need access to a DNS server that will resolve names for internal addresses. You'll also need a way to resolve external addresses. One option is to communicate with a DNS server that performs name resolution for external addresses; another is providing connectivity to the ISA server firewall or Web proxy services, which may act as a DNS proxy.

Routing

Ensure that your ISA server has routes to all internal networks. For a complex network, define a route on your ISA server for all network segments on your internal network. You can manually populate the routing table using the ROUTE ADD command or by using a dynamic routing protocol, such as Routing Information Protocol (RIP).

Disabling Socket Pooling

When any of the following services are running on the ISA server, you should disable socket pooling and configure each of the services to listen only on the internal interface:

- IIS Web Publishing service
- IIS SMTP service
- IIS FTP service
- IIS NNTP service
- Exchange 2000 POP3 service
- Exchange 2000 IMAP4 service

Note Windows Server 2003—At the time of publication, procedures to disable socket pooling on IIS6 were available only for the Web service. Technical support was creating a Microsoft Knowledge Base article to explain how to disable socket pooling for the other services. Visit *http://support.microsoft.com* and type in **"socket pooling" and IIS6 and *servicename*** to search for the relevant articles. You can also visit *http://www.microsoft.com/isaserver/setupserver2003.asp* to see the most current information about how to make ISA Server 2000 work with Windows Server 2003.

Chapter 10 Common Web and Server Publishing Scenarios | 173

To disable socket pooling for IIS Web and FTP services in Windows 2000, follow these steps:

1. Open a command prompt and change the directory to the \Inetpub\Adminscripts folder.
2. Type **net stop msftpsvc** and press Enter to stop the IIS FTP service. Type **net stop w3svc** and press Enter to stop the IIS Web Publishing service.
3. Type the following: **cscript adsutil.vbs set msftpsvc/disablesocketpooling true** (to disable socket pooling for the FTP service) or **cscript adsutil.vbs set w3svc/disablesocketpooling true** (to disable socket pooling for the IIS Web Publishing service), and then press Enter.
4. Restart the IIS FTP service by typing **net start msftpsvc** and pressing Enter or restart the IIS Web Publishing service by typing **net start w3svc** and pressing Enter at the command prompt.
5. Type **exit** to close the Command Prompt window.

Note To verify that the services are listening only on the internal interface, type **netstat-na** at a command prompt.

To disable socket pooling for the IIS Web service on Windows 2003, follow these steps:

1. Install the Windows Server 2003 Support Tools by inserting the Windows Server 2003 CD or accessing the media on a network share. Open the Support Folder and then double-click on the SUPTOOLS.MSI file. Follow the on-screen instructions to install the tools.
2. Open a command prompt.
3. Type **httpcfg delete iplisten -I 0.0.0.0** and press Enter to stop all listening.
4. Type **httpcfg set iplisten -i** and the internal IP Address of your ISA server and press Enter to allow only the internal IP address to listen.
5. Type **net stop http** and press Enter to stop the IIS6 HTTP service.
6. Type **net stop w3proxy** and press Enter to stop the IIS Web proxy service.
7. Type **net start http** and press Enter to start the IIS6 HTTP service.
8. Type **net start w3proxy** and press Enter to start the IIS6 Web proxy service.

Note Be sure that you repeat these steps for all IP addresses that need to listen.

To disable socket pooling for IIS SMTP service on Windows 2000, follow these steps:

1. Copy the Mdutil.ex_ file from the I386 folder on the Microsoft Windows 2000 CD-ROM to the InetPub\Adminscripts folder on your local hard disk.
2. Open a command prompt, change the location to the InetPub\Adminscripts folder, and then type **expand mdutil.ex_ mdutil.exe** and press Enter.
3. Type **mdutil.exe enum -path:smtpsvc** at the command prompt and then press Enter.

4. Type **mdutil set -path smtpsvc/*number* -value 1 -dtype 1 -prop 1029 -attrib 1** at the command prompt, where *number* is the SMTP Service number for which you want to disable socket pooling, and then press Enter.

> **Note** Repeat Step 4 for each SMTP virtual server using a different value for *number*.

To disable socket pooling for IIS Network News Transport Protocol (NNTP) service on Windows 2000, follow these steps:

1. Copy the Mdutil.ex_ file from the I386 folder on the Windows 2000 CD-ROM to the InetPub\Adminscripts folder on your local hard disk.

2. Open a command prompt, change the location to the folder in which you copied the Mdutil.ex_ file, and then type **expand mdutil.ex_ mdutil.exe** and then press Enter.

> **Note** Steps 1 and 2 aren't necessary if you have completed the procedure above for disabling socket pooling for the IIS SMTP service.

3. Type **mdutil.exe enum -path:nntpsvc** at the command prompt and then press Enter.

4. Type the command **mdutil set -path nntpsvc/*number* -value 1 -dtype 1 -prop 1029 -attrib 1** at the command prompt, where *number* is the NNTP Service number for which you want to disable socket pooling, and then press Enter.

> **Note** Repeat Step 4 for each NNTP virtual server with a different value for *number*.

Publishing Web Server

Almost all administrators need to publish a Web site behind the ISA server. We cover the two most common configurations required: publishing a Web server located behind the ISA server and publishing a Web server that's collocated, or installed on the ISA server itself.

Publishing a Web Site Behind the ISA Server

To publish a Web server behind the ISA server, you'll need to configure a destination set, create a Web listener, and then create a Web publishing rule.

Creating a Destination Set

The first step to publishing a Web server is to create a destination set based on the Web site's fully qualified domain name (FQDN). The FQDN will be mapped to the external network interface on the ISA server and will be what users type in their browsers to access the site.

To create a destination set, see Chapter 7, "Configuring ISA Policy Elements."

Creating a Web Listener for Incoming Web Requests

The second step to publishing a Web server is to create an incoming Web listener for incoming Web requests. You can configure a listener in a variety of ways so that you can control how ISA Server receives and processes these requests.

To create an incoming listener, see Chapter 9, "Publishing Fundamentals."

Creating a Web Publishing Rule

The third step to publishing a Web server is to create a Web publishing rule. Your Web publishing rule will make your Web server available to external clients by associating the internal Web site with the ISA server's external interface and allowing requests for content to be returned to external clients.

To create a Web publishing rule, follow these steps:

1. Open the ISA Management console.
2. In the left pane, expand your ISA server node, expand the Publishing node, right-click Web Publishing Rules, click New, and then click Rule.
3. Type a name to be given to the rule and then click Next.
4. On the Destination Sets page, click the drop-down list and select Specified Destination Set. Select the destinations you created above specifically for this rule, and then click Next.
5. On the Client Type page, select the types of client requests that will be applied to this rule and then click Next. The options include:
   - **Any Request** Applies to any request from any client.

Note If you configured ISA Server to always authenticate users on the Incoming Web Requests tab of the ISA Server properties, the rule will apply only to authenticated users.

   - **Specific Computers (Client Address Sets)** The wizard will prompt you to add client sets. Click Add to create a new client set, add or create the client sets, and click OK. After returning to the Client Sets page, select the desired client sets, and then click Next to go to Step 6.
   - **Specific Users and Groups** The wizard will prompt you to add a user or group. Click Add, type the name of the user or group, click OK, and then click Next to go to Step 6.
6. On the Rule Action page, select Redirect The Request To This Internal Web Server and type the IP address of the internal Web server to be published. If using host headers, select the Send The Original Host Header To The Publishing Server Instead Of The Actual One check box. Click Next to continue.
7. Review the rule configuration and click Finish.

Publishing a Web Site on the ISA Server

Because of space or financial considerations, you might have your ISA server and Web server colocated on the same server. While this configuration can make your life as an administrator a lot more difficult, it's still supportable. Follow the steps below to publish collocated ISA and Web servers.

Modifying Web Site Properties in IIS

1. Open the Internet Services Manager console.
2. In the left pane, expand your server node, right-click the Default Web Site and then click Properties. If you are using Microsoft Windows Server 2003, the Default Web Site node is located within Web Sites.
3. Click the drop-down list for IP Address and select the IP address bound to the ISA server's internal interface.
4. In the TCP Port box, type a port number that's not currently in use by the ISA server.

> **Note** To determine which ports are taken, open a command prompt window and type **netstat-na**.

5. Click OK to close the Default Web Site Properties page.
6. Right-click the server node, select All Tasks, and click Restart IIS.

Creating a Web Publishing Rule

You can follow the same steps as shown for publishing a Web server behind an ISA server, with a few exceptions.

- On the Rule Action page, select Redirect The Request To This Internal Web Server.
- When publishing a Web site on the ISA server, set the Connect To This Port When Bridging Request As HTTP option to the TCP port number defined for the Web site. This is explained in the preceding section, "Modifying Web Site Properties in IIS."

Publishing Secured Web Site (HTTPS)

This scenario describes publishing a Secure Sockets Layer (SSL) site using server publishing rules. The following components are necessary for publishing a Hypertext Transfer Protocol Secure (HTTPS) Web site:

- Certificate installed on Web server
- Incoming listener
- Protocol definition
- Server publishing rule

Web Server Certificate

Using the HTTPS protocol definition and a server publishing rule requires that the Web server have a certificate installed to provide SSL connectivity. Requesting a certificate from a Certificate Authority (CA) and installing the certificate on the Web server are Internet Information Server (IIS) procedures.

More Info To perform certificate administration, see the *Microsoft Windows 2000 Administrator's Pocket Consultant, IIS 5.0 Administrator's Pocket Consultant* (Microsoft Press, 2001), or *Microsoft IIS 6.0 Administrator's Pocket Consultant* (Microsoft Press, 2003), all by William R. Stanek. Also see the Microsoft Knowledge Base article "HOW TO: Enable SSL for All Customers Who Interact with Your Web Site in Internet Information Services" at *http://support.microsoft.com/view/tn.asp?kb=298805*.

Creating an Incoming Listener

To effectively use server publishing rules and prevent possible port contention on the external interface on the ISA server, you should create a unique incoming listener. To create an incoming listener, see Chapter 9.

Using the Predefined HTTPS Protocol Definition

ISA Server includes a predefined protocol definition, HTTPS Server, which allows inbound requests on port 443. The settings for HTTPS Server protocol definition are as follows:

- Port Number: 443
- Protocol Type: TCP
- Direction: Inbound
- Secondary Connections: None

Creating an HTTPS (SSL) Server Publishing Rule

To create a server publishing rule, follow these steps:

1. Open the ISA Management console.
2. In the left pane, expand your ISA server node, expand the Publishing node, right-click Server Publishing Rules, click New, and then click Rule.
3. Type a name to be given to the rule and then click Next.
4. On the Address Mapping page, specify the external and internal IP addresses you'll associate with this rule. In the IP Address Of Internal Server field, type the IP address of the internal Web server to be published. You may, in addition, click Find, and on the Find Internal IP Address page, type the name of the server. If you don't know the name of the server, click Browse, select the internal server, and then click Find to display the available internal IP addresses for that server. Select the IP address and then click OK. In the

External IP Address On ISA Server field, type the IP address assigned to the external interface of the ISA server to be associated with the rule. Optionally, you can click Browse, select the IP address, and then click OK. Click Next to continue.

5. On the Protocol Settings page, click the drop-down list to select the HTTPS Server protocol definition to apply to the initial inbound connections, as shown in Figure 10-1, and then click Next.

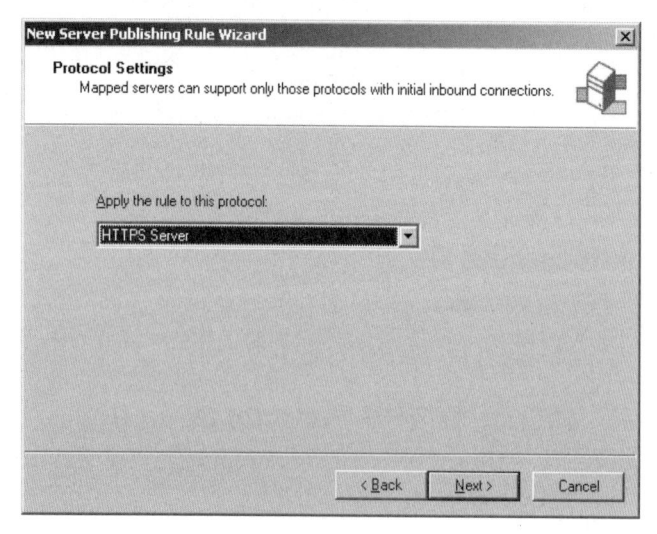

Figure 10-1. *Choose the HTTPS Server protocol definition.*

6. On the Client Type page, select the types of client requests that will be applied to this rule, and then click Next. The options include:

- **Any Request**
- **Specific Computers (Client Address Sets)** The wizard will prompt you to add client sets. Click Add to create a new client set, add or create the client sets, and then click OK. After returning to the Client Sets page, select the desired client sets, and then click Next to go to Step 7.

7. Review the rule configuration and then click Finish.

Publishing FTP Server

Two commonly used methods to make your FTP servers available to clients on the Internet are to use either packet filters or server publishing rules. As we know from previous chapters, packet filters provide more widespread access than server publishing rules but are sometimes necessary when services on the ISA server itself must be published.

Chapter 10 Common Web and Server Publishing Scenarios | 179

Using Packet Filters to Provide FTP Services

As we described in previous chapters, you must have IP Packet Filtering enabled in order for your ISA server to properly function as a firewall. If you're using a colocated FTP and ISA server configuration, you can simply create specific packet filters to enable external clients to access FTP services. Follow the steps below to configure packet filters for FTP.

To create an inbound packet filter for port 21, complete the following steps:

1. Open the ISA Management console.
2. In the left pane, expand your ISA server node, expand Access Policy, right-click IP Packet filters, select New, and then click Filter.
3. Type a name for the IP Packet Filter and then click Next.
4. Click the Allow Packet Transmission button on the Filter Mode page and then click Next.
5. Select the Custom option on the Filter Type page and then click Next.
6. On the Filter Settings page, choose the following options:
   - IP Protocol: TCP
   - Direction: Inbound
   - Local Port: Fixed Port (21)
   - Remote Port: All ports

   Click Next.
7. On the Local Computer page, select This ISA Server's External IP Address and then type the IP Address of the ISA server's external interface. If your ISA server has multiple network interfaces, select the Default IP Addresses For Each External Interface On The ISA Server Computer option button. Click Next.
8. Select All Remote Computers on the Remote Computers page and then click Next.
9. Review your settings for accuracy and then click Finish.

To create an outbound packet filter for port 20, complete the following steps:

1. Open the ISA Management console.
2. In the left pane, expand your ISA server node, expand Access Policy, right-click IP Packet filters, select New, and then click Filter.
3. Type a name for the IP Packet Filter and then click Next.
4. Select the Allow Packet Transmission button on the Filter Mode page and then click Next.
5. Select the Custom option on the Filter Type page and then click Next.
6. On the Filter Settings page, choose the options as follows:
   - IP Protocol: TCP
   - Direction: Outbound

- Local Port: Fixed Port (20)
- Remote Port: All ports

Click Next.

7. On the Local Computer page, select This ISA Server's External IP Address and then type the IP Address of the ISA server's external interface. If your ISA server has multiple network interfaces, select the Default IP Addresses For Each External Interface On The ISA Server Computer option button. Click Next.
8. Select All Remote Computers on the Remote Computers page and click Next.
9. Review your rule configuration and then click Finish.

Configuring FTP Packet Filters to Allow PASV Clients

If Internet Explorer clients have the Enable Folder View For FTP Sites option selected in their Advanced Internet Options tab, they connect in passive (PASV) mode, which might be rejected if you have packet filters enabled for your FTP client. You can either clear that check box on clients that connect, or you can enable PASV mode on your ISA server (this option isn't recommended, as it decreases the level of security) by following these steps:

1. Open Regedit.exe.
2. Navigate to HKEY_LOCAL_MACHINE/SYSTEM/CurrentControlSet/Services/W3Proxy/Parameters.
3. Right-click the NonPassiveFTPTransfer DWORD value and then click Modify.
4. Type **0** in the Value Data box (the default value is 1) and click OK.
5. Restart the ISA Server Web Proxy Service.

Publishing FTP Using ISA Server

Publishing your FTP server provides a more secure implementation than using packet filters, plus you have the added bonus of allowing both active and passive mode clients to access FTP services. You may publish FTP if the FTP services are on the ISA server itself or use packet filters, as described above. If, however, your FTP services are behind the ISA server, you should always choose to use publishing over packet filters.

To use server publishing to allow external clients to access your FTP server, perform the steps below.

Disabling Socket Pooling

By default, Internet Information Services (IIS) 5.0 uses a feature called Socket Pooling to listen on all external interfaces. Disable this feature using the steps shown at the beginning of this chapter.

Configuring FTP Server to Listen on the Internal Interface

You now need to configure your FTP server to listen on the internal interface of the ISA server by following these steps:

1. Open the Internet Information Services Manager and expand your server's node. If you're using Windows Server 2003, expand FTP Sites.
2. Right-click the Default FTP Site, select Properties, and then select the FTP Site tab.
3. The default IP Address setting is All Unassigned. Change it to the internal IP Address of the ISA server and then click OK.

Disabling Port Attack Mechanism

If your FTP site is located on the ISA server itself and you're using Windows 2000 Server, you'll need to disable the FTP port attack mechanism. This option was implemented to prevent certain FTP exploits; however, it also prevents ISA Server from properly publishing the FTP server. You can configure this parameter by following these steps:

1. Open the Registry Editor by typing **regedit.exe** in the Run command.
2. Work your way down to HKEY_LOCAL_MACHINE\SYSTEM\CurrentControlSet\Services\Msftpsvc\Parameters\.
3. Right-click the EnablePortAttack value in the right pane and then choose Modify.
4. Change the value to **1**.
5. Exit the Registry Editor and then restart the FTP service.

Configuring the Server Publishing Rule

Finally, you'll create and configure the server publishing rule that enables FTP access by following these steps:

1. Open the ISA Management console.
2. In the left pane, expand your ISA server node, expand the Publishing node, right-click Server Publishing Rules, click New, and then click Rule.
3. Type a name to be given to the rule, such as **Local FTP Server**, and then click Next.
4. Enter the internal IP address of the FTP Server specified in IIS.
5. Enter the IP address of the ISA server's external interface and click Next.

6. Select the FTP Server option in the Protocol Settings dialog box and click Next.
7. Review your rule configuration and then click Finish.

Enabling the FTP Access Filter

The FTP Access Application Filter is enabled by default. It's necessary for ISA Server to dynamically open packet filters for client sessions, so you should ensure its status by following these steps:

1. Open the ISA Management console.
2. In the left pane, expand your ISA server node, expand the Extensions node, and then click Application Filters.
3. In the right pane, right-click the FTP Access Filter. If the Enable option shows in the context menu, choose it.

> **Note** To enforce authentication for your published FTP server, you'll need to perform some additional steps. For detailed information, see Microsoft Knowledge Base article 310110, "HOW TO: Secure FTP Directory Access by Using Internet Security and Acceleration Server 2000" at *http://support.microsoft.com/?kbid=310110*.

Publishing Exchange Server

One of the most common activities in business today is making one's Exchange server available to external clients. A typical publishing scenario for Exchange on ISA server is to locate the Exchange server behind the ISA server; the steps below assume that architecture. We recognize that for financial reasons you might need to have ISA Server and Exchange Server located on the same server, and so we provide a section devoted to special requirements for this configuration. For even more information on this type of implementation, refer to the ISA Server Feature Pack 1 documentation.

> **Note** We assume in this chapter that you already have Exchange Server 2000 installed and running in your environment and that your ISA Server 2000 has Service Pack 1 (SP1) with the ISA Feature Pack 1 (FP1) installed, along with the most current patches. If you don't have this ISA Server configuration, see Chapter 2 for more information on how to install and configure both SP1 and FP1.

You can make your Exchange server available to external clients in three ways:

- **Mail-only access using POP3 or IMAP4 clients** You may use the Secure Mail Server Publishing Wizard to configure this scenario.
- **Message Application Programming Interface (MAPI) client access** This allows users to take full advantage of all Outlook features, including calendars and new mail notification; you can use the RPC Publishing Wizard for this scenario.

- **Web-based access using OWA** You can use the OWA Publishing Wizard for this scenario.

We'll provide step-by-step instructions on how to configure each of these scenarios.

Publishing a Mail Server Located Behind ISA Server

To successfully publish an internal Exchange Server behind an ISA Server computer, ensure that you configure the prerequisites outlined at the beginning of this chapter, and then follow the steps listed below.

Configuring DNS Resolution

To ensure that your Exchange server will be able to contact external mail servers and vice versa, confirm that DNS is on your network and can resolve Internet domain names. Use this checklist to verify that resolution is taking place correctly:

- Assign a public IP address provided by your Internet service provider (ISP), public vendor, or host site to your ISA server's external network adapter.
- Define your public Mail Exchange (MX) and Host (A) records and map them to the ISA server's external IP address.
- Verify that your external domain is registered publicly—that is, you can look it up at a site like *http://www.internic.net/whois.html*.

Configuring Server Client Type

Be sure to configure your Exchange Server as a SecureNAT client. See Chapter 3, "Installing and Configuring Microsoft ISA Server 2000 Clients," for detailed instructions. As long as your Exchange server and ISA server are installed on the same machine, it's possible to install the firewall client; however, it's not recommended.

Note that if you're in a complex network, your ISA server must have routes for all the networks in your environment. Use the ROUTE ADD command to configure routes if you don't have a dynamic routing protocol such as RIP enabled. See the Windows 2000 Help or Windows Server 2003 Help and Support Center documentation for more information.

Creating Client Address Sets

You'll need to create a client address set that defines your internal Exchange and DNS server or servers; the protocol rules that allow Exchange traffic to communicate with external clients will in turn use this policy element.

To create a client address set, follow the steps outlined in Chapter 7. Configure one client address set with the IP address of your Exchange server and another with that of your DNS server.

Creating Protocol Definitions

Before your Exchange server can communicate beyond the ISA Server firewall, you'll need to define a protocol rule that allows SMTP and DNS traffic. Without these rules, your Exchange servers can neither transmit e-mail nor resolve the FQDNs of external mail servers.

To create these protocol definitions, follow the steps defined in Chapter 7, and configure them with the settings described in Table 10-1.

Table 10-1. Protocol Rules Required for Exchange POP3 and IMAP Communications

Rule Name	Allow or Deny	Protocol Rule	Applies To
Allow SMTP Traffic	Allow	SMTP	Client address set defined for your Exchange server above
Allow DNS Traffic	Allow	DNS Query DNS Zone Transfer	Client address set configured for your DNS server as defined above

Note To publish multiple internal Exchange servers with server publishing rules, you need to add multiple IPs to the external interface or add multiple external interfaces with an IP bound to each. Remember, when using server publishing rules, after you bind an external IP to a specific port (for example, SMTP port 25), you can't configure additional server publishing rules to use the same port.

Running the Secure Mail Publishing Wizard

ISA Server provides the Mail Server Security Wizard, which will contain a protocol rule for the mail service, the external IP address of the ISA server, and the internal IP address of the Exchange server to which the external IP will map.

Note If you have both ISA Server and Exchange on the same server, the Mail Server Security Wizard creates packet filters rather than protocol rules.

To run the Mail Server Security Wizard, follow these steps:

1. Open the ISA Management console.
2. In the left pane, expand your ISA server node, expand the Publishing node, right-click Server Publishing Rules, and then click Secure Mail Server.
3. On the Welcome page, click Next.
4. On the Mail Services Selection page, select the following check boxes:
   - Incoming SMTP
   - Outgoing SMTP
   - Incoming POP3
   - Incoming IMAP4

5. On the ISA Server's External IP Address page, type the ISA Server computer's external IP address and then click Next.
6. On the Internal Mail Server page, click At This IP Address, type the internal IP address of the Exchange server, and then click Next.
7. Verify that the information is correct and then click Finish to complete the wizard.

The new rules that the wizard creates are all named with the prefix Mail wizard rule.

In summary, the Secure Mail Publishing Wizard automatically created the following items:

- The necessary server publishing rules for the protocols chosen (POP3, IMAP4, SMTP-Inbound)
- A single protocol rule for the SMTP client protocol (SMTP-Outbound)
- A client address set that contains your internal Exchange server's IP address

Publishing Exchange Using the RPC Publishing Wizard for Outlook Clients

You might need to configure your Exchange server so that remote clients using Outlook can connect back to the Exchange server across the Internet. Although configuring a virtual private network (VPN) is an option, it's much faster and more convenient for users to be able to connect through a standard Internet connection. You enable and configure the RPC filter to provide this functionality.

Note This configuration isn't available when your Exchange and ISA servers are colocated (both installed on the same server) or on an Exchange front-end server.

Configuring DNS Resolution Configure Server Client Type

You need to follow the basic steps described above to configure DNS. One additional consideration is that if the Exchange server's internal host name is different from the Exchange server's host name in the public Internet DNS database, you should create an entry in the Hosts file on the client computers that resolves the name for the Exchange server with the external IP address for the ISA Server computer.

Creating a Site and Content Rule

If you haven't done this already, create a site and content rule that will allow access to all Internet sites and content. For details on how to configure such a rule, refer to Chapter 8, "Configuring ISA Access Policy."

Configuring Client Address Sets

Follow the instructions given in the section of this chapter entitled "Publishing a Mail Server Located Behind ISA Server."

Creating Protocol Rules

To allow your internal Exchange server to communicate outward to clients and other mail servers, create protocol rules that allow this. Configure the protocol rules as defined above in Table 10-1.

Enabling Client Authentication

By default, external clients aren't able to authenticate directly with a Domain Controller on the internal network. You must configure the Exchange server to act as a proxy for these clients. To configure the Exchange server as a proxy for the Outlook client, complete the following steps:

1. On the Exchange Server computer, click the Start button and then click Run.
2. Type **regedit** and then click OK.
3. Go to the HKEY_LOCAL_MACHINE\SYSTEM\CurrentControlSet\Services\MSExchangeSA\Parameters key.
4. Right-click the Parameters key.
5. Choose the New option and then choose DWORD Value.
6. Type **No RFR Service**.
7. Double-click the new value and set Value Data to 1. Click OK.

Creating a Server Publishing Rule

ISA Server uses server publishing rules allowing external clients access to internal services. Your next step is to create such a server publishing rule to publish your Exchange server by following these steps:

1. Open the ISA Management console.
2. In the left pane, expand your ISA server node, expand the Publishing node, right-click Server Publishing Rules, click New, and then click Rule.
3. Type a Server Publishing Rule Name and then click Next.
4. In the Address Mapping page, type the internal and external address of the ISA Server computer in the appropriate fields.
5. In the Protocol Settings dialog box, for the Apply The Rule To This Protocol option, choose the Exchange RPC Server protocol, and then click Next.
6. Choose the default Any Request option and then click Next.
7. Review your rule configuration and then click Finish.

Configuring the Outlook Clients

By publishing the Exchange server, clients can use the same configuration when connecting by means of the Internet as they would when connecting locally.

However, if the internal and external names of the Exchange server differ, you might need to create a separate profile. For detailed steps on how to configure the different Outlook clients, refer to the ISA Server FP1 documentation.

Enabling Access to Exchange Servers Outside ISA Server

ISA Server FP1 also gives Outlook clients behind an ISA server the ability to access external Exchange servers through the use of Outbound RPC access. This option creates a more flexible environment to allow mail access across campuses through the Internet, and without the configuration of dedicated VPN connections or tunnels.

To enable Outlook clients to access Exchange servers outside the ISA server, follow these steps:

1. Open the ISA Management console.
2. In the left pane, expand your ISA server node, expand Access Policy, right-click Protocol Rules, click New, and then click Rule.
3. Type a name for the protocol rule and click Next.
4. On the Rule Action page, select Allow and click Next.
5. On the Protocols page, select Selected Protocols for the Apply This Rule To option. Select RPC in the Protocols list and click Next.
6. On the Schedule page, select the appropriate schedule and click Next.
7. On the Client Type page, select the appropriate client type and click Next.
8. Review your rule configuration and then click Finish.

Publishing an OWA Server

One of the most common and popular ways to access Exchange services is through the use of OWA, which provides Exchange clients' e-mail through a Web interface. To publish OWA through an ISA server, follow the steps below.

Prerequisites

Make sure you configure some items before you'll be able to publish OWA successfully:

- **DNS infrastructure** Configure your Exchange server's SMTP properties to use a Smart Host or configure the OWA server's internal network interface to use an internal DNS server that forwards requests to the ISP's DNS server.
- **ISA Server client configuration** Set up your OWA server as a SecureNAT client.
- **Authentication method** Change Authentication within IIS to use Basic Authentication. For more information, see the ISA Server FP1 documentation.

188 | Part II Microsoft ISA Server 2000 Policy Management and Publishing Services

- **Exchange mailbox configuration** If users have a mailbox, they should be able to use OWA. However, there's a property that can revoke access using Hypertext Transfer Protocol (HTTP) that's set in users account properties. If it was cleared, users can't connect.

Using a Web Publishing Rule

Once your infrastructure is in place, you can create a Web publishing rule for OWA by completing the following instructions.

Creating a Destination Set To create the Destination Set, perform the following steps:

1. Open the ISA Management console.
2. Expand the Policy Elements node, right-click Destination Sets, select New, and then select Set.
3. Type a name for the destination set and type a description if you want.
4. Click Add.
5. On the Add/Edit Destination page, type the FQDN or IP address of the external interface of ISA Server to which external users will connect.
6. In the Path field, type **/exchange/*** and then click OK.
7. Repeat Steps 4 and 5, in the path box type **/exchweb/***, and click OK.
8. Repeat Steps 4 and 5, in the path box type **/public/***, and click OK.
9. Click OK to finish.

Creating a Web Publishing Rule Perform the following steps to publish the server:

1. Open the ISA Management console.
2. In the left pane, expand your ISA server node, expand the Publishing node, right-click Web Publishing Rules, click New, and then click Rule.
3. Type a name to be given to the rule and then click Next.
4. On the Destination Sets page, click the drop-down list to select Specified Destination Set.
5. In the Name field, select the destination set you created above specifically for this rule, and then click Next.
6. On the Client Type page, select the types of client requests that will be applied to this rule and then click Next. The options include:
   - **Any Request** Applies to any request from any client.

   > **Note** If you configured ISA Server to always authenticate users on the Incoming Web Requests tab of the ISA Server properties, the rule will apply only to authenticated users.

   - **Specific Computers (Client Address Sets)** The wizard will prompt you to add client sets. Click Add to create a new client set, add or create the client sets, and then click OK. After returning to the Client Sets page, select the desired client sets and then click Next to go to Step 6.

- **Specific Users And Groups** The wizard will prompt you to add a user or group. Click Add, type the name of the user or group, click OK, and then click Next to go to Step 6.

7. On the Rule Action page, select Redirect The Request To This Internal Web Server and type the name or IP address of the internal Web server to be published. If using host headers, select the Send The Original Host Header To The Publishing Server Instead Of The Actual One check box. Click Next to continue.
8. Review the rule configuration and then click Finish.

Using the OWA Web Publishing Wizard

The OWA Wizard installs a listener to accept incoming requests, defines an OWA-specific destination set, and creates a Web publishing rule. To run the OWA, follow these steps:

1. Open the ISA Management console.
2. In the left pane, expand your ISA server node, expand the Publishing node, right-click Web Publishing Rules, click New, and then click Publish Outlook Web Access Server.
3. Type in a name for the rule and then click Next.
4. Type in the FQDN of the OWA server and then click Next.
5. Type in the FQDN external clients will use to access OWA and then click Next.
6. Select the Enable SSL check box. Click Select, select your SSL certificate, and then click OK. Click Next.
7. Review your rule configuration and then click Finish. Click Save Changes And Restart The Services and then click OK.

Publishing SQL Server

The optimal way to publish an internal SQL server located behind an ISA server is to use a server publishing rule. The following components are necessary for publishing a SQL server:

- Incoming listener
- Protocol definition
- Server publishing rule

Creating an Incoming Listener

To effectively use server publishing rules and prevent possible port contention on the external interface on the ISA server, create a unique incoming listener. To do this, see Chapter 9.

Using the Predefined Protocol Definition

Server publishing rules use predefined or custom protocol definitions to make a specific protocol or set of protocols available through the ISA server. A SQL server uses TCP port 1433 for communication, and ISA Server includes a predefined protocol definition called Microsoft SQL Server. The settings for the Microsoft SQL Server protocol definition are as follows:

- Port Number: 1433
- Protocol Type: TCP
- Direction: Inbound
- Secondary Connections: None

Creating a SQL Server Publishing Rule

To create a server publishing rule, follow these steps:

1. Open the ISA Management console.
2. In the left pane, expand your ISA server node, expand the Publishing node, right-click Server Publishing Rules, click New, and then click Rule.
3. Type a name to be given to the rule and click Next.
4. On the Address Mapping page, specify the external and internal IP addresses you'll associate with this rule. In the IP Address Of Internal Server field, type the IP address of the internal SQL server to be published. You may, in addition, click Find, and on the Find Internal IP Address page, type the name of the server. If you don't know the name of the server, click Browse, select the internal server, and then click Find to display the available internal IP addresses for that server. Select the IP address and then click OK. In the External IP Address On ISA Server field, type the IP address assigned to the external interface of the ISA server to be associated with the rule. Optionally, you can click Browse, select the IP address, and then click OK. Click Next to continue.
5. On the Protocol Settings page, click the drop-down list to select the Microsoft SQL Server protocol definition to apply to the initial inbound connections as shown in Figure 10-2, and then click Next.
6. On the Client Type page, select the types of client requests that will be applied to this rule and then click Next. The options include:
    - **Any Request**
    - **Specific Computers (Client Address Sets)**   The wizard will prompt you to add client sets. Click Add to create a new client set, add or create the client sets, and then click OK. After returning to the Client Sets page, select the desired client sets, and then click Next to go to Step 7.
7. Review the rule configuration and click Finish.

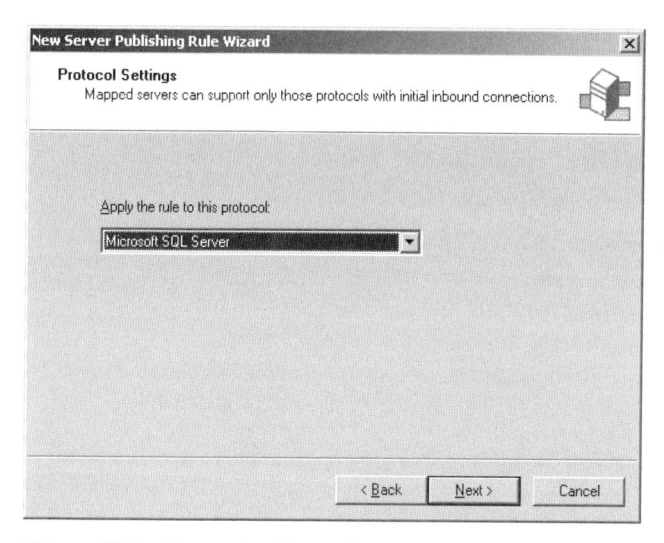

Figure 10-2. *Choose the Microsoft SQL Server protocol definition.*

Publishing Remote Desktop or a Terminal Server

Publishing Remote Desktop is appropriate when you, as a network administrator, want to remotely administer a server using Remote Desktop when you're away from the console. The procedure for publishing Remote Desktop is identical to the procedure for publishing a Terminal Server, because both Remote Desktop and Terminal Server use the same Remote Desktop Protocol (RDP). This scenario describes how to publish RDP from the internal network behind an ISA server by using a server publishing rule.

Creating an RDP Protocol Definition

Terminal services and Remote Desktop rely on RDP for communications. RDP is responsible for carrying the keyboard and mouse inputs, along with the screen shots across the network during a remote desktop session.

To create an RDP protocol definition, follow these steps:

1. Open the ISA Management console.
2. In the left pane, expand the Policy Elements node, right-click Protocol Definitions, select New, and then click Definition.
3. Type a name for the protocol definition and then click Next.
4. Type **3389** for the Port Number, select TCP for the Protocol Type, select Inbound as the Direction, and then select Next.

5. On the Secondary Connections page, keep the default setting of No because the RDP protocol doesn't require secondary connections. Click Next to continue.
6. Review the configuration and click Finish to complete.

Creating a RDP Publishing Rule

To create a server publishing rule, follow these steps:

1. Open the ISA Management console.
2. In the left pane, expand your ISA server node, expand the Publishing node, right-click Server Publishing Rules, click New, and then click Rule.
3. Type a name to be given to the rule, and click Next.
4. On the Address Mapping page, specify the external and internal IP addresses you'll associate with this rule. In the IP Address Of Internal Server field, type the IP address of the internal server to be published. You may, in addition, click Find, and on the Find Internal IP Address page, type the name of the server. If you don't know the name of the server, click Browse, select the internal server, and then click Find to display the available internal IP addresses for that server. Select the IP address and then click OK. In the External IP Address On ISA Server field, type the IP address assigned to the external interface of the ISA server to be associated with the rule. Optionally, you can click Browse, select the IP address, and then click OK. Click Next to continue.
5. On the Protocol Settings page, click the drop-down list to select the RDP protocol definition you created to apply to the initial inbound connections, and then click Next.
6. On the Client Type page, select the types of client requests that will be applied to this rule, and then click Next. The options include:
   - **Any Request**
   - **Specific Computers (Client Address Sets)** The wizard will prompt you to add client sets. Click Add to create a new client set, add or create the client sets, and then click OK. After returning to the Client Sets page, select the desired client sets, and then click Next to go to Step 7.
7. Review the rule configuration and then click Finish.

Publishing a Citrix Server

A Citrix server's functionality is very similar to that of a Microsoft Terminal server. Both commonly provide remote administration capabilities, and so actions to publish a Citrix server located behind an ISA server are detailed below:

- Configuring the Citrix server as a SecureNAT client
- Creating a Protocol Definition

- Creating a Server Publishing rule
- Configuring the Citrix server
- Configuring the Citrix clients

Configuring the Citrix Server as a SecureNAT Client

You should configure the Citrix server to be published as a SecureNAT client by following the steps explained in Chapter 3.

Creating a Citrix ICA Protocol Definition

The Citrix ICA protocol definition is necessary for allowing the ICA protocol to be published. To create a protocol definition, follow these steps:

1. Open the ISA Management console.
2. In the left pane, expand the Policy Elements node, right-click Protocol Definitions, select New, and then click Definition.
3. Type a name for the protocol definition and then click Next.
4. Type **1494** for the Port Number, select TCP for the Protocol Type, select Inbound as the Direction, and then select Next.
5. On the Secondary Connections page, keep the default setting of No, as the ICA protocol doesn't require secondary connections. Click Next to continue.
6. Review the configuration and then click Finish to complete.

Creating a Citrix Server Publishing Rule

The server publishing rule will map the IP address assigned to the external interface on the ISA server to the internal IP address used by the Citrix server. The rule will also use the protocol definition created for the Citrix ICA protocol above.

To create a server publishing rule to publish a Citrix server, follow these steps:

1. Open the ISA Management console.
2. In the left pane, expand your ISA server node, expand the Publishing node, right-click Server Publishing Rules, click New, and then click Rule.
3. Type a name to be given to the rule and then click Next.
4. On the Address Mapping page, specify the external and internal IP addresses you'll associate with this rule. In the IP Address Of Internal Server field, type the IP address of the internal Citrix server to be published. You may, in addition, click Find, and on the Find Internal IP Address page, type the name of the Citrix server. If you don't know the name of the server, click Browse, select the internal server, and then click Find to display the available internal IP addresses for that server. Select the IP address and then click OK. In the External IP Address On ISA Server field, type the IP address assigned to the external interface of the ISA server to be associated with the rule. Optionally, you can click Browse, select the IP address, and then click OK. Click Next to continue.

5. On the Protocol Settings page, click the drop-down list to select the protocol definition you created for the Citrix ICA protocol to apply to the initial inbound connections, and then click Next.
6. On the Client Type page, select the types of client requests that will be applied to this rule, and then click Next. The options include:
   - **Any Request**
   - **Specific Computers (Client Address Sets)** The wizard will prompt you to add client sets. Click Add to create a new client set, add or create the client sets, and then click OK. After returning to the Client Sets page, select the desired client sets, and then click Next to go to Step 7.
7. Review the rule configuration and then click Finish.

Configuring the Citrix Server

You must configure an alternate address on the Citrix server. The ALTADDR command allows the ICA Brower to listen for requests on more than one IP address. To configure the alternate address, follow these steps:

1. Open a command prompt window.
2. Type **altaddr /set *ip address***, where ip address is the external IP address on the ISA server used in Step 4 of the section of this chapter entitled "Creating a Citrix Server Publishing Rule," and then press Enter.
3. Type **exit** to close the command prompt window.
4. Restart the Citrix server.

Configuring the Citrix Clients

For ICA clients to connect to the published server, the ICA client software must be configured with the IP address of the external interface on the ISA server. This IP address is the address used in the server publishing rule and by the ALTADDR command.

Publishing a DNS Server

There might be times when you need to publish the DNS service located on the ISA server or a DNS server located behind the ISA server. Two options you have in publishing a DNS server include using either packet filters or server publishing rules.

> **Note** Before continuing, see Microsoft Knowledge Base article 331065, "A Problem In the ISA Server DNS Intrusion Detection Filter May Cause Denial Of Service" at *http://support.microsoft.com/?kbid=331065* to download and install the patch before publishing a DNS server.

Publishing a Public DNS Server Located Behind an ISA Server

In this scenario you can use server publishing rules to make your public DNS server available to receive and send DNS requests from external clients.

The following components are necessary for publishing a DNS server:

- Incoming listener
- Protocol definition(s)
- Server publishing rule(s)

Creating an Incoming Listener

To effectively use server publishing rules and prevent possible port contention on the external interface on the ISA server, you should create a unique incoming listener.

To create an incoming listener, see Chapter 9.

Using the Predefined Protocol Definition

ISA Server includes two predefined protocol definitions for the DNS service: DNS Query Server and DNS Zone Transfer Server. The settings for the DNS Query Server protocol definition are as follows:

- Port Number: 53
- Protocol Type: UDP
- Direction: Receive Send
- Secondary Connections: None

The settings for the DNS Zone Transfer Server protocol definition are as follows:

- Port Number: 53
- Protocol Type: TCP
- Direction: Inbound
- Secondary Connections: None

Creating a DNS Server Publishing Rule

To create a server publishing rule, follow these steps:

1. Open the ISA Management console.
2. In the left pane, expand your ISA server node, expand the Publishing node, right-click Server Publishing Rules, click New, and then click Rule.
3. Type a name to be given to the rule and then click Next.
4. On the Address Mapping page, specify the external and internal IP addresses you'll associate with this rule. In the IP Address Of Internal Server field, type the IP address of the internal DNS server to be published. You may, in addition, click Find, and on the Find Internal IP Address page, type the name of

the server. If you don't know the name of the server, click Browse, select the internal server, and then click Find to display the available internal IP addresses for that server. Select the IP address and then click OK. In the External IP Address On ISA Server field, type the IP address assigned to the external interface of the ISA server to be associated with the rule. Optionally, you can click Browse, select the IP address, and then click OK. Click Next to continue.

5. On the Protocol Settings page, click the drop-down list to select the DNS Query Server protocol definition to apply to the initial inbound connections, and then click Next.

6. On the Client Type page, select the types of client requests that will be applied to this rule and then click Next. The options include:
   - **Any Request**
   - **Specific Computers (Client Address Sets)**   The wizard will prompt you to add client sets. Click Add to create a new client set, add or create the client sets, and then click OK. After returning to the Client Sets page, select the desired client sets, and then click Next to go to Step 7.

7. Review the rule configuration and then click Finish.

8. If you need to allow DNS zone transfers to a secondary DNS server on the Internet, repeat Steps 1–7, but this time in Step 5 select the DNS Zone Transfer Server protocol definition.

Publishing a Public DNS Server on the ISA Server

This scenario describes how to publish the DNS service running on the ISA server by using packet filters. You need to create two custom packet filters, and you also need to utilize a predefined packet filter.

Using the Predefined DNS Query Packet Filter

ISA Server includes a packet filter for DNS queries that allows the ISA server to send DNS queries to an external DNS server and then in return receive responses from that DNS server. The DNS Filter settings are as follows:

- Name: DNS Filter
- Filter Type: Predefined
- Protocol: UDP
- Direction: Send Receive
- Local Port: All ports
- Remote Port: Fixed port, 53
- Local Computer: Default IP address on the external interface(s)
- Remote Computer: All remote computers

Creating Two DNS Server Packet Filters

You need to create two custom packet filters to allow the DNS server on the ISA server to receive incoming DNS queries from external clients (DNS Query filter) and to allow the DNS server to perform zone transfers with configured secondary DNS servers located on the Internet (DNS Zone Transfer filter).

To create a DNS Query packet filter, complete the following steps:

1. Open the ISA Management console.
2. In the left pane, expand your ISA Server node, expand Access Policy, right-click IP Packet Filters, click New, and then click Filter.
3. Type a name to be given to the IP Packet Filter and then click Next.
4. If you have an array of servers, you'll see the Servers page. Set whether the filter should be used by all ISA Server Computers In The Array or select the Only This Server option button and select the ISA server. Click Next to continue.
5. On the Filter Mode page, select Allow Packet Transmission and then click Next.
6. On the Filter Type page, choose Custom and then click Next.
7. On the Filter Settings page, type the following information as shown in Table 10-2. Click Next after you've entered the appropriate information.

Table 10-2. DNS Query Packet Filter Settings

Setting	Value
IP Protocol	UDP
Direction	Receive Send
Local Port	Fixed Port, 53
Remote Port	All Ports

8. On the Local Computer page, specify the IP address to which the packet filter applies. Click Next.
9. On the Remote Computers page, select the remote computers the packet filter applies to. Select All Remote Computers and then click Next to continue.
10. Review the IP packet filter configuration and click Finish to complete.

To create a DNS Zone Transfer packet filter, repeat Steps 1–10 while substituting the values for Step 7, as shown in Table 10-3:

Table 10-3. DNS Zone Transfer Packet Filter Settings

Setting	Value
IP Protocol	TCP
Direction	Both
Local Port	Fixed Port, 53
Remote Port	All Ports

Additional Resources

You can find additional information and resources about common scenarios and troubleshooting specific issues below:

General Scenario-Based References

- ISA Server 2000 Help documentation
- ISA Server Feature Pack 1 (FP1) documentation at *http://www.microsoft.com/isaserver/featurepack1/*
- Shinder, Tom and Debra Littlejohn Shinder. *ISA Server and Beyond*. Rockland, MA: Syngress, 2003

Microsoft Knowledge Base References

The Microsoft Knowledge Base provides many helpful articles that provide necessary background and additional steps that we can't cover in this book. Look up the articles and other topics of interest below at *http://support.microsoft.com/*.

- Article 303426, "ISA Server Publishing Rule Does Not Include SMTP Outbound Check Boxes"
- Article 304948, "RPC Interfaces That Are Exposed by Secure Mail Publishing in ISA Server 2000"
- Article 280437, "Exchange 2000 Server Exchange System Manager Cannot Open Public Folders"
- Article 296614, "Differences Between Exchange 2000 Standard and Enterprise Versions"
- Article 263237, "Windows 2000 and Exchange 2000 SMTP Use TCP DNS Queries"
- Article 224196, "Restricting Active Directory Replication Traffic to a Specific Port"
- Article 246739, "Exchange 2000 Server Front-End/ Back-End Terminology and Implementation"
- Article 291662, "How to Publish Domain Name System Servers with Internet Security and Acceleration Server"
- Article 269556, "DNS Queries Generated When Static Packet Filter Is Removed"
- If your organization doesn't have default routes out to the Internet, it's likely that your ISA server will drop FTP and RPC requests. See Article 311777, "How to Enable Translating Client Source Address in Server Publishing."

Part III
Microsoft ISA Server 2000 and Enterprise Systems Administration

Part III covers how to integrate Microsoft's ISA Server into enterprise environments. Chapter 11 reviews the differences between a stand-alone ISA server and an ISA array and then details how to install and configure ISA Server arrays. Chapter 12 focuses on enterprise and array policies and how those policies are applied to ISA Server arrays. Chapter 13 addresses the various enterprise technologies included with ISA Server, including Cache Array Routing Protocol (CARP), network load balancing, virtual private network (VPN) services, and the H.323 gatekeeper.

Chapter 11

Managing ISA Server and Windows Active Directory

This chapter reviews the concept of stand-alone server and array implementations of Microsoft ISA Server, and then explains how to install and configure ISA Server arrays in Microsoft Windows domains. The first section focuses on requirements for stand-alone versus array members. The next section outlines how to create ISA Server arrays in a Microsoft Windows 2000 and Microsoft Windows Server 2003 Active Directory directory service environment. The last section explains how to implement ISA Server in alternative domain environments to provide other levels of security.

Stand-Alone Versus Array Members

As we explained in Chapter 1, "Overview of Microsoft ISA Server 2000 Administration," Microsoft ISA Server 2000 Standard Edition allows only the option of installing a stand-alone server, which you must administer on an individual basis. Microsoft ISA Server 2000 Enterprise Edition provides the option of installing an individual ISA server into what is known as an array, from which you can administer many ISA servers using a single policy.

Note Even though you can install ISA Server 2000 Enterprise Edition as a stand-alone server, install the first ISA server as an array member to provide more flexibility, even if you'll have only one ISA server on your network.

Characteristics of a Stand-Alone ISA Server

You can install a stand-alone ISA server using either the Standard or Enterprise edition of ISA Server. Each stand-alone server has unique policies that you must administer on an individual basis; each server also stores its configuration information in the local registry (as compared to array members, which store ISA Server configuration data in Active Directory). Without Active Directory, you can use other products, such as Microsoft Application Center 2000, or write scripts to manage multiple stand-alone ISA servers; however, you'll need similar hardware and configurations (in the case of Application Center 2000), and additional effort to ensure standardization (in the case of scripts). You can promote a stand-alone server to an array member by following the steps provided in Chapter 2, "Installing and Configuring Microsoft ISA Server 2000."

Characteristics of an ISA Server Array Member

Installing an array member requires ISA Server 2000 Enterprise Edition and an implementation of the Active Directory, where all array data are stored. When you create an array, the name of the first server becomes the name of the array; you have no limit to the number of servers that can participate in the array.

> **Tip** You can rename an array using the ISA Management snap-in by right-clicking the array, selecting Properties, and then typing the new name in the Name field. Click OK to complete renaming the array.

An array utilizes enterprise-wide policies that you can easily distribute among multiple ISA servers, which helps provide valued fault tolerance capabilities for ISA Server. Enterprise and array policies are the focus of Chapter 12, "Using Enterprise and Array Policies."

Active Directory Interoperability

In general, most array configuration is stored within Active Directory, whereas a stand-alone server stores configuration information within the registry. There are, however, some exceptions in which data are stored on individual servers. These exceptions include:

- Static filters
- Cache content and activity logs
- Generated reports (settings exist on all members, but the reports themselves are stored on one)

> **Note** When you back up ISA Server arrays, server-specific information isn't included.

Creating and Configuring ISA Server Arrays

Creating and configuring ISA Server arrays gives you the ability to better manage groups of ISA Server computers. You'll need to know the criteria required to install an array. This section describes those criteria and additional security requirements, and then provides detailed steps for installing and configuring arrays.

ISA Server Array Criteria

To use ISA Server arrays, you should understand the criteria for ISA Server arrays:

- You must use ISA Server 2000 Enterprise Edition.
- Active Directory must be installed on the network.
- All array members must belong to the same Windows 2000 or Windows Server 2003 domain.
- All array members must belong to the same site.
- All array members must be installed in the same mode (cache, firewall, or integrated).
- An array can contain one or more members.
- You must install the same add-ins (such as application filters, Web filters, and so on) on all array members for consistent functionality.

Administrative Requirements for ISA Server Arrays

See Table 11-1 for a description of the administrative requirements to install or configure stand-alone servers and arrays.

Table 11-1. Administrative Requirements for Stand-Alone Servers and Array Members

Action	Administrative Membership
Create stand-alone ISA server	Administrators group on the local server (which should, of course, include Domain Admins)
Modify the Active Directory schema (by running the Enterprise Initialization tool)	Enterprise Admins and Schema Admins group of the forest to which the servers belong
Promote an existing stand-alone ISA server to an array member	Domain Admin or Enterprise Admin for the domain or forest, or both, to which the server belongs

Creating the Array Environment

To prepare your ISA Server environment to support arrays, you'll need to ensure that you've completed the tasks we described in other places in this book:

- Update the schema by using the Enterprise Initialization Tool. For information on this, see Chapter 2, "Running the Enterprise Initialization Tool."
- Ensure that the schema extensions have been updated and replicated to all domain controllers. See Chapter 2, "Verifying Schema Extensions."
- Configure enterprise policy settings. See Chapter 2, "Configuring Enterprise Policy Settings" and "Enterprise and Array Policies Explained," and Chapter 12, "Using Enterprise and Array Policies."
- Promote any stand-alone servers into the array. See Chapter 2, "Promoting a Stand-Alone Server to an Array Member."

Creating a New Array

Once you've configured your environment, you might need to configure a new array to manage a set of ISA servers. To create a new array, follow these steps:

1. Open the ISA Management console.
2. In the left pane, right-click Servers And Arrays, click New, and then click Array.
3. Type a name for the array and then click Next.
4. On the Domain Name page, click the top drop-down list to select the site the server is a part of, click the bottom drop-down list to select the domain, and then click Next.
5. On the Create Or Copy An Array page, you have the option to create a new array or copy an existing array. If you select Copy This Array, click the drop-down list to select the array to be copied, and then click Next.

Note If you copy an existing array, after clicking Next the wizard is complete. Review the configuration and then click Finish.

6. On the Enterprise Policy Settings page, you can define whether enterprise policies should be enabled for the array. The options are explained in Table 11-2.

Table 11-2. Enterprise Policy Options

Options	Explanation
Do Not Use Enterprise Policy	Select this option if you choose not to use an enterprise policy.
Use Default Enterprise Policy Settings	Select this option to use default values. If you choose this option, continue to Step 8.
Use Custom Enterprise Policy Settings	Select this option to specify custom values for an enterprise policy.
Allow Array Policy	This option is available when you choose Use Custom Enterprise Policy Settings.

Click Next to continue.

7. On the Array Policy Options At Enterprise Level page, if you choose to allow publishing rules to be created on the array or wish to force packet filtering on the array, select the respective check boxes and then click Next.
8. On the Array Type page, select the mode (Cache, Firewall Only, or Integrated) to be used by the array member and then click Next.

Note The mode must be the same for all members of the same array.

9. Review the configuration and then click Finish.

Adding or Removing Array Members

When you add or remove array members, remember that the information stored in Active Directory must replicate to all other domain controllers in the domain. Be sure to back up your array configuration before you make changes to array membership; this easy step will save you a lot of time should anything go awry.

Backing Up and Restoring an Array Configuration Backing up an array member is a process that's similar to backing up an ISA stand-alone server. Both types of backups use the procedures below and will be saved with a .bif file name extension. To back up an array, follow these steps:

1. Open the ISA Management console.
2. In the left pane, right-click your array and then click Back Up.
3. In the Backup Array window, in the Store Backup Configuration In This Location field, type the full path and name for the backup file you're creating. You may type a description in the Comment field to provide any additional information you'd like to keep regarding the backup.

Note Although the ISA Help file states that the path should be a local NTFS drive, you can create a backup file and store it on a remote computer on the network.

4. Click OK to complete. Click OK again when the Backup Array dialog box notifies you that the array data has been successfully backed up.

To restore an array configuration, follow these steps:

1. Open the ISA Management console.
2. In the left pane, right-click your array and then click Restore.
3. When prompted to confirm the replacement of the existing configuration as shown in Figure 11-1, click Yes.

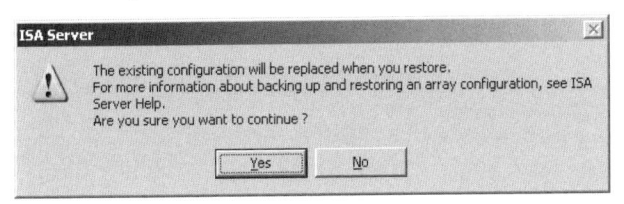

Figure 11-1. *Restoring an array configuration with a previous backup file overwrites the existing configuration.*

4. In the Restore Array dialog box, in the Restore Array Configuration From The Following Backup (.BIF) File field, type the full path for the backup file and then click OK.

Note The backup file selected must be the backup file for the same array you're planning to restore. You can't use a backup file from a different array during a restore, nor can you restore an array to a stand-alone server.

5. Click OK. Click OK at the Restore Array dialog box to verify the backup file selected and to complete the restore. Click OK again when you're notified that the array data has been restored successfully.

Removing an Array Member When you delete all servers from an array, the last server deleted removes the array itself. To remove an ISA server from an array, follow these steps:

1. Open the ISA Management console.
2. In the left pane, expand your ISA server node and then click Computers.
3. In the right pane, right-click the ISA server to be removed from the array and click Delete.
4. Click Yes to confirm the deletion as shown in Figure 11-2.

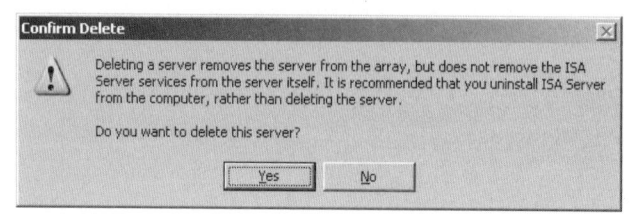

Figure 11-2. *When you remove an ISA server from an array, you're asked to confirm the deletion.*

Adding an Array Member To add a server to an array, you must either install or reinstall ISA Server, as joining an existing array is an option available during initial ISA Server installation. Remember that the mode—cache, firewall, or integrated—of the server joining the array must match that of the other array members.

Moving an ISA Array Member to a Different Array

To move a server to a different array, you must uninstall and then reinstall ISA Server, as joining a different array is an available option during initial ISA Server installation (as long as you've run the enterprise initialization tool and multiple arrays are already configured). Follow the steps shown in Chapter 2 to uninstall and then install a new ISA server.

Configuring Array Permissions

To grant additional administrators the permissions to manage an array, follow these steps:

1. Open the ISA Management console.
2. In the left pane, right-click the array and then click Properties.
3. Click the Security tab.
4. Click Add to grant a new user or group permissions to manage the array and then the appropriate permissions. Click Remove to deny a user or group the permissions to manage the array.
5. Click OK to complete.

ISA Server 2000 and Domain Integration

Environments in which companies haven't yet implemented the use of Active Directory, or in which separate forests must share resources, present special considerations for ISA Server implementations. You'll have several options available to you; however, in all designs the members of an ISA Server array must reside within the same domain and be a part of the same physical site.

Managing a Multidomain Configuration and Trust Relationships

The ISA Server implementations we've shown so far were installed into an existing domain; ISA Server is flexible enough to also reside in a domain created specifically for ISA servers. Usually, you'll need to install ISA Server into its own domain when ISA Server can't be integrated with Active Directory or where ISA Server must accommodate clients from different Windows domains.

ISA Server and Windows NT 4.0 domains

ISA Server can be a member of a Microsoft Windows NT 4.0 domain but can only be installed in stand-alone mode. The reason, as noted earlier, is because ISA Server is dependent upon Active Directory for establishing an ISA Server array. If you need an ISA Server array and your company's domain is still operating with Windows NT 4.0, you have the choice of upgrading your Windows NT 4.0 domain to a Windows 2000 or Windows Server 2003 domain or creating a new Windows 2000 or Windows Server 2003 domain.

Upgrading Your Windows NT 4.0 Domain If you haven't already done so, you probably have plans to upgrade your Windows NT 4.0 domain to a Windows 2000 or Windows Server 2003 domain. If you don't have plans to upgrade, we would recommend doing so soon, as support for Windows NT 4.0 is near its end. This option gives you the opportunity to upgrade your infrastructure and the ability to promote a stand-alone ISA server to an array member, once you've modified the schema by running the enterprise initialization tool. For links to articles on upgrading your domain, see "Additional Resources" at the end of this chapter.

Creating a New Windows 2000 or Windows Server 2003 Domain If your company has no plans to upgrade the Windows NT 4.0 domain to Windows 2000 or Windows Server 2003, you can create a new domain for the sole purpose of hosting ISA Server. The ISA server will be a member of the new domain, and you'll need to configure a trust relationship in which the new domain trusts the existing Windows NT 4.0 domain, as shown in Figure 11-3. Creating this trust allows the users in the NT 4.0 domain the capability to authenticate to the ISA server for outbound access.

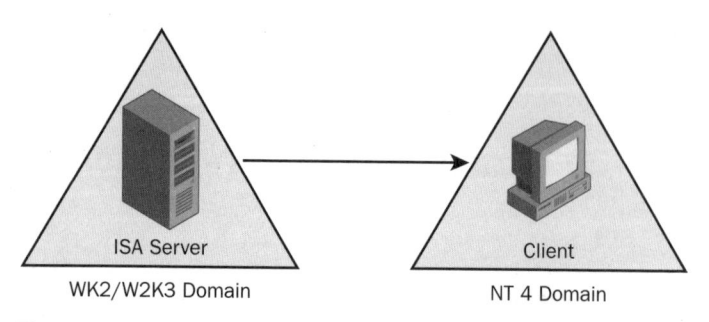

Figure 11-3. *The Windows 2000 and the Windows Server 2003 domains trust the Windows NT 4.0 domain so that its clients can use ISA Server services.*

ISA Server and Windows 2000 and Windows Server 2003 Domains

When ISA Server is a member of Windows 2000 or Windows Server 2003 domains, you have the most options for configuring the ISA server as a stand-alone server or an array member.

ISA Server in a Single Domain In a single domain environment, you can either join the ISA server to the existing domain and then configure it as an array member or create a new domain specifically for the ISA server. Creating a new domain in the existing forest provides an additional level of security, as a domain is, by definition, a security boundary. Because Windows 2000 or Windows Server 2003 implement two-way transitive trusts between all domains in a forest, creating a new domain automatically establishes the necessary trusts for the users to be authenticated during outbound access

To provide another level of security, you could create a new domain in a separate forest; this would require you to manually configure an implicit, one-way trust, which helps to ensure that only specified personnel are granted rights to administer ISA Server in the new domain. In Windows Server 2003, you could easily use a new feature known as a two-way forest trust to establish the trust between the two domains in different forests. For more information, see the "Additional Resources" section at the end of this chapter.

ISA Server in Multiple Domains with Trusts If you're using ISA Server in a multiple domain environment, trust relationships are key. If you place an ISA server within a domain in a Windows 2000 or Windows Server 2003 forest, you must establish implicit two-way trusts between each domain. If you want to place ISA Server within a new domain outside your existing forest, there's no implicit trust between two domains in separate forests. You'll need to create an explicit one-way trust from the domain that ISA Server is in, trusting the domain in the other forest where your users and computer accounts reside. The benefit of creating an ISA server in an isolated forest is security. But with the added security comes additional management of both establishing explicit trusts and connecting to the ISA server.

More Info For detailed step-by-step explanations of trust administration, see *Microsoft Windows 2000 Administrator's Pocket Consultant* or *Microsoft Windows Server 2003 Administrator's Pocket Consultant*, both published by Microsoft Press and written by William R. Stanek.

Additional Resources

- "Upgrading Windows NT 4.0 Domains to Windows Server 2003" in the Windows Server 2003 Resource Kit at *http://www.microsoft.com/technet/prodtechnol/windowsserver2003/evaluate/cpp/reskit/adsec/part1/rkpdswnt.asp*.
- There are several relevant articles in the Microsoft Knowledge Base. You can find them by going to *http://support.microsoft.com/?kbid=**article number*** (insert the correct number at the end of the URL).
    - Article 296480, "HOW TO: Upgrade a Windows NT4.0-Based PDC to a Windows 2000-Based Domain Controller"
    - Article 295654, "Windows 2000 Server Cannot Join Existing ISA Array"
    - Article 296657, 'The Computer Cannot Join an Array' Error Message and Error Code 0x8007203a Logged When You Try to Install ISA Server 2000 Enterprise Edition"
    - Article 323774, "ISA Server Services Are Unavailable for an Array Partner"
    - Article 284761, "Error Message 'Could Not Register Smtpfltr.dll' Occurs When You Attempt to Install ISA Server in an Array"
    - Article KB288214, "The ISA Server Array Configuration Cannot Be Restored"

Chapter 12

Using Enterprise and Array Policies

One of the many reasons Microsoft ISA Server 2000 can easily scale to enterprise-size environments is its ability to centrally administer and enforce policies. This chapter focuses on the administration and management of enterprise and array policies, which you can push down to a number of ISA servers from a central console, making the administration of ISA Server easier than ever.

Enterprise and Array Policies Explained

In order to use enterprise policies and arrays, you must install ISA Server Enterprise Edition and the ISA server must be a member of a Microsoft Windows 2000 Server or Microsoft Windows Server 2003 domain. To configure policies, you must have sufficient rights to administer them; normally, you must be a member of the Enterprise Administrators group to administer enterprise policies and a member of the Domain Administrators group to administer array policies (although you can configure security for policies using the procedures shown later in this chapter). You can create many enterprise policies that are applicable to one or many arrays.

Note Enterprise and array policies aren't available in ISA Server Standard edition. For more information about the differences between the versions of ISA Server, see Chapter 1, "Overview of ISA Server 2000 Administration."

An array consists of one or several ISA servers that you administer with the same set of policies. An enterprise policy consists of site and content rules as well as protocol rules that are then applied to arrays. You may also create policy elements at the enterprise level that propagate down to all ISA servers in the organization. For a comparison of enterprise and array policies, see Table 12-1.

Table 12-1. Comparing Enterprise and Array Policies

Policy Setting	Enterprise Policy	Array Policy
Applies policies to all arrays in the enterprise	Yes	No
Applies policies to individual members of an array	No	Yes
Can only further restrict an enterprise policy	No	Yes

Enterprise policies apply to all servers in the targeted array; you can then configure and apply array policies to further restrict the ISA server configuration.

Enterprise and Array Decisions

Enterprise policies provide the baseline configuration for the policies available in your environment; you must choose how restrictive you want that baseline to be. When using array policies in conjunction with enterprise policies, remember that array policies can only impose further restrictions; at the array level you won't be able to open up any rights restricted by the enterprise policy.

You may be as strict or lenient as your business case requires. For example, you could set your enterprise policy to apply to all ISA servers and restrict any configuration of array policies. Alternatively, you may allow array administrators to configure any and all rules. Most administrators choose a hybrid approach where they create basic restrictions in the enterprise policy—such as restricting access to pornography or gambling sites by denying access to certain destination sets—and then allow administrators to further configure settings at the array level. See Table 12-2 for a description of what you can configure in enterprise and array policies.

Table 12-2. Configurable Options in Enterprise and Array Policies

	Enterprise Policy	Array Policy
Policy Elements	Create	Create if allowed by enterprise policy
Site and Content Rules	Create	Create if allowed by enterprise policy
Protocol Rules	Create	Create if allowed by enterprise policy
Web and Server Publishing Rules	Not available	Create
IP Packet Filters	Not available	Create

Your ISA Server mode affects the extent to which enterprise policies operate. Cache mode only supports an access policy for Hypertext Transfer Protocol (HTTP) traffic, whereas integrated or firewall modes allow full use of all policies and rules.

Configuring Enterprise Policy Settings

You have three options for applying an enterprise policy at the array level:

- **Enterprise Policy Only** This option allows only the preferred enterprise policy to apply at the array level; you can't configure any array policies.
- **Combined Enterprise And Array Policy** This option ensures that the enterprise policy applies by default, and an array policy can further restrict (but can't override) the enterprise policy settings.
- **Array Policy Only** No enterprise policy applies to arrays, which allows the array administrator full control of creating and configuring any array policy.

If you wish to change the default enterprise policy settings, you must ensure that all arrays' policy settings are set at the default setting of Use Custom Enterprise Policy Settings. To change an array policy so that you can use custom enterprise policy settings, follow these steps:

1. Open the ISA Management console.
2. In the left pane, expand the Servers And Arrays node, right-click the applicable array, and then click Properties.
3. Select the Policies tab.
4. Select Use Custom Enterprise Policy Settings and then click OK.

Caution Use caution when changing enterprise policies, as they change the rules configured at the array level.

Enterprise Policy Administration

This section explains how to perform administrative tasks related to managing an enterprise, paying special attention to enterprise policies. We start by describing how to create and configure enterprise policies. Before we go over the process for deleting policies, we explain how to back up and restore enterprise settings. After a brief discussion of how to administer enterprise-level permissions, we'll cover how to connect to remote ISA Server enterprises or arrays, or both. Finally, we'll illustratehow to set a default enterprise policy.

Note Remember that you must be a member of the Enterprise Administrators group to create and configure enterprise policies.

Creating Enterprise Policies

You'll use enterprise policies when you want to manage all the arrays in your environment from a central location. You can configure site and content rules, protocol rules, and policy elements through an enterprise policy; to create one, follow these steps:

1. Open the ISA Management console.
2. In the left pane, expand the Enterprise node, right-click Policies, click New, and then click Policy.
3. Type a name for the policy and then click Next.
4. Click Finish to complete the creation of the enterprise policy.

Configuring Enterprise Policies

To set the default configurations for all the ISA Server arrays in your enterprise environment, you'll need to complete the following steps:

1. Open the ISA Management console.
2. In the left pane, right-click the Enterprise node and then click Set Defaults.
3. In the Set Defaults dialog box, you can choose to modify the default enterprise policy settings as shown in Table 12-3.

Table 12-3. Default Enterprise Policy Settings

Enterprise Settings	Explanation
Use Array Policy Only	This option configures the array to use its own policy.
Use This Enterprise Policy	This option configures the selected arrays to use the configuration defined in an enterprise policy.
Allow Array-Level Access Rules That Restrict Enterprise Policy	This option is available only when choosing Use This Enterprise Policy. This option allows array administrators to create array level rules, but won't actually create any rules itself.
Allow Publishing Rules	This option allows an array to publish servers. You can't create publishing rules at the enterprise level.
Force Packet Filtering On The Array	This option allows an array administrator the ability to choose the enforce packet filtering option at the array level, but does not actually set packet filtering details for all arrays. This option forces the selection of the Enable Packet Filtering check box in the General tab of the IP Packet Filters properties at the array level.

4. Click OK to complete.

Backing Up and Restoring an Enterprise Configuration

Before you make major changes to your enterprise environment, you should back up the enterprise configuration. This backup process will save all enterprise policies, enterprise policy elements, and the relationships between arrays and enterprise policies into a file that you can store in a directory of your choosing. It doesn't, however, save any array-specific information; after you back up your enterprise configuration, you should then perform the steps outlined in Chapter 11, "Managing ISA Server and Windows Active Directory," to backup each array configuration affected by your enterprise policy.

To back up an enterprise configuration, complete the following steps:

1. Open the ISA Management console.
2. In the left pane, right-click the Enterprise node and then click Back Up.
3. In the Backup Enterprise Configuration dialog box, type the full path and name for the backup file to be created in the Store Backup Configuration In This Location field. You may type a description in the Comment field to provide any additional information you'd like to keep regarding the backup.

Tip Although the ISA Help file states that the path should be a local NTFS drive, you can create a backup file and store it on a remote computer on the network.

4. Click OK to initiate the backup.
5. Click OK after the backup is complete.

When you restore your enterprise configurations, you should also be sure to restore each array configuration by following the instructions discussed in Chapter 11.

To restore an enterprise configuration, follow these steps:

1. Open the ISA Management console.
2. In the left pane, right-click the Enterprise node and then click Restore.
3. When prompted to confirm the replacement of the existing configuration, as shown in Figure 12-1, click Yes.

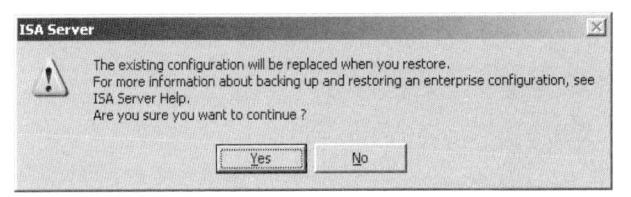

Figure 12-1. *You're prompted to confirm the replacement of the existing enterprise configuration.*

4. In the Restore Enterprise Configuration dialog box, type the full path for the backup file in the Restore Array Configuration From The Following Backup (.BEF) File field, and then click OK.
5. Click OK to verify the backup file selected and to complete the restore.
6. Click OK after the restore is complete.

Deleting Enterprise Policies

When you no longer require an enterprise policy, it's best to delete the policy by following these steps:

1. Open the ISA Management console.
2. In the left pane, expand the Enterprise node and then expand the Policies node.
3. Right-click the applicable enterprise policy and then click Delete.
4. When prompted to confirm the deletion, click Yes to remove the policy.

Enterprise Administration and Permissions

By default, only Enterprise Administrators have permissions to modify enterprise configurations and policies. To configure these enterprise permissions, follow these steps:

1. Open the ISA Management console.
2. In the left pane, right-click the Enterprise node and then click Properties.
3. In the Security tab, click Add to grant a new user or group permissions to modify the enterprise policy configuration. Next, apply the the appropriate permissions, and follow the prompts. To deny a user or group the permissions to modify the enterprise policy configuration, click Remove and follow the prompts.
4. Click OK to complete.

To configure enterprise policy permissions, follow these steps:

1. Open the ISA Management console.
2. In the left pane, expand the Enterprise node and then expand the Policies node.
3. Right-click the applicable enterprise policy and then click Properties.
4. In the Security tab, click Add to grant a new user or group permissions to modify the enterprise policy configuration. Next, apply the appropriate permissions, and follow the prompts. To deny a user or group the permissions to modify the enterprise policy configuration, click Remove and follow the prompts.
5. Click OK to complete the process.

Connecting to Remote Enterprise and Arrays

The ISA Management console gives you the ability to manage any enterprise and array in a network environment.

To connect to remote enterprise and arrays, follow these steps:

1. Open the ISA Management console.
2. In the left pane, right-click Internet Security and Acceleration Server and then click Connect To.
3. In the Connect To dialog box, click Connect To Enterprise And Arrays, as shown in Figure 12-2. Click OK.

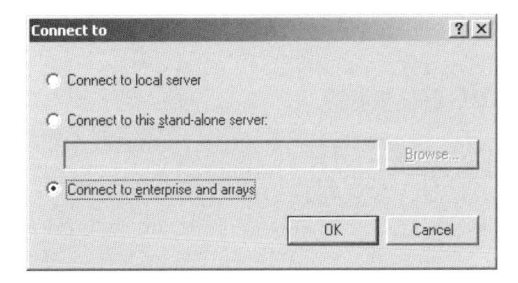

Figure 12-2. *Use the Connect To dialog box to connect to another enterprise and array for remote administration.*

Applying an Enterprise Policy to Selective Arrays

In an enterprise environment, you might be managing multiple arrays and enterprise policies and require the ability to determine which enterprise policies apply to certain arrays.

To apply an enterprise policy to arrays selectively, follow these steps:

1. Open the ISA Management console.
2. In the left pane, expand the Enterprise node, expand the Policies node, right-click the applicable enterprise policy, and then click Properties.
3. Select the Arrays tab.
4. Check the specific arrays to assign this policy to.
5. Click OK.
6. Click OK again if you're warned about incompatible backup files.

Note If you're applying an enterprise policy to an array that currently doesn't use any type of enterprise policy, all rules that allow access will be deleted from the array.

Setting a Default Enterprise Policy

With the capability of defining multiple enterprise policies, you'll probably want to change the default enterprise policy at some point.

To set a default enterprise policy, follow these steps:

1. Open the ISA Management console.
2. In the left pane, expand the Enterprise node, expand the Policies node, right-click the applicable enterprise policy, and then click Set As Default Policy.

Array Policy Administration

Administration at the array level varies according to the options you choose for the enterprise policy. An array policy used in conjunction with an enterprise policy will only further restrict the settings imposed. An array policy manages the way in which outbound communication for ISA Server clients works, and it includes the potential to create and configure site and content rules, Internet Protocol (IP) packet filters, Web publishing rules, and server publishing rules. If an array policy isn't tied to an enterprise policy, the array policy rules might allow and deny access based on the needs of the array administrator.

Allowing Array Policies

Before you create an array policy, you must first allow array policies to be applied. To allow array policies, follow these steps:

1. Open the ISA Management console.
2. In the left pane, right-click the Enterprise node and then click Set Defaults.
3. Select Use Array Policy Only and then click OK.

Note The option to Use Array Policy Only is also presented during the enterprise initialization. This selection doesn't prevent you from creating an enterprise policy, only from applying it to the array.

Configuring Array Policies

You have several options if you want to enforce settings on arrays from the enterprise, which we discuss in the following sections. For in-depth information about how to administer individual arrays, see Chapter 11.

Forcing Packet Filtering for an Array

If your default enterprise settings force packet filtering, then your array will have packet filtering enabled. If, however, this setting is not enforced at the enterprise level, you may enforce it at the array level. This selection helps to ensure that packet filtering, which drops any unauthorized packets, is enabled and protecting your network.

To enforce packet filtering at the array level, follow these steps:

1. Open the ISA Management console.
2. In the left pane, right-click the applicable array and then click Properties.
3. Select the Policies tab.
4. Select the Force Packet Filtering On The Array check box and then click OK.

Allowing Publishing Rules in an Array

You can't create publishing rules at the enterprise level. In order to publish an internal server, you must enable publishing at the array level.

To allow publishing rules in an array, follow these steps:

1. Open the ISA Management console.
2. In the left pane, right-click the applicable array and then click Properties.
3. Select the Policies tab.
4. Select the Allow Publishing Rules check box and then click OK.
5. Click OK again if you're warned about incompatible backup files.

Configuring Enterprise Policy Settings for an Array

To apply an enterprise policy to an array, follow these steps:

1. Open the ISA Management console.
2. In the left pane, expand the Servers And Arrays node, right-click the applicable array, and then click Properties.
3. Select the Policies tab.

4. Using Table 12-3, choose the appropriate selections, and then click OK. The Policies tab is shown in Figure 12-3.

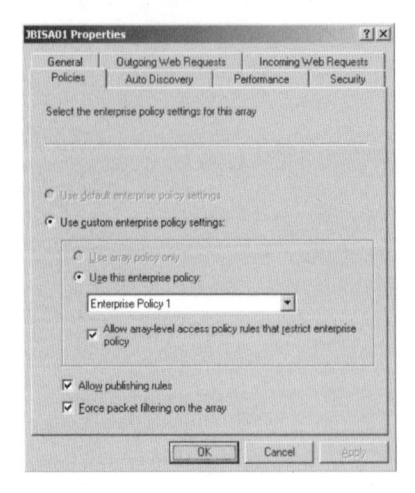

Figure 12-3. *The Policies tab allows you to determine how settings will apply to the array.*

Note Which options are available depends on the default settings configured at the enterprise level.

Backing Up, Restoring and Deleting an Array Configuration

Before you make any modifications to an array, you should back it up. If any problems result from your change, you can then restore the original configuration and avoid the time-consuming processes of diagnosing, fixing, and sometimes even recreating your ISA Server arrays.

The backup process for arrays will save most information, but a few configurations aren't saved. See Table 12-4 for a summary of what is saved in an array backup.

Table 12-4. ISA Server Array Backup Configuration

Configuration Information	Backed Up?
Access policy rules	Yes
Publishing rules	Yes
Policy elements	Yes
Alert configuration	Yes

Table 12-4. ISA Server Array Backup Configuration

Configuration Information	Backed Up?
Cache configuration	Yes
Array properties	Yes
Cache content	No
Activity logs reports	No
Effective enterprise policy	No

You won't be able to restore an array backup to an array other than the one that was originally backed up. To back up, restore, or delete an array, follow the procedures outlined in Chapter 11.

Additional Resources

- Microsoft Knowledge Base has several articles that might be of interest to you. Go to *http://support.microsoft.com/?kbid*=article number to find them.
    - Article 262366, "The Enterprise or Array Policies Restricting Internet Access Do Not Seem to Work"
    - Article 315667, "HOW TO: Configure an Enterprise Policy in ISA Server"
    - Article 284835, "Cannot Connect to the Enterprise Administration Console"
    - Article 317238, "How to Grant Administrator Rights to a User or a Group in ISA Server"
- For tools that will help to automate the backup and restore of enterprise and array configurations, visit the ISA Server script and tool site managed by ISA Server Sustained Engineering team members and ISA tool expert Jim Harrison at *http://www.isatools.org*.

Chapter 13

Working with Enterprise Technologies and ISA Server 2000

If you work in an enterprise (usually defined as a mid-sized to large company), you'll need to support many clients using a range of different technologies. Don't be thrown off, however, by the term "enterprise technology." Smaller companies also use such technologies, as is the case with virtual private networks, or VPNs, which many small companies employ to support geographically distributed sites and roaming clients. Below is a list of the technologies we'll cover in this chapter:

- **Cache Array Routing Protocol (CARP)** A large internet content cache that is distributed throughout different servers in the organization
- **Network Load Balancing** Redundancy for your Microsoft ISA servers
- **Virtual private networks (VPNs)** Clients that connect to your network remotely and securely
- **H.323 gatekeeper** Audio, video, and data collaboration traffic

We explain these technologies briefly and then provide steps that outline how to install, configure, and monitor each one.

Cache Array Routing Protocol (CARP)

CARP allows your clients access to a Web cache distributed across multiple ISA servers. For details on how CARP works, see "Cache Array Routing Protocol" in the ISA Server 2000 Help documentation. For our purposes, you simply need to know that enabling CARP means you can use the hard disk space available on all the servers in an array to create a single logical cache. ISA Server uses CARP to keep track of which servers use what content.

Only ISA Server 2000 Enterprise edition supports CARP, as ISA Server 2000 Standard edition doesn't support arrays.

Enabling CARP for Outgoing and Incoming Web Requests

You can configure ISA Server to process CARP requests for either outgoing or incoming Web requests. By default, ISA Server enables CARP for outgoing requests and disables CARP for incoming requests. The steps below explain how to confirm that your ISA Server array runs CARP for outgoing and incoming Web requests.

To enable Cache Array Routing Protocol for outgoing Web requests, complete the following steps:

1. Open the ISA Management console.
2. In the left pane, expand the Servers And Arrays node, right-click the applicable array, and then click Properties.
3. Select the Outgoing Web Requests tab.
4. Select the Resolve Requests Within Array Before Routing check box.

Note This option won't be present if your ISA server is configured as a stand-alone server. The check box is selected by default for outgoing requests.

5. Click OK.
6. When prompted, you can choose the option Save The Changes, But Don't Restart The Services or the option Save The Changes And Restart The Services. Select the appropriate option button based on your needs and then click OK.

Note Both the Web proxy service and Scheduled Content Download service will require that you restart the services.

To enable Cache Array Routing Protocol for incoming Web requests, complete the following steps:

1. Open the ISA Management console.
2. In the left pane, expand the Servers And Arrays node, right-click the applicable array, and then click Properties.
3. Select the Incoming Web Requests tab.
4. Select the Resolve Requests Within Array Before Routing check box.

Note This option won't be present if your ISA server is configured as a stand-alone server.

5. An ISA Server Configuration message box will appear, as shown in Figure 13-1. Click OK to accept and continue.

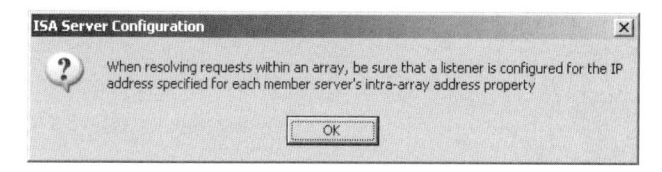

Figure 13-1. *You'll require a listener to match the intra-array Internet Protocol (IP) address for array requests to resolve properly.*

6. Click OK.
7. When prompted, you can choose the option Save The Changes, But Don't Restart The Services or the option Save The Changes And Restart The Services. Select the appropriate option button based on your needs and then click OK.

Configuring Intra-Array Communication

The IP address used for intra-array communication among ISA Server array members must be an internal IP address defined in the Local Address Table (LAT). In addition, you must create a listener for the internal IP address. When dealing with incoming Web requests, the configured listener should also use the same port configured for all incoming requests.

To configure intra-array communication, follow these steps:

1. Open the ISA Management console.
2. In the left pane, expand the Servers And Arrays node, expand the applicable array, and then click the Computers node.
3. In the right pane, right-click the applicable ISA server and then click Properties.
4. Select the Array Membership tab.
5. Type the internal IP address to be used for intra-array communication. You can also click Find, select the correct internal IP address, and then click OK.
6. Click OK.

Configuring the CARP Load Factor

The load factor apprises the ISA Server array members of how much load (that is, how many requests) each member can handle. The default load factor is 100. The value can be configured anywhere between 1 and 2147483647.

To configure the load factor, follow these steps:

1. Open the ISA Management console.
2. In the left pane, expand the Servers And Arrays node, expand the applicable array, and then click the Computers node.

3. In the right pane, right-click the applicable ISA server and then click Properties.
4. Select the Array Membership tab.
5. Type a value to determine how ISA Server array members should divide the load for Web requests.
6. Click OK.

If you attempt to type a value outside of the acceptable range for the load factor value, you'll be presented with the warning shown in Figure 13-2.

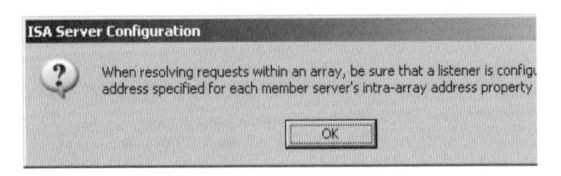

Figure 13-2. *The load factor value must be within ISA supported limits (1–2147483647).*

CARP and Scheduled Content Download

If you configured a scheduled content download job, CARP will distribute its downloaded content across the array for both incoming and outgoing Web requests. You must disable CARP if you wish to make available scheduled content on all servers in an array.

Network Load Balancing

Internet connectivity keeps many businesses running. If your company depends on keeping Internet content available to internal or external clients, you'll probably want the redundancy provided by Network Load Balancing. This technology allows several ISA servers to share a single IP address while maintaining a unique, shared IP address as well. This group of computers is known as a cluster. One important feature of a cluster is that Network Load Balancing distributes the workload among all participating servers. It also prevents interruption of service by ensuring that, should one server fail, others will continue providing service seamlessly.

Prerequisites

Before you can install Network Load Balancing and configure your ISA servers as a cluster, make sure you've met the following prerequisites:

- Your ISA servers are running Microsoft Windows 2000 Advanced and Datacenter Servers or Windows Server 2003, Standard, Enterprise, or Datacenter editions—standard Windows 2000 Server doesn't support Network Load Balancing.
- You've obtained an IP address for the cluster (also known as the Primary IP address) in addition to an IP address assigned to each member of the cluster (known as Dedicated IP Addresses).
- You've installed all ISA servers in the same mode.

Installing and Configuring Network Load Balancing

Once you've completed the prerequisites for Network Load Balancing, you'll need to configure the internal network adapters to support your cluster. By default, the Network Load Balancing Service is available, but not enabled, on a Windows 2000 server; if for some reason the service isn't available, follow these steps to install the service:

1. Open the Control Panel and double-click Network And Dial-up Connections.
2. Right-click the applicable internal network interface and then click Properties.
3. Click Install, click Service, and then click Add.
4. Click Network Load Balancing and then click OK.

Note Remember that if the service isn't available, you're probably running the Standard version of Windows 2000 Server.

To configure Network Load Balancing, complete the following steps:

1. Open the Control Panel and double-click Network And Dial-up Connections.
2. Right-click the applicable internal network interface and then click Properties.
3. Select the Network Load Balancing check box and then click Properties.
4. In the Cluster Parameters tab, you'll need to provide the following information about the cluster, as shown in Table 13-1.

Table 13-1. Configuring the Cluster Parameters

Cluster Parameters	Explanation
IP Address	This address is the cluster IP address, which must be set identically for all hosts in the cluster. This address is often referred to as the virtual IP address or VIP. This IP address must be configured in the Internet Protocol (TCP/IP) Properties.
Subnet Mask	This parameter denotes the subnet mask for the cluster IP address.

(continued)

Table 13-1. Configuring the Cluster Parameters *(continued)*

Cluster Parameters	Explanation
Full Internet Name	This is the full internet name that identifies the cluster. This parameter should be the same on all members of the cluster.
Cluster Operation Mode (Windows Server 2003 only)	This parameter specifies whether or not a multicast Media Access Control (MAC) address should be used for cluster operations.
Remote Control (Allow Remote Control on Windows Server 2003)	This parameter specifies whether remote control operations are enabled. By default, they're not. If you do enable them on Windows Server 2003, you must also provide a password.

5. Select the Host Parameters tab. Provide the following information about the host, as shown in Table 13-2.

Table 13-2. Configuring the Host Parameters

Host Parameters	Explanation
Priority	Assign a unique priority to each ISA server in the cluster.
Dedicated IP Address (IP Address on Windows Server 2003)	This IP address is assigned to the internal network interface of the ISA server to individually address each host in the cluster. This IP address must be configured in the Internet Protocol (TCP/IP) Properties.
Subnet Mask	This parameter denotes the subnet mask for the dedicated IP address.
Initial Host State (Windows Server 2003 only)	This parameter controls the starting of Network Load Balancing and whether the host will immediately join the cluster when the operating system is started.
Retain Suspended State After Computer Restarts (Windows Server 2003 only)	If Retain Suspended State After Computer Restarts is selected, this option will configure the host to stay in a suspended state if the computer restarts.

6. Select the Port Rules tab. By default, all Transmission Control Protocol (TCP) or User Datagram Protocol (UDP) traffic directed to the cluster IP address on ports 0 through 65535 is equally load balanced. You can add, edit, or remove port rules by clicking the appropriate buttons. The Windows Server 2003 default view of the Port Rules tab is shown in Figure 13-3.
7. Click OK twice and then click Close to complete.

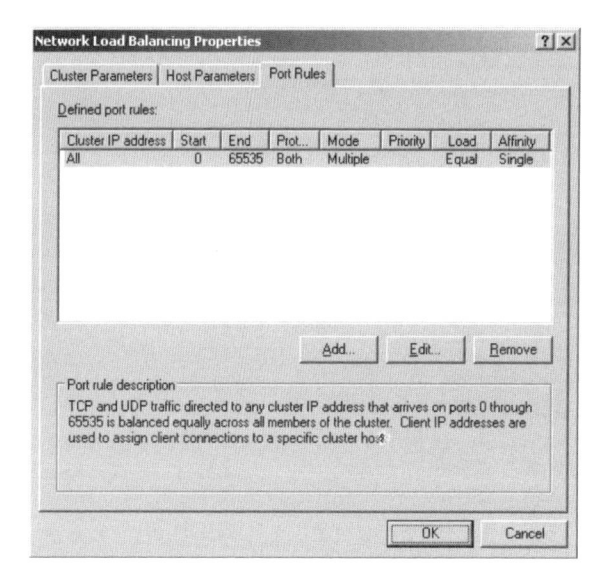

Chapter 13 Working with Enterprise Technologies and ISA Server 2000 | 229

Figure 13-3. *This is the default view of the Port Rules tab when you're configuring Network Load Balancing.*

To install the Network Load Balancing Service on a Windows Server 2003, Enterprise edition server, follow these steps:

1. Open the Control Panel and double-click Network Connections.
2. Right-click the applicable internal network interface and then click Properties.
3. Select the Network Load Balancing check box and then click Properties.

Note Remember that Network Load Balancing isn't available on Windows 2000 Server but on Windows 2000 Advanced Server and all versions of Windows Server 2003.

The options to configure Network Load Balancing on a Windows Server 2003, Enterprise Edition server are identical to the Windows 2000 server steps described above.

Additional Configuration for ISA Server and Network Load Balancing

To create the most efficient environment for Network Load Balancing, be sure you've performed the following actions:

- Ensure that all SecureNAT clients take advantage of the Network Load Balancing functionality by setting the default gateway of these clients to the primary (virtual) IP address of the cluster, rather than the dedicated IP address of an individual ISA server.

- If your server operates with only one network adapter, configure two separate IP addresses. Set the priority of the dedicated IP address to a value lower than that of the primary (virtual) IP address.
- If your server operates with two network adapters, set the priority of the dedicated IP address to a value lower than that of the primary (virtual) IP address; this configuration sets the priority of the dedicated IP address to be higher than that of the primary IP address.

Tip You can configure the priority of IP addresses by opening your network adapter's properties, selecting the Network Load Balancing service, and clicking Properties. Select the Host Parameters tab and then set the priority.

Server Publishing and Network Load Balancing

When clustering ISA servers, most Web publishing scenarios require that Network Load Balancing binds only to external network adapters. Server publishing, however, can't support Network Load Balancing on Windows 2000 Server installations, because server publishing requires Network Load Balancing to bind to both internal and external network adapters. This creates the potential for traffic sent from published servers to be received by an internal network adapter—the response stalls there.

Tip If you require Network Load Balancing and server publishing on Windows 2000, you can either use a hardware-based solution or Stonesoft's StoneBeat FullCluster, which is available at *http://www.stonesoft.com/isaserver.*

Windows Server 2003 supports Network Load Balancing and server publishing through a technology called bidirectional affinity. This feature creates multiple instances of Network Load Balancing on the server to ensure that the internal and external network adapters send and receive the appropriate traffic.

Using DNS Round Robin

You can also load balance ISA servers by configuring Domain Name System (DNS) round robin. DNS round robin is just as feasible as Network Load Balancing, and you can implement it with fewer configurations; however, it's not as efficient as Network Load Balancing in providing load balancing and fault tolerance services. See the Windows Server Help documentation for more information on configuring DNS round robin.

Virtual Private Networks (VPNs)

A VPN allows computers to communicate across a shared, public network (most often the Internet) using secured communications. This communication takes place across Point-to-Point Tunneling Protocol (PPTP) or Layer Two Tunneling Protocol (L2TP) connections. If you want to allow clients to access your network resources by connecting across the Internet or if you wish to connect two of your company's offices using the Internet, you'll use VPN to make these scenarios possible.

Using ISA Server as a VPN Server

ISA Server provides three wizards—shown in Table 13-3—that you can use to establish VPN connections.

Table 13-3. ISA Server VPN Wizards Explained

ISA VPN Wizards	Explanation
Local ISA VPN Wizard Remote ISA VPN Wizard	These two wizards create a gateway-to-gateway configuration, allowing two networks to initiate and receive connections.
ISA Virtual Private Network Configuration Wizard	This wizard allows mobile clients to connect to the internal network.

Configuring a Gateway-to-Gateway VPN

If you wish to join two offices using a VPN, you'll create a gateway-to-gateway configuration, which requires that both the local and remote VPN servers run in either firewall or integrated mode.

Configuring the Local VPN Server

The Local ISA VPN Wizard will configure the ISA server to respond to requests sent from the remote VPN server. Running the Local ISA VPN Wizard creates the following components:

- Dial-on demand interfaces, which allows the local VPN server to accept incoming connections from the remote network
- Static packet filters and static routes, which forward traffic between the local and remote networks
- A VPN configuration file, which is required when running the Remote ISA VPN Wizard

To configure a local VPN server, follow these steps:

1. Open the ISA Management console.
2. In the left pane, expand your server or array, right-click Network Configuration, and then click Set Up Local ISA VPN Server.

Note If you're using Taskpad view, you can also click the Configure A Local Virtual Private Network (VPN) icon to initiate this wizard.

3. Click Next to continue.
4. If the Routing And Remote Access service isn't running, you'll be prompted to start the service in order to continue with the wizard. Click Yes to start the service.
5. On the ISA Virtual Private Network (VPN) Identification page, type a name to identify the local and remote networks and then click Next.

Note A VPN connection will be created in the RRAS console with a naming format of local network_remote network.

6. On the ISA Virtual Private Network (VPN) Protocol page, select the protocols to be used for VPN communication between the two gateways. The options are:
   - Use L2TP Over IPSec
   - Use PPTP
   - Use L2TP Over IPSec, If Available, Otherwise, Use PPTP

   Click Next to continue.

7. On the Two-Way Communication page, select the Both The Local And Remote ISA VPN Computers Can Initiate Communication check box if you want both ends of the VPN to be able to initiate the connection. Type the fully qualified domain name (FQDN) or IP address of the remote VPN server, and then type the remote VPN computer name or domain name for authentication purposes, as shown in Figure 13-4.

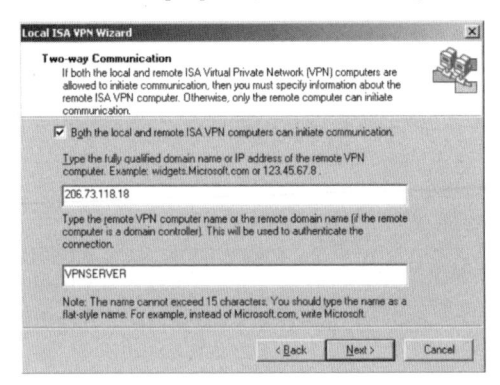

Figure 13-4. *You configure two-way communication between the local and remote VPN servers on the Two-Way Communication page.*

Click Next to continue.

Note If the remote computer is a domain controller, type the NetBIOS name of the domain, and not the FQDN.

8. On the Remote Virtual Private Network (VPN) Network Page, click Add to enter the range of IP addresses on the remote network to which the local VPN server can gain access, click OK, and then click Next.
9. On the Local Virtual Private Network (VPN) Network page, select the IP address of the local computer to which the remote ISA VPN server will connect. Click Add, Remove, or Restore to change the configured range of addresses on the local network to which computers on the remote network can connect. Click OK and then click Next.
10. On the ISA VPN Computer Configuration File page, type a name and path to save the ISA VPN configuration file, and then type a password to be assigned to protect the file. Click Next to continue.

Note You'll require the VPN configuration file during the execution of the Remote ISA VPN Wizard.

11. On the Completing The ISA VPN Setup Page, click Details to review the configuration, click Back, and then click Finish to complete the wizard.

Configuring the Remote VPN Server

After completing the Local ISA VPN Wizard, you'll next need to configure the remote VPN server to complete the gateway-to-gateway configuration. The remote VPN server will initiate the connections to the local VPN server. Running the Remote ISA VPN Wizard creates the following components:

- Dial-on demand interfaces that allow the remote VPN server to initiate connections to the specific local VPN server
- Static packet filters and static routes that forward traffic between the local and remote networks

Before starting the wizard, you'll need the VPN configuration file created during the Local ISA VPN Wizard. Typically, the administrator of the local network will copy the VPN configuration file to a floppy disk or e-mail the file to the administrator of the remote network (the file is very small). Once you obtain the VPN configuration file, you can begin the Remote ISA VPN Wizard.

To configure a remote VPN server, follow these steps:

1. Open the ISA Management console.
2. In the left pane, expand your server or array, right-click Network Configuration, and then click Set Up Remote ISA VPN Server.

Note If you're using Taskpad view, you can also click the Configure A Remote Virtual Private Network (VPN) icon to initiate this wizard.

3. Click Next to continue.
4. On the ISA VPN Computer Configuration File page, type the filename and path for the VPC file, or click Browse to select the VPN configuration file. Type the password assigned to the file by the administrator of the local VPN server and then click Next.
5. On the Completing The ISA VPN Configuration Wizard page, click Details to review the configuration, click Back, and then click Finish to complete the wizard.

Confirming the Gateway-to-Gateway Configuration

Now that you have created both a local and remote ISA VPN server, you'll want to confirm that you can initiate communications between the two networks. In the following steps you'll use the Routing And Remote Access console to verify connectivity by checking the status of the demand-dial interface created during the execution of the wizards:

1. Open the Routing And Remote Access console.
2. In the left pane, expand your Routing and Remote Access Service (RRAS) server node and then click Network Interfaces.
3. In the right pane, select the interface created by the Local ISA VPN Wizard and then check the status in the Connection Status column. The status will be either connected, disconnected, or unreachable.

Note The name of the demand-dial interface will be in the format *local network_remote network*.

Connecting Remote Clients Using VPN

In order for clients to connect back to your network across the Internet, ensure that the following prerequisites are in place:

- Install the ISA server in integrated mode as a stand-alone server
- Configure the ISA server as a VPN server
- Provide the client some means of connecting to the Internet

Next, follow the steps shown in the remainder of this section.

Configuring a Client Virtual Private Network (VPN)

The VPN Client Wizard configures a VPN server on the ISA Server computer to allow external clients the ability to dial in to the internal network. The VPN Client wizard will establish static packet filters on the ISA server for PPTP and L2TP support:

- Allow PPTP protocol packets (client)
- Allow PPTP protocol packets (server)
- Allow L2TP protocol Internet Key Exchange (IKE) packets
- Allow L2TP protocol packets

The RRAS will be configured to open 128 ports for each protocol, PPTP and L2TP. To change the number of configured ports after running the VPN client wizard, follow these steps:

1. Open the Routing And Remote Access console.
2. In the left pane, expand your RRAS server node, right-click Ports, and then click Properties.
3. Select WAN Miniport (PPTP) and then click Configure.
4. Set the Maximum Port setting to the desired number of PPTP ports to be configured for supporting your external client base, as shown in Figure 13-5.

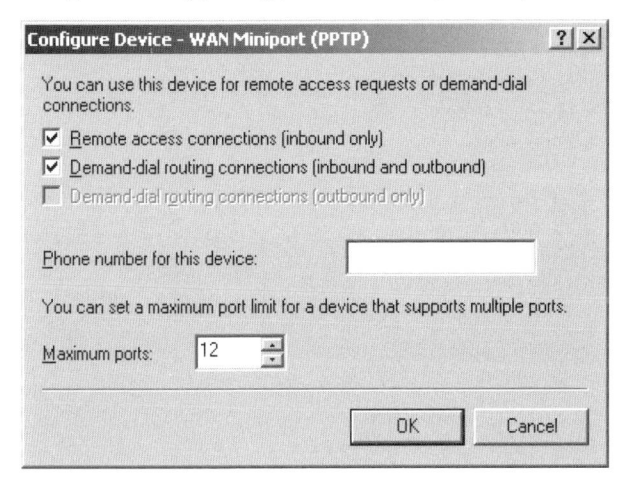

Figure 13-5. *You use the Maximum Port setting to configure the number of maximum PPTP ports for your VPN server.*

Click OK to continue.

5. Select WAN Miniport (L2TP) and then click Configure.
6. Set the Maximum Port setting to the desired number of L2TP ports to be configured for supporting your external client base, and then click OK.
7. Click OK and then close the Routing And Remote Access console.

To set up ISA Server as a VPN server to accept incoming requests from external VPN clients, follow these steps:

1. Open the ISA Management console.
2. In the left pane, expand your server or array, right-click Network Configuration, and then click Allow VPN Client Connections.

Note If you're using Taskpad view, in the right pane you can also click the Configure A Client Virtual Private Network (VPN) icon to launch the same wizard.

3. Click Next to begin the wizard.
4. Click Details to see the configuration that will be created when completing this wizard, review the settings, and then click Back. Figure 13-6 illustrates the ISA Virtual Private Network (VPN) Server Summary page.

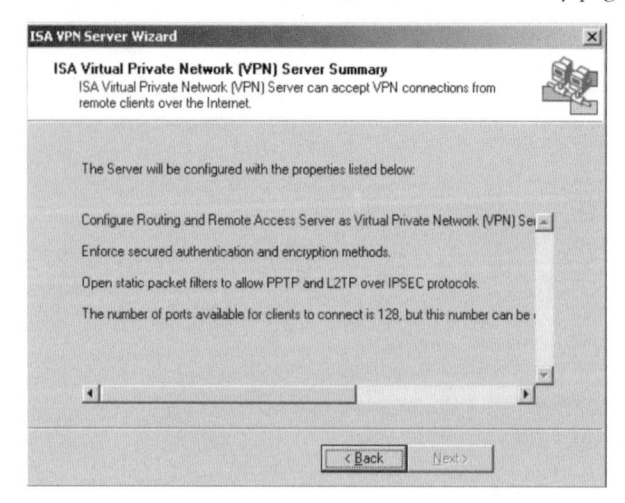

Figure 13-6. *The ISA Virtual Private Network (VPN) Server Summary page gives you a summary of the Client VPN Wizard details.*

5. Click Finish.
6. If RRAS isn't enabled on the ISA server, you'll be asked if the wizard should start the RRAS service. If RRAS is enabled, you'll be asked if the wizard should restart the RRAS service. Click Yes.

Configuring a VPN Connectoid

Once you've set up the ISA VPN server, you'll configure a connectoid on the client for connecting to the VPN server. The following steps explain how to create a VPN connection on Windows 2000 and Windows XP computers.

To configure a Windows 2000 VPN client connectoid, follow these steps:

1. Open the Control Panel and double-click Network And Dial-up Connections.
2. Double-click Make New Connection.
3. If prompted for your area code, type the area code, and then click OK twice.
4. On the Welcome To The Network Connection Wizard page, click Next.
5. On the Network Connection Type page, select Connect To A Private Network Through The Internet and then click Next.

Chapter 13 Working with Enterprise Technologies and ISA Server 2000

6. On the Destination Address page, type the external IP address on the ISA VPN server and then click Next.
7. On the Connection Availability page, select whether this connection is to be used by only you or by all users, and then click Next.
8. On the Internet Connection Sharing page, click Next to continue.

Note Don't select the Internet Connection Sharing check box.

9. Click Finish to complete.

To configure a Windows XP VPN client connectoid, follow these steps:

1. Open the Control Panel and click Network And Internet Connections.
2. Click Network Connections.
3. Click Create A New Connection.
4. On the Welcome To The Network Connection Wizard page, click Next.
5. On the Network Connection Type page, select Connect To The Network At My Workplace and then click Next.
6. On the Network Connection page, select Virtual Private Network Connection and then click Next.
7. On the Connection Name page, type a name for the connection and then click Next.
8. On the VPN Server Selection page, type the FQDN or external IP address of the ISA VPN server and then click Next.
9. Click Finish to complete.

Note If you've changed your default Windows XP settings, your screens may appear slightly different from those described above.

Configuring VPN Pass-Through

In order for internal clients to connect to VPN servers located outside of networks you control, you must configure the ISA server to allow PPTP traffic to pass through.

To configure PPTP traffic through ISA server, follow these steps:

1. Open the ISA Management console.
2. In the left pane, expand your server or array node, expand Access Policy, right-click IP Packet Filters, and then click Properties.
3. Select the PPTP tab.
4. Select the PPTP Through ISA Firewall check box and then click OK.

Manually Configuring the VPN

After your initial configuration of the VPN, you might find it necessary to add additional protocols by following the steps below.

Adding Support for Additional VPN Protocols To reconfigure a VPN to use an additional protocol, follow these steps:

1. Open the Routing And Remote Access console.
2. In the left pane, expand your RRAS server node and click Network Interfaces.
3. In the right pane, right-click the applicable demand-dial interface and click Properties.
4. Select the Networking tab.
5. In the drop-down list for Type Of VPN, select the appropriate protocol (Automatic, PPTP VPN, L2TP IPSec VPN), and then click OK.
6. Close the Routing And Remote Access console.

Creating a PPTP Packet Filter In order to manually add support for the PPTP protocol, you'll need to create two packet filters: PPTP call and PPTP receive.

To manually create the necessary PPTP packet filters for your VPN server, follow these steps:

1. Open the ISA Management console.
2. In the left pane, expand your ISA Server node and expand Access Policy. Then right-click IP Packet Filters, select New, and select Filter.
3. Type a name to be given to the IP Packet Filter and then click Next.
4. If your have an array of servers, you'll see the Servers page. Set whether the filter should be used by all ISA Server Computers In The Array or select the Only This Server option and select the ISA server. Click Next to continue.
5. On the Filter Mode page, select Allow Packet Transmission and then click Next.
6. On the Filter Type page, select the Predefined option and select the PPTP Call protocol. Click Next to continue.

Note When creating the second PPTP packet filter, the PPTP Receive protocol should be selected.

7. On the Local Computer page, specify the IP address on the external interface of the local ISA VPN server. Click Next.
8. On the Remote Computers page, select Only This Remote Computer, type the IP address of the remote ISA VPN server, and click Next to continue.
9. Review the IP packet filter configuration and click Finish to complete.

Creating an L2TP Packet Filter In order to manually add support for the L2TP protocol, you'll need to create two custom packet filters that allow User Datagram Protocol (UDP) port 500 and UDP port 1701 connections.

To manually create the necessary L2TP packet filter for UDP port 500 traffic, follow these steps:

1. Open the ISA Management console.
2. In the left pane, expand your ISA Server node and expand Access Policy. Then right-click IP Packet Filters, select New, and select Filter.
3. Type a name to be given to the IP Packet Filter and then click Next.
4. If your have an array of servers, you'll see the Servers page. Set whether the filter should be used by all ISA Server Computers In The Array or select the Only This Server option button and select the ISA server. Click Next to continue.
5. On the Filter Mode page, select Allow Packet Transmission and then click Next.
6. On the Filter Type page, select the Custom option button and then click Next.
7. On the Filter Settings page, type the information in each field as shown in Figure 13-7. Click Next.

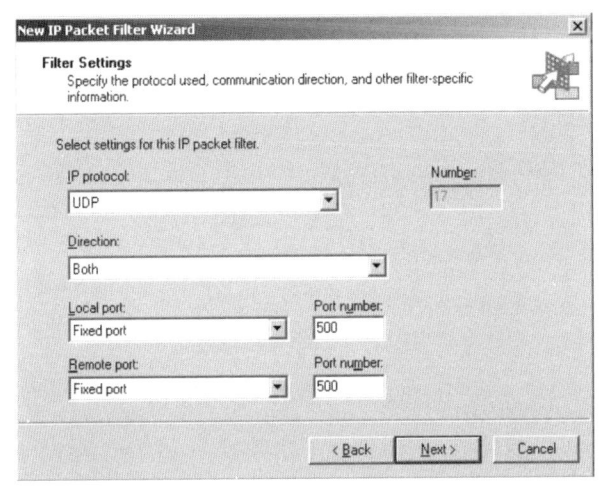

Figure 13-7. *You can use the Filter Settings page to configure the filter settings necessary for creating an L2TP packet filter for UDP port 500 traffic.*

8. On the Local Computer page, specify the IP address on the external interface of the local ISA VPN server. Click Next.
9. On the Remote Computers page, select Only This Remote Computer, type the IP address of the remote ISA VPN server, and click Next to continue.
10. Review the IP packet filter configuration and click Finish to complete.

240 | **Part III** Microsoft ISA Server 2000 and Enterprise Systems Administration

To manually create the necessary L2TP packet filter for UDP port 1701 traffic, follow these steps:

1. Open the ISA Management console.
2. In the left pane, expand your ISA Server node and expand Access Policy. Then right-click IP Packet Filters, select New, and select Filter.
3. Type a name to be given to the IP Packet Filter and then click Next.
4. If your have an array of servers, you'll see the Servers page. Set whether the filter should be used by all ISA Server Computers In The Array or select the Only This Server option button and select the ISA server. Click Next to continue.
5. On the Filter Mode page, select Allow Packet Transmission and then click Next.
6. On the Filter Type page, select the Custom option button and then click Next.
7. On the Filter Settings page, type the information in each field as shown in Figure 13-8.

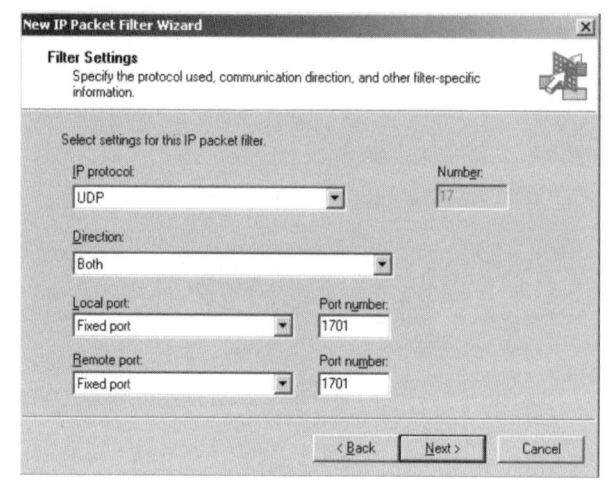

Figure 13-8. *You can use the Filter Settings page to configure the filter settings necessary for creating an L2TP packet filter for UDP port 1701 traffic.*

8. On the Local Computer page, specify the IP address on the external interface of the local ISA VPN server. Click Next.
9. On the Remote Computers page, select Only This Remote Computer, type the IP address of the remote ISA VPN server, and click Next to continue.
10. Review the IP packet filter configuration and click Finish to complete.

Tip By default, IPSec VPN client traffic can't pass through an ISA server (or any other Network Address Translation [NAT] configuration) because of the way authentication takes place. You can, however, configure your ISA server to support a process called IPSec NAT Transversal. For detailed steps on how to configure this on your ISA server, see Stefaan Pouseele's article "How to Pass IPSec Traffic Through ISA Server" at *http://www.isaserver.org/articles/IPSec_Passthrough.html*.

H.323 Gatekeeper

Once the realm of consumers, more and more companies require the use of audio, video, and data conferencing tools like RealNetworks, Microsoft NetMeeting, MSN Messenger, and the like. H.323 is an International Telecommunication Union Telecommunication (ITU-T) Standard for multimedia transmissions across packet-switched networks. H.323 communications supported by ISA include the components listed below:

- **Terminals** Usually a PC or stand-alone device (like a smart webcam) that runs the audio, video, and so on.
- **Gateways** Usually a server that translates from a different standard to the H.323 format.
- **Gatekeepers** Usually a server acting as the manager through which all H.323 traffic flows; it provides addressing and authentication for H.323 traffic.
- **Multipoint Control Units (MCUs)** Usually a server or client that negotiates the sharings of data among three or more clients.

ISA Server functions primarily as an H.323 gatekeeper, which authorizes and routes H.323 traffic to clients. It also functions as an H.323 proxy. In the following section, you'll learn how to install the H.323 Gatekeeper service and configure it for use in your environment.

Prerequisites

You'll need to take a few steps to ensure that your network supports H.323 traffic. First, ensure that clients can find the gatekeeper by creating a DNS service record. Next, create a protocol rule that allows H.323 traffic into and out of your network.

Create a DNS Service Record for the H.323 Gatekeeper

In order for internal clients to successfully locate the gatekeeper, create a DNS service (SRV) record. DNS service (SRV) records are defined on Windows 2000 and Windows Server 2003 DNS servers—they locate services on the network.

To create the Q931 SRV record for the H.323 gatekeeper on a Windows 2000 DNS server, follow these steps:

1. Open the DNS console.

2. In the left pane, expand the DNS server node, expand Forward Lookup Zones, right-click the domain, and then click Other New Records.
3. In the Resource Record Type window, select Service Location, and then click Create Record.
4. In the New Resource Record dialog box, type the following information for each field as listed.
   - Service: _q931
   - Protocol: _tcp
   - Port Number: 1720
   - Host Offering This Service: type the FQDN of your ISA server's external interface
5. Click OK and then click Done to complete.

To create the Q931 SRV record for the H.323 gatekeeper on a Windows Server 2003 DNS server, follow these steps:

1. Open the DNS console.
2. In the left pane, expand the DNS server node, expand Forward Lookup Zone, and select your domain. Right-click the domain, and then click Other New Records.
3. In the Resource Record Type window, select Service Location (SRV), and then click Create Record.
4. In the New Resource Record window, type the following information for each field as listed.
   - Service: _q931
   - Protocol: _tcp
   - Port Number: 1720
   - Host Offering This Service: type the FQDN of your ISA server's external interface
5. Click OK and then click Done to complete.

Defining Access to the H.323 Protocol

In order to control access to the H.323 protocol, you must create a protocol rule by completing the following steps:

1. Open the ISA Management console.
2. In the left pane, expand your ISA server or array node and expand Access Policy. Right-click Protocol Rules, select New, and then select Rule.
3. Type a name to be given to the rule and then click Next.
4. On the Rule Action page, select Allow and then click Next.
5. On the Protocols page, select Selected Protocols, select the H.323 Protocol, and then click Next.
6. On the Schedule page, select a schedule and then click Next.

7. On the Client Type page, select the types of clients to which this rule applies by selecting Any Request, Specific Computers, or Specific Users And Groups. Click Next to continue.
8. Review the rule configuration and then click Finish to complete.

Installing and Configuring the H.323 Gatekeeper

During the ISA Server installation, you have the option to perform a Typical, Full, or Custom installation as described in Chapter 2, "Installing and Configuring Microsoft ISA Server 2000." The H.323 Gatekeeper service is automatically installed only when you choose a full installation.

If you didn't perform a full installation during the initial build of ISA Server, you can add the H.323 Gatekeeper service by following these steps:

1. Open the Control Panel and then double-click Add/Remove Programs.
2. Under Currently Installed Programs, select Microsoft Internet Security And Acceleration Server and then click Change.
3. Click Add/Remove.
4. Select Add-In Services and then click Change Option.
5. Select the Install H.323 Gatekeeper Service check box and then click OK.
6. Select Administration Tools and then click Change Option.
7. Select the H.323 Gatekeeper Administration Tool check box and then click OK.

Note The H.323 Gatekeeper administration tool is necessary for administering the gatekeeper within the ISA Management console.

8. Click Continue. Follow the prompts to progress through the ISA Server installation.

Note Refer to Chapter 2 for more information if necessary.

Installing the H.323 Gatekeeper Service Management Console

Installing only the H.323 Gatekeeper service and not the H.323 gatekeeper administration tool installs the service but doesn't allow you to add a gatekeeper from within the ISA Management console. You'll then find the entire H.323 gatekeeper node within the ISA Management console missing! Ensure that you choose to install both the H.323 Gatekeeper service and the administration tool to enable remote administration of the H.323 service from your ISA Management console.

Enabling the H.323 Filter

The installation of the H.323 Gatekeeper service includes the H.323 application filter. This filter enables users to interact with other H.323 clients using applications that require video, audio, application sharing functionality, or all three, over the Internet.

To enable and configure the H.323 filter, see the section entitled "H.323 Filter" in Chapter 9, "Publishing Fundamentals."

Adding an H.323 Gatekeeper

To add an H.323 Gatekeeper to ISA Server, follow these steps:

1. Open the ISA Management console.
2. In the left pane, right-click H.323 Gatekeepers and click Add Gatekeeper.
3. In the Add Gatekeeper dialog box, select either This Computer or Another Computer to specify which ISA server will host the gatekeeper. If you select Another Computer, you must type the name of the ISA server.
4. Click OK.

Note After you click OK in Step 4, a new server node in the left pane will appear beneath H.323 Gatekeepers; this node represents the added gatekeeper.

Configuring H.323 Gatekeeper Properties

The H.323 Gatekeeper Properties allow you to configure the settings explained in Table 13-4 for each gatekeeper in your environment.

Table 13-4. H.323 Gatekeeper Properties

Tab	Property	Explanation
General	Gatekeeper Description	Add a description for the gatekeeper here.
Network	Network Adapters	Select the check box next to the network adapter that should listen for call requests.
Advanced	Registration Expiration Time	Determine the number of seconds registered clients should remain in the Gatekeeper database.
	Active Call Expiration Time	Enter the number of seconds of no activity before calls expire.
	Compact Database	Click here to compact the gatekeeper database.
Security	Standard security dialog boxes	Configure the users and groups that have access to the H.323 service.

Configuring H.323 Gatekeeper Permissions

To configure H.323 Gatekeeper permissions, complete the following steps:

1. Open the ISA Management console.
2. In the left pane, expand the H.323 Gatekeepers node, right-click the applicable H.323 gatekeeper server, and then click Properties.
3. Select the Security tab.
4. Click Add to grant a new user or group permissions to modify the gatekeeper configuration and then apply the appropriate permissions. Click Remove to deny a user or group the permissions to modify the gatekeeper configuration.
5. Click OK to complete.

Enable IP Routing to Improve H.323 Performance

All ISA Server's application filters support a function called "kernel-mode data pumping," which increases data throughput for protocols—like H.323 and File Transfer Protocol (FTP)—that use secondary connections. This function is available, however, only if you've enabled IP Routing on your ISA server. To enable kernel-mode data pumping, complete the following steps:

1. Open the ISA Management console.
2. In the left pane, expand your ISA server or array node, expand Access Policy, right-click IP Packet Filters, and then click Properties.
3. In the General tab, select the Enable Packet Filtering and Enable IP Routing check boxes and then click OK.

Configure Call Routing Rules

Call routing rules tell your ISA server where to send requests for H.323 traffic. ISA Server routes each request to a destination based on the rules you configure.

Creating a Call Routing Rule

Various types of rules are associated with call routing. You can create the following types of call routing rules:

- Phone number rules
- E-mail address rules
- IP address rules

Creating a Phone Number Rule To create a phone number rule, follow these steps:

1. Open the ISA Management console.
2. In the left pane, expand the H.323 Gatekeepers node, expand the applicable H.323 gatekeeper server, and then expand Call Routing.
3. Right-click Phone Number Rules and then click Add Routing Rule.

246 | Part III Microsoft ISA Server 2000 and Enterprise Systems Administration

4. Click Next to continue.
5. On the Name And Description page, type a name for this rule; you may also provide a description. Click Next to continue.
6. On the Prefix Or Phone Number page, type either the prefix or entire telephone number for this routing rule.

Note If you type the entire phone number, clear the Route All Phone Numbers Using This Prefix check box.

Click Next to continue.

7. On the Destination Type page, select the destination type to be used by this routing rule. The options to select from are shown in Figure 13-9.

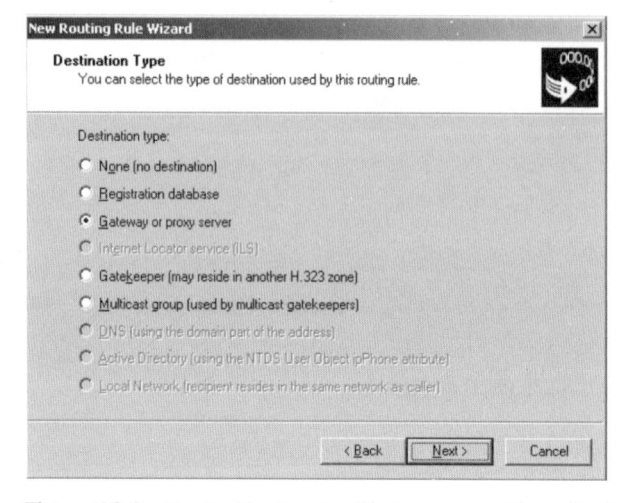

Figure 13-9. *On the Destination Type page, you'll see the destination types available for a phone number routing rule.*

Note If None (No Destination) or Registration Database is selected, the wizard's next page will be the Routing Rule Metric page, as explained in Step 10.

8. On the Destination Name page, select the appropriate destination and then click Next.
9. On the Change A Phone Number page, select the type of action to perform before sending the phone number to the destination. The options are shown in Table 13-5.

Table 13-5. Options for Changing a Phone Number

Actions	Explanation
Discard Digits	This option removes numbers from the beginning of a phone number (like an area code) before it's routed to the next proxy or gateway.
Add Prefix	This option adds numbers to the beginning of a phone number (like a 9) before it's routed to the next proxy or gateway.

Click Next to continue.

10. On the Routing Rule Metric page, type a number to define the metric used by this routing rule. The metric is used to determine the most preferred route. Click Next to continue.
11. Click Finish to complete.

Creating an E-Mail Address Rule To create an e-mail address rule, follow these steps:

1. Open the ISA Management console.
2. In the left pane, expand the H.323 Gatekeepers node, expand the applicable H.323 gatekeeper server, and expand Call Routing.
3. Right-click E-Mail Address Rules and then click Add Routing Rule.
4. Click Next to continue.
5. On the Name And Description page, type a name for this rule, and optionally provide a description. Click Next to continue.
6. On the Domain Name Suffix page, type the domain suffix to be used by the rule. If you type a specific address, clear Route All E-Mail Addresses That Include This General DNS Domain Name, and then click Next.
7. On the Destination Type page, select the destination type to be used by this routing rule and then click Next.

Note If None (No Destination), Registration Database, DNS (Using The Domain Part of The Address), or Active Directory (Using The NTDS Object IpPhone Attribute) is selected, the next page of the wizard will be the Routing Rule Metric page, as explained in Step 9.

8. On the Destination Name page, select the appropriate destination and then click Next.
9. On the Routing Rule Metric page, type a number to define the metric used by this routing rule. The rule uses this metric to determine the most preferred route. Click Next to continue.
10. Click Finish to complete.

Creating an IP Address Rule To create an IP address rule, follow these steps:

1. Open the ISA Management console.
2. In the left pane, expand the H.323 Gatekeepers node, expand the applicable H.323 gatekeeper server, and expand Call Routing.
3. Right-click IP Address Rules and click Add Routing Rule.
4. Click Next to continue.
5. On the Name And Description page, type a name for this rule, and optionally provide a description. Click Next to continue.
6. On the IP Address Pattern page, type the IP address and subnet mask and then click Next.
7. On the Destination Type page, select the destination type to be used by this routing rule and then click Next.

> **Note** If None (No Destination) or Local Network (Recipient Resides In The Same Network As Caller) is selected, the next page of the wizard will be the Routing Rule Metric page, as explained in Step 9.

8. On the Destination Name page, select the appropriate destination and then click Next.
9. On the Routing Rule Metric page, type a number to define the metric used by this routing rule. The metric is used to determine the most preferred route. Click Next to continue.
10. Click Finish to complete.

Configuring an Internal NetMeeting Client to Use an H.323 Gatekeeper

NetMeeting allows clients to collaborate using audio, video, chat, and other useful tools like remote control and whiteboard sharing. You can better support the NetMeeting clients in your environment by configuring them to use a central gatekeeper.

To configure an internal NetMeeting client to use the H.323 gatekeeper, follow these steps:

1. Open NetMeeting.
2. Click the Tools menu and then click Options.
3. In the General tab, click Advanced Calling.
4. In the Advanced Calling Options dialog box, select each of the options as shown in Table 13-6.

Table 13-6. Advanced Calling Options for Internal NetMeeting Clients

Gatekeeper Settings	Explanation
Use A Gatekeeper To Place Calls	Select this option and type the name or internal IP address of the H.323 gatekeeper.
Log On Using My Account Name	Select this option and type your user name or e-mail address to register with the H.323 gatekeeper.
Log On Using My Phone Number	Select this option and type your telephone number to register with the H.323 gatekeeper.

5. Click OK twice to close the NetMeeting dialog boxes.

Configuring an External NetMeeting Client to Use an H.323 Gatekeeper

To configure an external NetMeeting client to dial the external interface of the H.323 gatekeeper, complete the following steps:

1. Open NetMeeting.
2. Click the Tools menu and then click Options.
3. In the General tab, click Advanced Calling.
4. In the Advanced Calling Options dialog box, select Use A Gatekeeper To Place Calls, type the FQDN, which resolves to the external interface of the ISA server, and then click OK twice.

Additional Resources

- The Microsoft Knowledge Base provides many helpful articles that provide necessary background and additional information that supplements this chapter. Look up the articles at *http://support.microsoft.com/?kbid*=article number, where *article number* is the number for the particular article.
  - Article 328428, "Web Server Cannot Handle HTTP Request Made with ISA Array."
  - Article 240997, "Configuring Network Load Balancing."
  - Article 288574, "Cannot Perform Load Balancing with Network Load Balancing and Server Publishing Enabled."
  - Article 317506, "You May Not Be Able to Log On to the Domain with VPN If a Winsock Proxy Is Enabled."
  - Article 318419, "Connections Are Dropped If You Add VPN Connections to ISA Server."
  - Article 303530, "VPN Clients May Not Work on ISA Server Perimeter Networks."
  - Article 311777, "How to Enable Translating Client Source Address in Server Publishing."

- Article 303530, "VPN Clients May Not Work on ISA Server Perimeter Networks."
- Article 284651, "The Virtual Private Network Wizard for Client Access Does Not Seem to Change the Number of Available Virtual Private Network Ports."
- Article 303503, "How to Join or Access an Internal Domain from an External Client Using ISA Server and VPN."
- Article 818033. "ISA Server 2000 VPN Tunnel Drops Large Packets as Malformed."
- Article 313433, "VPN Dial-up Connections Are Not Filtered by ISA Server."

- You may also want to go to the VPN Section of ISAserver.org at *http://www.isaserver.org/pages/search.asp?query=VPN.*
- "Scale-Out Caching with ISA Server 2000" at *http://www.microsoft.com/isaserver/techinfo/deployment/ScaleOutCachingwithISA.asp*
- Pouseele, Stefaan. "How to Pass IPSec Traffic Through ISA Server" at *http://www.isaserver.org/articles/IPSec_Passthrough.html.*
- Shinder, Tom. "IPSec NAT Transversal" at *http://newsletters.cramsession.com/Newsletters/NewsletterArchive/Netadmin/november-20-2002netadmin.html#feature.*
- "Achieving Site-to-Site Virtual Private Networking and Perimeter Security in a High Availability Environment with Microsoft ISA Server and RRAS" at *http://www.microsoft.com/isaserver/techinfo/deployment/2000/avanadevpn.asp.*
- International Engineering Consortium. "H.323 Tutorial" at *http://www.iec.org/online/tutorials/h323/topic01.html.*
- Shahid, Vic Singh. "H.323 Gatekeeper" white paper available at *www.isatools.org.*

Part IV

Microsoft ISA Server 2000 Security Management

Companies require protection from malicious attackers, corporate spies, worms, and viruses. With the increasing use of the Internet to make information and content available to customers and to share and better leverage corporate resources, the danger of valuable company resources being exposed—intentionally or not—to outside influences becomes greater. This section explains how you can configure Microsoft ISA Server to deny access to malicious attackers while providing authorized access to your friendly resources.

Chapter 14 illustrates how to configure two different types of perimeter networks and describes a variety of publishing procedures for making resources available in the perimeter network. Chapter 15 explains how to secure all the aspects of the ISA server, from locking down permissions to disabling unnecessary services.

Chapter 14

Microsoft ISA Server 2000 and Perimeter Networks

In this chapter we'll show you how to configure Microsoft ISA Server in a perimeter network, explain the key benefits and limitations of the trihomed and back-to-back perimeter networks, and walk through several perimeter network publishing scenarios, including Web, File Transfer Protocol (FTP), and Simple Mail Transfer Protocol (SMTP) services.

Perimeter Networks Explained

The function of perimeter networks is to separate computers that must make contact with external clients from your internal network. A perimeter network (also known as DMZ, demilitarized zone, and screened subnet) uses a unique range of Internet Protocol (IP) addresses to separate and make available computers that must serve content to clients connecting from an unprotected network like the Internet.

ISA Server supports most common perimeter network types; this chapter focuses on the two most widely used scenarios, as follows:

- **Trihomed ISA Server perimeter network**   Use one ISA server with three network interface cards to connect with the internal, external, and perimeter networks, separating them through the use of the Local Address Table (LAT) and network IDs.

- **Back-to-back perimeter network**   Use two ISA servers, connecting one to the Internet and the other to the internal network.

Note   In a back-to-back perimeter network, you could also use a third-party firewall for one of the two firewalls, but throughout this chapter we're referring to two ISA servers.

The back-to-back scenario provides a much more secure configuration than the trihomed scenario, but it can be more expensive. In the following sections you'll learn how to configure both types of perimeter networks using ISA Server.

Trihomed ISA Server Perimeter Networks

In a trihomed perimeter network, you'll configure the ISA server with three network interfaces:

- One network interface connects to the internal network and should use a private IP address.
- The second network interface connects to the servers located in the perimeter network and must use a public IP address.
- The third network interface connects to the Internet and should use a public IP address that is different from that used for the perimeter network.

An illustration of a trihomed perimeter network is shown in Figure 14-1.

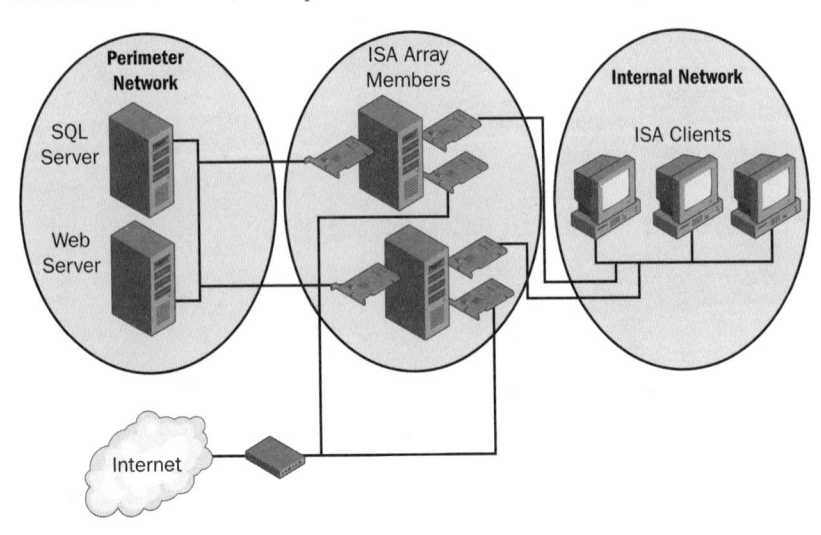

Figure 14-1. *This illustration shows a trihomed ISA Server perimeter network.*

Configuring the Trihomed ISA Server Network Interfaces

To configure the three network interfaces, follow these steps:

1. Install the first network interface with a public IP address (usually provided by your Internet service provider) that's directly connected to the Internet.
2. Install the second network interface with the public IP address that will be used for the perimeter network. This public IP address is an IP address segmented from a block of IP addresses provided by your Internet service provider (ISP).

Note If you're unfamiliar with variable subnetting or supernetting, refer to Microsoft Knowledge Base article 164015, which can be found at *http://support.microsoft.com*.

3. Install the third network interface with a private IP address that will be used for the private, internal network.

Caution Be certain your LAT doesn't contain the IP address used for the perimeter network.

Configuring the Trihomed Perimeter Network

To configure a trihomed perimeter network with ISA Server, complete the following steps:

1. Open the ISA Management console.
2. In the left pane, expand your ISA server or array, expand the Network Configuration node, right-click Local Address Table (LAT), and click Construct LAT.
3. In the Construct LAT dialog box, select the appropriate options to reflect all the IP address ranges in your internal network and then click OK.

Caution Do not include any IP addresses for servers in the perimeter network in the LAT.

4. In the left pane, expand the Access Policy node, right-click IP Packet Filters, and then click Properties.

Note A trihomed perimeter network can't support Web or server publishing rules, site and content rules, or protocol rules. In a trihomed scenario, ISA Server routes the packets rather than translating them (as is the case with publishing); therefore, you must use static packet filters to publish the perimeter network servers.

5. In the General tab, select the Enable Packet Filtering and Enable IP Routing check boxes and click OK.

Note Enabling packet filtering and IP routing is a necessary step for publishing servers located in the perimeter network. You can now create the necessary static packet filters for the servers that will provide content to external users on the Internet.

6. In the right pane, create a static IP packet filter for each server in the perimeter network. The static IP packet filters generally will be configured as shown in Table 14-1.

Table 14-1. Trihomed Perimeter Network IP Packet Filter Configuration Settings

IP Packet Filter Wizard Page	Required Selection(s)
Servers	Only This Server
Filter Mode	Allow
Filter Type	Custom
Filter Settings	Provide information for IP Protocol, Direction, Local Port and Port Number, Remote Port and Port Number
Local Computer	This Computer (On The Perimeter Network), and type the IP address of the published server
Remote Computer	All Remote Computers or Only This Remote Computer for limiting access

Note For more information on configuring packet filters, see the section entitled "Routing and IP Packet Filters" in Chapter 9, "Publishing Fundamentals."

Limitations of a Trihomed Perimeter Network

Because of the way traffic is routed to the perimeter network in a trihomed configuration, you'll find some substantial disadvantages to using a trihomed perimeter network configuration with ISA Server:

- You can't use Web or Server Publishing Rules to publish servers.
- Static packet filters control all access into and out of the perimeter network.
- Packet filters access control is limited to an IP address or a subnet.

Back-to-Back ISA Server Perimeter Networks

In a back-to-back network configuration, you need to set up two ISA Server computers to establish the perimeter network: an external ISA server that connects directly to the Internet and an internal ISA server that connects directly to the internal network. Locate the servers you wish to publish in the perimeter network between these two ISA servers to create the environment illustrated in Figure 14-2.

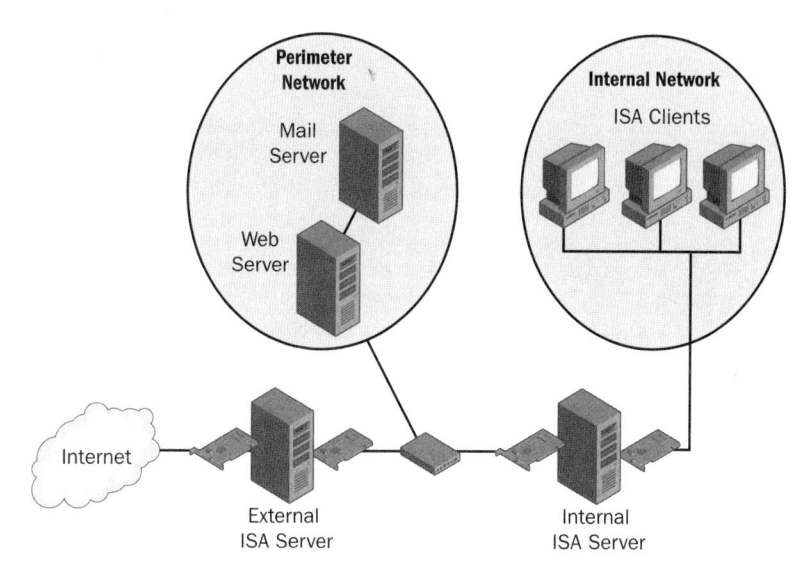

Figure 14-2. *This illustration shows a back-to-back ISA Server perimeter network.*

We'll discuss two back-to-back perimeter network configurations in this section: one uses private IP addresses for the perimeter network servers; the other uses public IP addresses for these servers. To start, however, we'll cover the basics of configuring your two ISA servers.

Configuring the Back-to-Back ISA Servers

Confirm that each ISA server meets the following prerequisites:

- Each server has two network interface adapters.
- If you're installing a private address back-to-back perimeter network, install the Microsoft Loopback Adapter on the external ISA server before installing ISA Server (see below for details).
- Install each server in integrated or firewall mode.

You can now configure the external and internal ISA servers.

Start by configuring the external ISA server (the server connected to the Internet) by following these steps:

1. Open the ISA Management console.
2. In the left pane, expand your server or array, expand the Network Configuration node, right-click Local Address Table (LAT), and click Construct LAT.

Note For more information on configuring the LAT, see Chapter 2, "Installing and Configuring Microsoft ISA Server 2000."

3. In the Construct LAT dialog box, configure the LAT to include the IP addresses for each server located in the perimeter network, including the IP address assigned to the internal ISA server's external network interface. Click OK.
4. Create the necessary Web and server publishing rules to make servers on the perimeter network available to external clients. To configure a Web or server publishing rule, see the sections of Chapter 9 entitled "Creating a Web Publishing Rule" and "Creating a Server Publishing Rule."

> **Note** The steps to publish either Web or server services are the same as those for a single ISA server configuration. See Chapter 9 for more details.

To configure the internal ISA server connected to the internal network, complete the following steps:

1. Open the ISA Management console.
2. In the left pane, expand your server or array, expand the Network Configuration node, right-click Local Address Table (LAT), and click Construct LAT.
3. In the Construct LAT dialog box, configure the LAT to include only the IP address ranges for each segment located in the internal network. Click OK.

> **Note** Do not put the perimeter network IP addresses in the internal ISA server's LAT.

4. Create the necessary Web and server publishing rules to allow perimeter network hosts to communicate with internal network clients. To configure a Web or server publishing rule, see the sections of Chapter 9 entitled "Creating a Web Publishing Rule" and "Creating a Server Publishing Rule."

Configuring Back-to-Back Perimeter Networks

You can configure a back-to-back ISA Server perimeter network so that the perimeter network segment uses either private or public IP addresses. Using private addresses for servers in the perimeter network allows you to publish the servers on the perimeter network using Web or server publishing rules, protocol rules, or site and content rules. Public address networks require that you use IP Packet filters to make services available—potentially a less secure configuration. Public address networks, however, do allow you to more completely make FTP services and H.323 services available to both external and internal clients.

> **Note** For more information on details about and the configuration of public and private address perimeter networks, see Tom and Debra Shinder's book, *ISA Server and Beyond* (Rockland, MA: Syngress Publishing Inc., 2002). They also cover several publishing scenarios—such as publishing virtual private networks (VPNs) in perimeter networks—that aren't found in this book because of space limitations.

In the following section we cover the steps necessary to configure both private and public address perimeter networks.

Configuring a Private Address Perimeter Network

A private address back-to-back perimeter network provides a secure configuration that segregates the private IP addresses used for your internal network and your perimeter network and also allows the external ISA server to use Web and server publishing (as opposed to IP packet filtering) to make services available to external clients.

Configure your private address back-to-back perimeter network as shown in Table 14-2.

Table 14-2. Configuration for a Private Address Back-to-Back Perimeter Network

Component	Configuration Required
External ISA server	Requires a network interface that connects to the Internet and another network interface that connects to the perimeter network. Requires the LAT to contain the private addresses assigned to all servers in the perimeter network.
Internal ISA server	Requires a network interface that connects to the perimeter network and another network interface that connects to the internal network. Requires the LAT to contain only the private addresses assigned to the internal network.

Configuring the External ISA Server for a Private Address Back-to-Back Perimeter Network Set up the external ISA server so that one network interface connects to the Internet and the other connects to the perimeter network. Assign the following IP addresses to the network interface adapters:

- A public, routable IP address assigned by an ISP to your network interface connected to the Internet.

- A private IP address to your network interface connected to the perimeter network. Include this address, along with the IP addresses of all perimeter network servers, in the external ISA server's LAT.

Configuring the Internal ISA Server for a Private Address Back-to-Back Perimeter Network Set up the internal ISA server so that one network interface connects to the perimeter network and the other connects to the internal network. Assign IP addresses to the network interface adapters as follows:

- On the perimeter network interface connected to the network, assign a private IP address from the perimeter network's scope.

- On the internal network interface, assign a private IP address from the internal network's scope.

> **Note** The private IP addressing scheme assigned to the perimeter network should be unique. The internal network should not include the private addressing scheme that the perimeter network uses.

Configuring Communication between the Perimeter Network and the Internal Network In order to control communication between servers located in the perimeter network and internal network, define publishing rules. The publishing rules should utilize client address sets to control from where clients can initiate certain types of communication. For example, if you have a Web server that's logging information to a SQL database server located on the internal network, you'd want to define a client address set with the IP address or range of IP addresses for the Web server. This will further limit the communication traffic sent between the perimeter network and the internal network.

Configuring Bidirectional Traffic from the Internal Network to the External Network When using a back-to-back perimeter network, the last configuration concern deals with defining how to configure inbound and outbound access between the internal network and external network. Use the following rules of thumb:

- Never use the external ISA server for outbound access control.
- Use only the external ISA server to control access from external clients to the perimeter network.
- Use the internal ISA server for controlling outbound access.
- Ensure that the internal ISA server is a member of a Microsoft Windows NT 4.0 or Windows 2000 domain for the purpose of user-level authentication.
- Ensure that the external ISA server is installed only in a workgroup, and not a domain. By creating two security contexts, you create a more secure environment. The only accounts and passwords available on the external ISA server are for the workgroup. To obtain access to the internal network, the attacker has to also penetrate the internal ISA server.

Configuring a Public Address Perimeter Network

A public address back-to-back perimeter network utilizes two separate public IP addresses for your external ISA server and your perimeter network, while maintaining private IP addresses only in your local network. This configuration requires that you use IP packet filtering to make services available to external clients—Web and server publishing are not available.

Configure the back-to-back public address perimeter network as shown in Table 14-3.

Table 14-3. Configuration for a Public Address Back-to-Back Perimeter Network

Component	Configuration Required
External ISA server	Requires that the external ISA Server have three network interfaces: external, perimeter, and the Microsoft Loopback Adapter
	Requires the use of packet filters to control access and communications to the perimeter network
Network Interfaces	Requires you to configure the Microsoft Loopback Adapter to trick ISA server so that you can define the LAT during setup
IP Addressing Scheme—LAT	Requires that the perimeter network not be configured on the external ISA server's LAT
	Requires you to use a block of public addresses for assignment to the perimeter network

Configuring the External ISA Server for a Public Address Back-to-Back Perimeter Network Set up the external ISA server so that one network interface connects to the Internet and the other connects to the perimeter network. Assign the following IP addresses to the network interface adapters:

- A public, routable IP address assigned by an ISP to your network interface connected to the Internet
- A public IP address (subnetted from your public address range to create a unique network ID) to the network interface connected to the perimeter network

Note If you're unfamiliar with variable subnetting or supernetting, refer to Microsoft Knowledge Base article 164015, which can be found at *http://support.microsoft.com*.

Configuring the Internal ISA Server for a Public Address Back-to-Back Perimeter Network Configure the internal ISA server so that one network interface connects to the perimeter network and the other connects to the internal network. Assign IP addresses to the network interface adapters as follows:

- A public IP address (from the subnet assigned to the perimeter network) to the network interface connected to the perimeter network
- A private IP address as assigned to the internal network to the network interface connected to the internal network
- The Microsoft Loopback Adapter, which you should install before installing ISA Server

Configuring the Microsoft Loopback Adapter The Microsoft Loopback Adapter is necessary because ISA Server doesn't support using only two external network interfaces (its purpose, of course, is to connect internal and external networks). You therefore must provide ISA Server with an internal network adapter for inclusion in the LAT.

> **Caution** Do not assign an IP address that is valid in your network to the Microsoft Loopback Adapter.

Add this address to the LAT of the external ISA server.

To install the Microsoft Loopback Adapter on a Windows 2000 Server, complete the following steps:

1. Open the Control Panel and double-click Add/Remove Hardware.
2. Click Next to continue.
3. Select Add/Troubleshoot A Device and click Next.
4. Select Add A New Device and click Next.
5. Select No, I Want To Select The Hardware From A List and click Next.
6. Select Network Adapters and click Next.
7. In the left pane, select Microsoft from the Manufacturers list. In the right pane, click Microsoft Loopback Adapter. Click Next to continue.
8. Click Next to install the adapter.
9. Click Finish to complete the wizard.

> **Note** For more information about the Microsoft Loopback Adapter, see the Microsoft Knowledge Base article 236869, "HOW TO: Install Microsoft Loopback Adapter in Windows 2000," which also provides steps for unattended installation. You can find the article at *http://support.microsoft.com*.

To install the Microsoft Loopback Adapter on a Windows Server 2003, complete the following steps:

1. Open the Control Panel and double-click Add Hardware.
2. Click Next to continue.
3. Select Yes, I Have Already Connected The Hardware and click Next.
4. Click Add A New Hardware Device and click Next.
5. Select Install The Hardware I Select Manually From A List and click Next.
6. Select Network Adapters and then click Next.
7. In the left pane, select Microsoft from the Manufacturers list. In the right pane, click Microsoft Loopback Adapter. Click Next to continue.
8. Click Next to start the installation of the network adapter.
9. Click Finish to complete the wizard.

Configuring Bidirectional Traffic from Both the Internal and Perimeter Networks to the External Network To control outbound and inbound access in a public address back-to-back environment, configure IP packet filters to allow communication between the following networks:

- Internal network to external network and vice versa
- Perimeter network to external network and vice versa

The configurations of the packet filters will vary based on the type of outbound and inbound access you wish to allow. Refer to the section "Publishing Services in Perimeter Networks" below for the different types of selections you can apply to the static packet filters.

Limitations of Perimeter Networks

As you've seen, perimeter networks provide greater protection, but each also comes with some limitations, as outlined in Table 14-4.

Table 14-4. Limitations of Back-to-Back Perimeter Networks

Perimeter Network Type	Limitations
Trihomed	Can't use Web or server publishing to publish servers. Requires the use of static IP packet filters, which filter traffic based only on an IP address or subnet.
Private address back-to-back	Requires VPN passthrough. Can't publish PORT mode FTP client using two ISA servers.
Public address back-to-back	Can't use Web or server publishing to publish servers. Requires the use of static IP packet filters, which filter traffic based only on an IP address or subnet. Requires the use of the Microsoft Loopback Adapter.

Publishing Services in Perimeter Networks

The main purpose of establishing a perimeter network is to make specific services available to external client requests while minimizing the risk to clients on the internal network. The servers are located in a separate network segment and should contain very selective corporate data. This segregation helps mitigate risk: if an intrusion were successful, little worth accessing would be available.

Depending on your perimeter network topology, you might be able to publish servers by using either IP packet filters or Web and server publishing rules. Use the following rules of thumb to remember when you must use packet filters:

- When you're publishing servers that are located in a trihomed perimeter network, use IP packet filters to make the servers accessible to external clients.
- When you're publishing servers or services located on the ISA Server computer itself, you must use IP packet filters.

Note Many of the scenarios described in this section of the chapter require the creation of new static IP packet filters, Web/server publishing rules, or LAT configuration modifications. Earlier in the book we discussed steps for creating each of these components, and so the procedures identified in the section will merely describe the unique options that you need to configure and not entire step-by-step procedures. Where appropriate, you'll find references to the chapters covering detailed, step-by-step procedures.

Publishing Web Servers

Publishing Web servers in a trihomed perimeter network configuration requires that you configure a static IP packet filter that allows access for external connections. In a back-to back scenario, you simply publish the server.

Configuring the Web Server in a Trihomed Perimeter Network

To publish a Web server, you need to create a custom, static packet filter with the options shown in Table 14-5.

Table 14-5. IP Packet Filter Settings for Publishing Web Services in a Trihomed Perimeter Network

IP Packet Filter Wizard Page	Required Selection(s)
Servers	Only This Server
Filter Mode	Allow
Filter Type	Custom
Filter Settings	IP Protocol: TCP
	Direction: Both
	Local Port and Port Number: Fixed Port, 80
	Remote Port: All Ports
Local Computer	This Computer, and type the IP address of the Web server
Remote Computer	All Remote Computers

The key benefit of using a packet filter and not Web publishing rules is that you retain the actual source IP address of the external client visiting the Web site.

Configuring the Web Server In a Back-to-Back Perimeter Network

Publishing a Web server located in a back-to-back ISA Server perimeter network is no different than publishing a Web server with a single ISA server. For information on publishing a Web server with a Web publishing rule, see the section of Chapter 9 entitled "Creating a Web Publishing Rule."

Publishing FTP Services

Publishing FTP in a trihomed environment is possible for PORT clients (and PASV clients if you poke holes in your firewall). With a back-to-back configuration, it's possible to publish FTP more securely because you can isolate the FTP server without having to open the firewall for internal resources, too. The following scenarios explain how to publish both types of FTP services—PORT and PASV.

Configuring the PORT Mode FTP Server in a Trihomed Perimeter Network

Two packet filters are required to publish a PORT mode FTP server. The options shown in Table 14-6 and Table 14-7 illustrate the required packet filter configurations.

Table 14-6. IP Packet Filter Settings for Publishing a PORT Mode FTP Server in a Trihomed Perimeter Network (Allowing Inbound Access to Port 21)

IP Packet Filter Wizard Page	Required Selection(s)
Servers	Only This Server
Filter Mode	Allow
Filter Type	Custom
Filter Settings	IP Protocol: TCP
	Direction: Both
	Local Port and Port Number: Fixed Port, 21
	Remote Port: All Ports
Local Computer	This Computer, and type the IP address of the FTP server
Remote Computer	All Remote Computers

Table 14-7. IP Packet Filter Settings for Publishing a PORT Mode FTP Server in a Trihomed Perimeter Network (Allowing Outbound Requests From Anyone From Port 20)

IP Packet Filter Wizard Page	Required Selection(s)
Servers	Only This Server
Filter Mode	Allow
Filter Type	Custom
Filter Settings	IP Protocol: TCP
	Direction: Both
	Local Port and Port Number: Fixed Port, 20
	Remote Port: All Ports
Local Computer	This Computer, and type the IP address of the FTP server
Remote Computer	All Remote Computers

Configuring the PASV Mode FTP Server in a Trihomed Perimeter Network

Clients connecting in PASV mode will also need two packet filters. The first packet filter establishes the command channel and is the same packet filter created for a PORT mode FTP server. The second packet filter allows all external clients to establish a connection to a high port listening on the FTP server.

Allowing inbound requests to port 21—the command channel—requires a packet filter identical to the first packet filter for a PORT mode FTP server. You should repeat the options identified in Table 14-5 here.

The second packet filter required isn't as secure as other packet filters, because you'll be configuring the ISA server to open any high port negotiated between the PASV FTP server and client. You'll be opening up a greater level of access to external clients, so ensure that the business reasons outweigh the potential risk. The selections required for this packet filter are shown in Table 14-8.

Table 14-8. IP Packet Filter Settings for Publishing a PASV Mode FTP Server in a Trihomed Perimeter Network (Allowing External Clients to Connect to a High Port)

IP Packet Filter Wizard Page	Required Selection(s)
Servers	Only This Server
Filter Mode	Allow
Filter Type	Custom
Filter Settings	IP Protocol: TCP
	Direction: Both
	Local Port: Dynamic
	Remote Port: All Ports
Local Computer	This Computer, and type the IP address of the FTP server
Remote Computer	All Remote Computers

Configuring FTP in a Back-to-Back Perimeter Network

Setting up an FTP server in a back-to-back perimeter network works in the same basic manner as explained in Chapter 10, "Common Web and Server Publishing Scenarios." You will, however, need to configure the external ISA server to allow access to external clients and the internal ISA server to allow access for internal clients.

Publishing SMTP Services in a Trihomed Perimeter Network

To publish an SMTP server in a trihomed perimeter network, you need to create a custom, static packet filter.

The predefined SMTP packet filter provided with ISA Server doesn't work because the predefined packet filters expect the designated service to listen on the ISA server's external interface. In a trihomed configuration, instead of listening on the ISA server's external interface, the SMTP service listens on the server in the perimeter network. This new packet filter allows inbound packets from any remote machine to communicate with port 25 on the SMTP server, and it allows outbound packets from port 25 on the SMTP server to communicate with any remote machine. Define this custom, static packet filter with the options illustrated in Table 14-9. For more information about configuring packet filters, see Chapter 10.

Table 14-9. IP Packet Filter Settings for Publishing an SMTP Server in a Trihomed Perimeter Network

IP Packet Filter Wizard Page	Required Selection(s)
Servers	Only This Server
Filter Mode	Allow
Filter Type	Custom
Filter Settings	IP Protocol: TCP
	Direction: Both
	Local Port and Port Number: Fixed Port, 25
	Remote Port: All Ports
Local Computer	This Computer, and type the IP address of the SMTP server
Remote Computer	All Remote Computers

Note Wondering about publishing in a back-to-back perimeter network scenario? You can do so using the same steps described in Chapter 10; however, if you wish to perform more advanced configurations—configuring an SMTP relay, for example—refer to Tom and Debra Shinder's book *ISA Server and Beyond* (Rockland: MA. Syngress Publishing Inc., 2002), which devotes an entire section to this subject.

Additional Resources

- There are several articles on the Microsoft Knowledge Base that provide useful information on topics covered in this chapter. You can find them by going to *http://support.microsoft.com/?kbid=article number* (insert the article number at the end of the URL).
  - Article 164015, "Understanding TCP/IP Addressing and Subnetting Basics."
  - Article 303530, "VPN Clients May Not Work on ISA Server Perimeter Networks."
  - Article 324972, "WebCast: Microsoft Internet Security and Acceleration Server 2000 and Perimeter Networks."
  - Article 313562, "HOW TO: Publish a Web Server on a Perimeter Network."
  - Article 313907, "The Allow All IP Packet Filter Does Not Work for ISA Server Perimeter Network Hosts."
  - Article 299959, "Cannot Access Mail Service That Is Installed Directly on ISA Server with a DMZ Network Adapter."
- Perimeter network resources are available at *http://www.isaserver.org*.
- Shinder, Tom and Debra Littlejohn Shinder. *ISA Server and Beyond: Real World Security Solutions for Microsoft Enterprise Networks* (Rockland, MA: Syngress Publishing Inc., 2002).

Chapter 15
Securing ISA Server 2000

The final chapter of this book focuses on one of the core functions of Microsoft ISA Server—security. We'll look first at how ISA Server fits into Microsoft's Trustworthy Computing model, and then we'll focus on intrusion detection. Next, we'll explain the purpose and procedures behind the Security Configuration Wizard. The last section of the chapter is dedicated to methods or ways to better optimize ISA servers, including disabling unnecessary services and configuring the network interface adapters.

Trustworthy Computing

Creating secure environments is part of Microsoft's Trustworthy Computing program, which reduces the risks of unauthorized and unwanted access to your computing data and systems. Named for its objectives and goals, this initiative—known as SD^3+C—is described in Table 15-1.

Table 15-1. Microsoft Trustworthy Computing Initiatives

Objective	Description
Secure by design	Before products ship, thoroughly check code for common vulnerabilities; add features that enhance security
Secure by default	Ship products so that they install in a secure state
Secure by deployment	Protect systems and data as they are used in day-to-day operations; security updates are easy to find and install; tools are available to assess and manage security risks across large organizations; attempted intrusions are detected
Communications	Disseminate security risks, fixes, and best practices to customers in a timely and comprehensible fashion

New products, such as Microsoft Office 2003 and Microsoft Windows 2003 Server, ship with more secure configurations than previous versions. Windows Update provides access to current patches and fixes. The Microsoft Security Response Center assembles teams to provide quick responses to problems. Newsletters, Web sites, and presentations at *http://www.microsoft.com/security* and at product sites provide better communication on how to securely configure your systems.

ISA Server plays a key role in Microsoft's Trustworthy Computing initiative, especially in helping to meet the objectives of the Secure by Deployment goal. ISA Server often serves as the gateway for corporate (and often sensitive) information flowing between your networks, other networks, and the Internet. ISA Server protects systems and data through the use of its firewall functionality—using ISA Server rules, you make services available to only the users and computers you specify. As you read in Chapter 6, "Monitoring and Reporting," ISA Server also uses filters to detect intrusions and to inspect and validate traffic on all ports, which can alert you to attacks and even automatically trigger actions to defend the environment when attacks begin.

Common Types of Attacks and Best Prevention Practices

We can classify common attacks against corporate networks into social and technical categories. For the most part, ISA Server won't help with social engineering attacks, but you can turn to books like Kevin Mitnick and William Simon's *The Art of Deception* (John Wiley & Sons, 2002) for more information on how to understand and prevent such intrusions.

Technical attacks fall into different classes, according to the authors of *Hack Proofing Your Network: Internet Tradecraft*, second edition (Syngress Media Inc., 2002) and *Hacking Exposed Windows 2000* by Joel Scambray and Stuart McClure (McGraw-Hill Osborne Media, 2001):

- Denial of service (DoS) attacks remove access to a resource through any means available, usually through overwhelming a resource's capacity—common DoS attacks include Distributed Denial-of-Service, Smurf, TCP Connect Flooding, and others.
- Information leakage attacks gather data exposed by your perimeter servers—common leakage occurs through finger or Domain Name System (DNS) requests, when port scanners find open Transmission Control Protocol (TCP) and User Datagram Protocol (UDP) connections, and through scans of your Web and mail servers.
- File system attacks seek access to the file system—common attacks include accessing and manipulating content directly, obtaining a copy of the Security Accounts Manager (SAM), and adding or modifying log files.
- Scripted attacks come in the form of viruses, worms, and Trojan horses that often self-propagate, and they can cause any number of possible nasty actions—well-known examples of these attacks include w32.Klez, Nimda, and CodeRed.

ISA Server helps to mitigate the risks presented by these attacks. Follow these best practices to help reduce your possible exposure:

1. Run ISA Server on a dedicated machine if possible, although it can be shared as long as it's configured correctly.
2. Configure your ISA Server environment with only those ports and services necessary to perform functions.
3. Harden your servers and use the security wizards to ensure the most locked-down environment possible.

Only the weakest security requirements will be fulfilled with a single security tool. Your ISA Server should be one part of your overall security plan that includes the following guidelines:

1. Establish a good understanding of security principles and practices by reading through the best practices available at *http://www.microsoft.com/technet/security/bestprac/* and by reading books such as Hacking Exposed Windows 2000, by Scambray and McClure.
2. Stay educated and up-to-date with the most current threats by reading the information available at sites like *www.microsoft.com/security*, *www.isaserver.org*, *www.ntbugtraq.com*, and *securityfocus.org*.
3. Document your settings so that you have a baseline against which you can measure any changes in the future—keep your documentation updated.
4. Be ever vigilant and audit your environment by checking the security of your systems, preferably using automated systems. Verify that no unnecessary ports are exposed. Use the Microsoft Baseline Security Analyzer to ensure that you have your servers are configured as you expect them to be and that you have applied all updates.
5. Protect yourself against viruses by using antivirus software—such as those solutions available at *http://www.microsoft.com/isaserver/partners/contentsecurity.asp*—and by following the steps outlined in articles available at *http://www.microsoft.com/isaserver/techinfo/prevent/*.

Intrusion Detection

Intrusion detection is a built-in component of ISA Server that allows you to easily identify a variety of attacks being made against your network, in addition to a variety of configurable actions to take when an attack is detected. The intrusion detection technology included with ISA Server is licensed from Internet Security Systems (ISS).

Intrusion detection allows your ISA server to detect an attack and provides notifications when the attack is being made against your ISA server.

Configuring Intrusion Detection

Intrusion detection isn't enabled by default on your ISA server. To protect yourself against some more common attacks, first enable intrusion detection and then determine the types of attacks you wish to filter and report against.

To enable intrusion detection, follow these steps:

1. Open the ISA Management console.
2. In the left pane, expand your ISA server or array node, expand the Access Policy node, right-click IP Packet Filters, and then click Properties.
3. In the General tab, select the Enable Intrusion Detection check box and then click OK.

> **Note** In order to select Enable Intrusion Detection, you must first select the Enable Packet Filtering check box.

To enable detection of particular attacks, complete the following steps:

1. Open the ISA Management console.
2. In the left pane, expand your ISA server or array node, expand the Access Policy node, right-click IP Packet Filters, and then click Properties.
3. Select the Intrusion Detection tab.
4. In the Intrusion Detection tab, select the types of attacks you'd like ISA Server to detect, as illustrated in Figure 15-1. Each attack is described in Table 15-2.

Table 15-2. Intrusion Attacks Explained

Type of Intrusion Attack	Description
Windows Out-Of-Band (WinNuke)	This type of attack is a DoS attack used to make a computer crash or a network interface unavailable.
LAND	This type of attack creates a spoofed IP address and source port to match the destination IP address and destination port. This process creates a loop to bring down the affected computer.
Ping Of Death	This type of attack causes a buffer overflow in the computer from the computer's attempts to continually respond to an extremely large IP packet.
IP Half Scan	This type of attack performs only a portion of the common three-step Transmission Control Protocol/Internet Protocol (TCP/IP) communication session to consume resources on the system that is being attacked.
UDP Bomb	This type of attack uses a maliciously configured UDP packet to create an operating system failure.
Port Scan	This type of probe detects open ports on a computer to identify potential vulnerabilities.

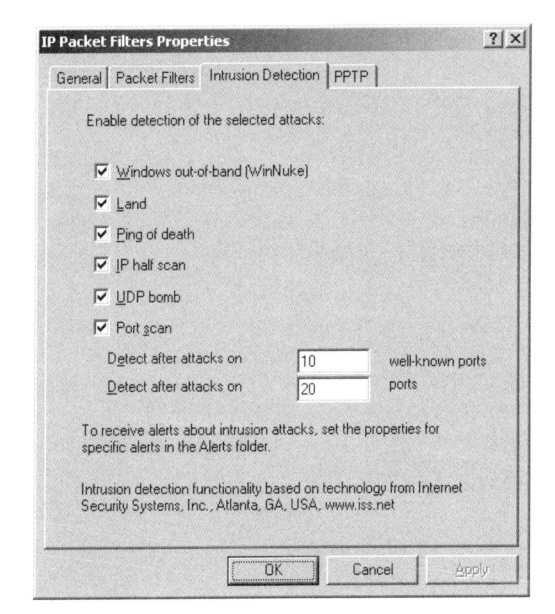

Figure 15-1. *You can monitor different types of intrusion attacks with ISA Server.*

5. Click OK.

ISA Server also includes the ability to track intrusion detection at the application level by using DNS and Post Office Protocol (POP) intrusion detection filters. By default, both the DNS and POP intrusion detection filters are enabled, regardless of whether you've enabled intrusion detection.

To enable detection of select DNS attacks, follow these steps:

1. Open the ISA Management console.
2. In the left pane, expand your ISA server or array node, expand Extensions, and then click Application Filters.
3. In the right pane, right-click DNS Intrusion Detection Filter and then click Properties.
4. Select the Attacks tab.
5. In the Attacks tab, select the types of attacks you'd like ISA Server to detect, as illustrated in Figure 15-2. Each attack is described in Table 15-3.

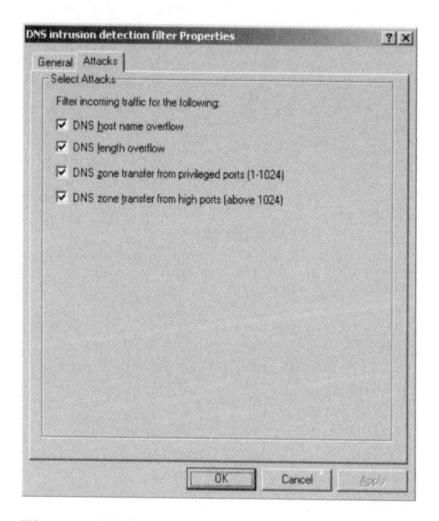

Figure 15-2. *You can monitor different types of DNS application-level attacks with ISA Server.*

Table 15-3. Application Level DNS Attacks Explained

Type of DNS Intrusion Attacks	Explained
DNS Hostname Overflow	This type of attack is a DNS response for a host name that exceeds a certain fixed length, causing an internal buffer overflow. This overflow allows a remote attacker to execute commands on the targeted computer.
DNS Length Overflow	This type of attack occurs when an IP address contains a length field larger than 4 bytes, causing an internal buffer overflow. This overflow allows a remote attacker to execute commands on the targeted computer.
DNS Zone Transfer From Privileged Ports (1-1024)	This type of attack occurs when a computer uses a DNS client application to transfer DNS zones from an internal DNS server to an external DNS server, which makes sensitive information about your network vulnerable to interception.
DNS Zone Transfer From High Ports (Above 1024)	This type of attack executes the same DNS zone transfer as the DNS Zone Transfer From Privileged Ports, but uses the unprivileged, high ports to conduct the transfer.

6. Click OK.

The POP Intrusion Detection filter includes only a single type of attack—the POP overflow buffer. This type of attack attempts to gain privileged access to certain versions of POP by exceeding the capacity of an internal buffer on the server. To ensure that the POP Intrusion Detection filter is enabled, follow these steps:

1. Open the ISA Management console.
2. In the left pane, expand your ISA server or array node, expand Extensions, and then click Application Filters.
3. In the right pane, right-click POP Intrusion Detection Filter and then click Properties.
4. In the General tab, verify that the Enable This Filter check box is selected.
5. Click OK.

Intrusion Detection Alerts and Actions

ISA Server includes alerts for intrusion detection, DNS intrusion, and POP intrusion. You may configure each of these alerts to perform a variety of actions when ISA Server detects an attack and triggers an alert:

- Stop selected services
- Start select services
- Send an e-mail message or page
- Run a previously specified program or script
- Write an event to the event log

Refer to the section of Chapter 6 entitled "Alerts" to see more detail about each of these actions.

ISA Server Security Wizards

The ISA Server Security Configuration Wizard provides an automated mechanism for locking down elements of your ISA server by applying a preconfigured security template. In this section we'll provide step-by-step procedures on how to run the wizard, explain the three different security levels available, and describe the security templates applied to your ISA server when you run the wizard.

The ISA Server Security Configuration Wizard uses preconfigured security templates, with three levels of security settings based on ISA Server's installation mode, and the server type—for example, whether the system is a member, stand-alone, or domain controller server, or hosts services like Internet Information Services (IIS) or Simple Mail Transfer Protocol (SMTP). Table 15-4 shows each security level, and the appropriate ISA Server mode and server type.

Table 15-4. Security Configuration Wizard Levels and Templates

Security Level	Preferred ISA Server Mode	Preferred Type of Server
Dedicated	Firewall only	No services other than ISA Server
Limited Services	Firewall and cache (integrated)	Domain controller
Secure	Firewall only	Web (IIS) server, SMTP server, or structured query language (SQL) server

Note Notice that the Secure option in the Security Configuration Wizard is actually the *least* secure setting available. The Dedicated option provides the highest level of security.

Security Templates

The preconfigured security templates determine the settings that will change. You can find the templates in the systemroot\security\templates folder on the ISA server.

To view the settings for a template, complete the following steps:

1. Open Windows Explorer and navigate to the *systemroot*\security\templates folder.
2. Right-click a template and then click Open. You should see settings similar to Figure 15-3.

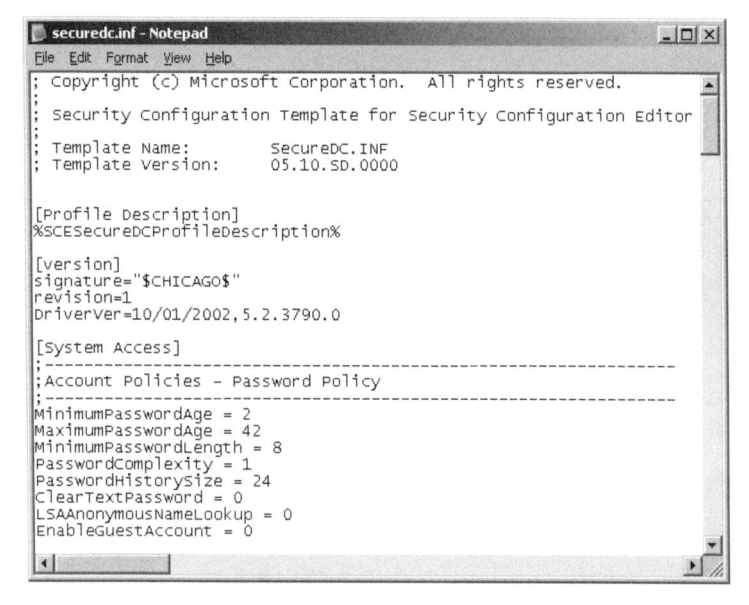

Figure 15-3. *You can view the settings for the securedc.inf security template by opening it with Notepad.*

Caution When you right-click the select template to open, you'll also see an option to Install. Be careful. If you click Install you won't be prompted or asked if you'd like to install the settings in the template; the security settings will be applied without prompts of any kind.

3. Close the template and Windows Explorer.

To run the Security Configuration Wizard, follow these steps:

1. Back up your server so that you can revert to your original configuration, if necessary.
2. Open the ISA Management console.
3. In the left pane, expand your ISA array or server node and click the Computers node.
4. In the right pane, right-click the ISA server that you wish to run the wizard against and click Secure.
5. Click Next to continue.

Caution The security templates that apply after running the Security Configuration Wizard aren't easy to undo. In fact, the wizard reminds you that the selections you make are irreversible. If you have a deep understanding of each of the settings configured in the security templates and a little luck, you might be able to revert back by painstakingly restoring settings one by one, or restoring from backup.

6. On the Select System Security Level page, select one of the three security levels to assign to the ISA server. The options are:
   - Dedicated
   - Limited Services
   - Secure

   Click Next to continue.
7. Review the configuration and then click Finish.

Optimizing ISA Server Security

ISA Server provides protection for your corporate network. Out of the box it's installed in a protected state, but taking a few additional steps to help shore up some potential soft spots provides an even more secure configuration. This section expands on methods to implement to further optimize ISA Server's security and performance. We'll start with a checklist describing steps to secure your ISA server, and then we'll provide details on how to perform these valuable activities:

- Securing the network interface adapters
- Disabling unnecessary server services
- Running ISA Server on a dedicated server
- Utilizing the URLScan tool and RSA SecureID authentication available with ISA Server Feature Pack 1

Checklist for Securing ISA Server 2000

Tom Shinder wrote two articles that culminate in a checklist for tightening the security of your ISA Server environment. Here is an adaptation of that checklist.

- Don't install or enable any unnecessary services or applications on your ISA server, and don't install ISA Server on a domain controller (unless, of course, you've created a separate forest and domain specifically for the ISA server).
- Ensure that only local IP addresses are in the Local Address Table (LAT) and local network domains are in the Local Domain Table (LDT).
- Use Group Policies to enforce complex passwords.
- Follow the steps to harden your server and keep it up-to-date with the most current patches and security updates.
- On the external interface disable File And Print Sharing and NetBIOS Over TCP/IP; be sure to select the Append These DNS Suffixes check box for your external interface and enter a local or false DNS suffix to prevent the resolution of unqualified requests from allowing access.
- For the internal interface, disable all clients, File And Printer Sharing, and NetBIOS if you don't require them.
- Select Enable Packet Filtering and Enable Intrusion Detection from the IP Packet Filters Properties dialog box; but unless it's unavoidable don't select Enable IP Routing. In the Packet Filters tab, select the Enable Filtering Of IP Fragments and Enable Filtering IP Options preferences.
- If you're not using Web publishing rules, remove all incoming Web listeners.
- Restrict access to your resources wherever possible.
    - Reduce the least restrictive site and content rule to the most secure group possible (for example, authenticated users or a global group that specifies who should have external access).

- Use and create protocol rules for required protocols; don't enable anything "just in case" you think you might need it some day.
- Use hardening techniques on published servers and allow access only to those who require it.
- Become familiar with the alerts available in ISA Server and configure the most important to perform actions that will help identify and mitigate problems quickly and accurately.
- Keep your logs on a dedicated disk, increase the number of log files saved, and set up a job to copy them each day to a backup location.
- In the Application Filters container, enable SMTP, POP, and DNS filters.

Note For more details about how to perform these steps, review the concepts in relevant chapters of this book or read Tom Shinder's excellent articles: "ISA Server Security Checklist - Part 1: Securing the Operating System and the Interface" available at *http://www.isaserver.org/pages/article_p.asp?id=200*; and "ISA Server Security Checklist - Part 2: Securing the ISA Server Configuration" available at *http://www.isaserver.org/tutorials/ISA_Server_Security_Checklist__Part_2_Securing_the_ISA_Server_Configuration.html*.

Securing the Network Interface Adapters

The configuration of the external and internal network interface adapters is critical to the security of your ISA server. You don't want external users to have the ability to attack open ports or to connect directly to your server because you unintentionally enabled File And Print Services on your external network interface. Configure the following settings for any ISA server that sits at the edge (perimeter) of your network.

For the external network interface:

- Unbind File And Printer Sharing for Microsoft Networks
- Unbind Client For Microsoft Networks
- Clear the Register This Connection's Addresses In DNS check box
- Select Disable NetBIOS Over TCP/IP

For the internal network interface:

- Bind at the top of the binding order
- Configure the default gateway

Note The following procedures are for a server running Windows 2000. We'll note any differences for a server running Windows Server 2003 as appropriate.

To configure the correct binding order for the network interface adapters, follow these steps:

1. Open Network And Dial-up Connections. On a server running Windows Server 2003, open Network Connections from the Control Panel.
2. Click the Advanced menu and then click Advanced Settings.
3. In the Adapters And Bindings tab, ensure that the internal network interface is at the top in the Connections box. If the internal network interface isn't listed first, select the interface, and the click the up arrow on the right until the interface is first in the list.

Note The binding order for network interface adapters is used for processing name resolution requests from internal clients. The ISA server will process client name resolution requests from top to bottom.

4. In the Adapters And Bindings tab, click the internal network interface in the Connections box and ensure that you've selected both the File And Printer Sharing For Microsoft Networks and Client For Microsoft Networks check boxes.
5. Click OK.

To disable the File And Printer Sharing For Microsoft Networks service and the Client For Microsoft Networks client on the external network interface, follow these steps:

1. Open Network And Dial-up Connections. On a server running Windows Server 2003, open Network Connections from the Control Panel.
2. Click the Advanced menu and then click Advanced Settings.
3. In the Adapters And Bindings tab, click the external network interface in the Connections box and clear both the File And Printer Sharing For Microsoft Networks and Client For Microsoft Networks check boxes.
4. Click OK.

To disable specific DNS and Windows Internet Name Service (WINS) settings on the external interface, follow these steps:

1. Open Network And Dial-up Connections. On a server running Windows Server 2003, open Network Connections from the Control Panel.
2. Right-click the external network interface and then click Properties.
3. Select Internet Protocol (TCP/IP) and then click Properties.
4. In the General tab, ensure that a Default Gateway address has been provided.

Note The external network interface should be the only network interface with a default gateway configured.

5. In the General tab, click the Advanced button.

6. Select the DNS tab.
7. In the DNS tab, clear the Register This Connection's Addresses In DNS check box.
8. Select the WINS tab.
9. In the WINS tab, select Disable NetBIOS Over TCP/IP and then click OK.

Caution If you're presented with a warning for an empty WINS address, click Yes to continue.

10. Click OK again. On Windows 2000 Server, click OK once more. On Windows Server 2003, click Close.

Disabling Services

Running services present potential security vulnerabilities on a server running Windows 2000 or Windows Server 2003. On an ISA server, disable unused services to reduce the likelihood that a security weakness in a running service will allow the server to be compromised.

The following list identifies some common services that you can disable on a server running Windows 2000 or a server running Windows Server 2003 with ISA Server. The services are in alphabetical order and will vary depending on the components you require running on the ISA server. For example, if you need IIS to run on the ISA server, you don't want to disable the IIS services. Your server may have unique requirements.

Note As a general rule, disable *all* services that are not needed.

The most common services that you can disable on a server include the following:

- Application Management
- DHCP Client
- Distributed Link Tracking Client
- Distributed Link Tracking Server
- Fax Service
- FTP Publishing Service
- Indexing Service
- IIS Admin Service
- Internet Connection Sharing (known as Internet Connection Firewall [ICF] / Internet Connection Sharing [ICS] on a server running Windows Server 2003 server)
- Intersite Messaging

- NetMeeting Remote Desktop Sharing (unless you're using this for remote control rather than Terminal Services/Remote Desktop)
- Network News Transport Protocol (NNTP)
- Remote Registry Service (unless you require this to manage your server)
- Simple Mail Transport Protocol (SMTP)
- Simple TCP/IP Services
- SNMP Service
- Telnet
- Utility Manager (Windows 2000 only)
- World Wide Web Publishing Service

Windows Server 2003 places more of an emphasis on security right out of the box; you'll find more services appear as Disabled, which reduces the number of services you need to stop. This allows your ISA server to obtain better performance from the hardware and provide increased security with fewer opportunities for exploits.

Running ISA Server on a Dedicated Server

Although ISA Server can run on servers configured as mail servers, Web servers, domain controllers, and so on, it functions best as a firewall product if you install it on a dedicated server whenever possible. There are times when this is unavoidable—as in the case when using Microsoft Small Business Server 2000, where ISA Server is a bundled product. No properly configured ISA server should have a problem running other applications; however, those other services require more vigilance and greater caution when you configure the ISA server. Greater complexity increases the risk of unintentionally poking a hole in your defenses. Simply put, the fewer functions your ISA server performs, the less chance you have of making mistakes and the greater protection you enjoy.

URLScan 2.5 for ISA Server

URLScan 2.5 is a tool included with ISA Server Feature Pack 1, and it was introduced to secure specific types of Hypertext Transfer Protocol (HTTP) requests processed by an IIS server. Since its release with the IIS Lockdown Tool, URLScan 2.5 has become an administrator favorite. You should utilize it to protect Web-related services like Outlook Web Access (OWA) that are published with ISA Server.

The URLScan tool consists of two files, Urlscan.dll and Urlscan.ini, which are bundled as Urlscan.exe. When the Web filter is installed, ISA server processes all incoming Web requests; it then filters each request based on the configuration of URLScan, determining whether it should pass the request on to the published Web server. URLScan filters only incoming requests.

Installing URLScan 2.5

The URLScan 2.5 Web filter installs in an enabled state and then applies to all Web publishing rules on the ISA server. To install URLScan 2.5, follow these steps:

1. Open Windows Explorer and open the directory where you downloaded the Feature Pack 1 source files.

Note ISA Server 2000 Feature Pack 1 is available from *http://www.microsoft.com/isaserver/featurepack1*.

2. Double-click the file Isafp1ur.exe to launch the installation.
3. Click I Agree to accept the End User License Agreement (EULA).
4. Click Yes to the Caution that some Web sites might be inaccessible to users after the installation is completed. The caution message is shown in Figure 15-4.

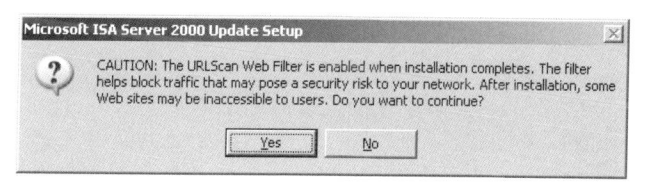

Figure 15-4. *Accept the URLScan installation warning message.*

5. Click Yes when prompted to use the optimized file for OWA as shown in Figure 15-5, which replaces the standard IIS file used by URLScan.

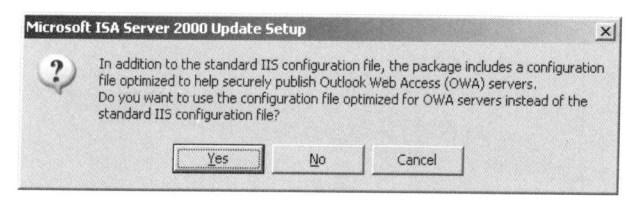

Figure 15-5. *If you use OWA, use the configuration file optimized for OWA.*

6. The Microsoft Web Proxy service stops, the updates are processed, and then the Microsoft Web Proxy service starts.
7. Click OK to complete the installation.

Note Clear the Read About The URLScan Web Filter check box if you don't wish to see the URLScan overview document.

Disabling the URLScan Web Filter

The URLScan Web filter installs in an enabled state. At some time you might want to confirm that access is working to a published Web server without URLScan interfering with the tests. To disable the URLScan Web filter, follow these steps:

1. Open the ISA Management console.
2. In the left pane, expand your ISA server or array node, expand the Extensions node, and then click Web Filters.
3. In the right pane, right-click URLScan Filter and click Disable.

Note You may also right-click URLScan Filter, click Properties, and in the General tab clear the Enable This Filter check box.

Configuring the Urlscan.ini File

The file Urlscan.ini contains the configuration options. Located in the ISA Server installation directory (by default, located in C:\Program Files\Microsoft ISA Server), the Urlscan.ini file contains to the criteria that determine the types of Web requests allowed to pass back to published Web servers. Included with URLScan 2.5 are two additional configuration files:

- **Urlscan_owa.ini** A configuration file that helps optimize the security for a published OWA server
- **Urlscan_iis.ini** A configuration file that helps optimize security for a typical Web server

Depending on the type of server being published (such as publishing an OWA server), you might want to edit the configuration of Urlscan.ini or apply the configuration file Urlscan_owa.ini. To edit the Urlscan.ini file, follow these steps:

1. Open Windows Explorer and browse to the ISA Server installation directory.
2. Locate and right-click the Urlscan.ini file and then click Open. The default settings for the Urlscan.ini file are shown in Figure 15-6.

Caution Incorrectly configuring the Urlscan.ini file could severely harm your operating ISA server. Take caution when proceeding to Step 3.

3. Make the desired changes to the file, click File, and then click Save.
4. Close Notepad and Windows Explorer.

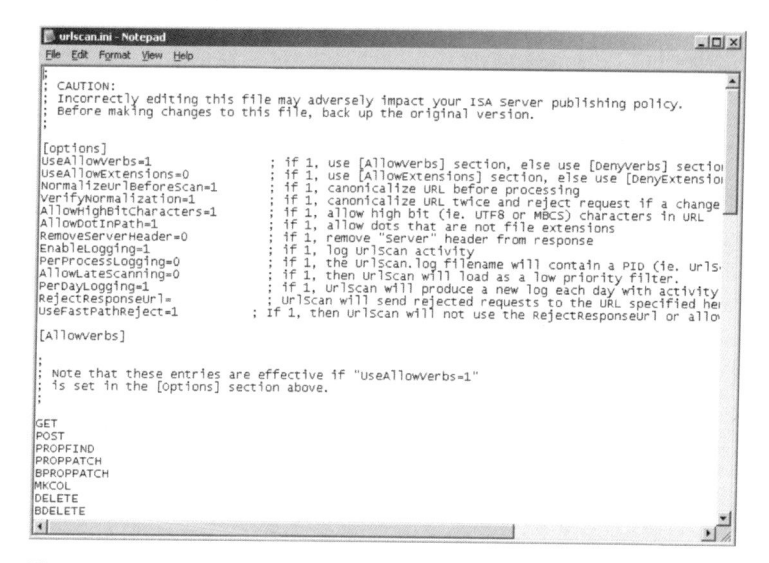

Figure 15-6. *The Urlscan.ini file available with ISA Server Feature Pack 1 contains default settings.*

Note You can find more information on the explanations of the options included in the Urlscan.ini file in the ISA Server Help file by searching for "About URLScan.ini." Remember that you must have installed ISA Feature Pack 1 to have this functionality available to you. You can find similar information in the Microsoft Knowledge Base article 326444, "HOW TO: Configure the URLScan Tool" located at *http://support.microsoft.com/?kbid=326444*.

A Look at Web Authentication with RSA SecurID

If you're using a product called SecurID—made by RSA Security, Inc.—ISA Server Feature Pack 1 includes a tool that supports two-factor authentication of Web and virtual private network (VPN) services. The inclusion of a Web filter for RSA SecurID provides increased authentication mechanisms (PIN numbers and secure tokens) when requiring authentication to published Web servers or access to ISA VPN servers.

In order to gain the functionality of the Web filter for RSA SecurID, you must be running an RSA ACE/Server on your network. Downloading the RSA Web filter in the Feature Pack and installing it on the ISA server without having the RSA ACE/Server won't provide any additional security.

Once you've purchased the RSA product, you can install the Web filter as shown in the following section, "Installing the RSA SecurID Web Filter."

Note You can find more information on the inner workings of RSA SecurID in the ISA Server Help file by searching for "About Authentication Support for RSA SecurID" after installing the Web filter for RSA SecurID. You can also see product information at *http://www.rsasecurity.com/products/securid/*.

Installing the RSA SecurID Web Filter

To install RSA SecurID, complete the following steps:

1. Open Windows Explorer and open the directory where you downloaded the Feature Pack 1 source files.

Note ISA Server 2000 Feature Pack 1 is available from *http://www.microsoft.com/isaserver/featurepack1*.

2. Double-click the file Isafp1sd.exe to launch the installation.
3. Click I Agree to accept the EULA.
4. Each of the ISA Server services is stopped, the updates are processed, and each of the ISA Server services is started.
5. Click OK to complete the installation.

Note Clear the Read About The Web Filter For RSA SecurID check box if you don't wish to see the RSA SecurID overview document.

Additional Resources

Security is a subject far too involved and vast for us to address completely in this book. The following resources provide more comprehensive information.

Security References

- Mitnick, Kevin D. and William L. Simon. *The Art of Deception*. Indianapolis, IN: John Wiley & Sons, 2002.
- Russell, Ryan, et al. *Hack Proofing Your Network*. Rockland, MA: Syngress Media, Inc., 2000.
- Scambray, Joel and Stuart McClure. *Hacking Exposed Windows 2000*. Berkeley, CA: McGraw-Hill Osbourne Media, 2001.
- Shinder, Tom and Debra Littlejohn Shinder. *Configuring ISA Server 2000: Building Firewalls for Windows 2000*. Rockland, MA: Syngress Media, Inc., 2001.

Trustworthy Computing

- *http://www.microsoft.com/presspass/exec/craig/10-02trustworthywp.asp*
- *http://www.microsoft.com/security/whitepapers/secure_platform.asp*

Securing ISA Server 2000

- ISA Feature Pack 1 at *www.microsoft.com/isaserver/featurepack1*.
- The RSA SecurID Read Me file from the Feature Pack 1 downloads available at *http://www.microsoft.com/isaserver*.
- The URLScan Web Filter Read Me file from the Feature Pack 1 downloads available at *http://www.microsoft.com/isaserver*.
- Shinder, Tom and Debra Littlejohn Shinder. *ISA Server and Beyond: Real World Security Solutions for Microsoft Enterprise Networks*. Rockland, MA: Syngress Media, Inc., 2002.

Index

A

access control filters
   inbound, 147, 166–69
   outbound, 141–44
access policies, 120–28, 128–40. *See also* policy elements
   application filters, 140–44
   bandwidth rules, 128–31
   defined, 119
   IP packet filters, 126–28
   outgoing Web requests, 135–40
   processing outgoing requests, 119–20
   protocol rules, 123–25
   routing rules, 131–35
   site and content rules, 120–23
   Web filters, 144
Access Policy folder, 14–15
Actions tab, alert configuration, 91–92
Active Caching, 5, 37
Active Directory directory service, 201–9
   arrays, 202–7
   domain integration, 207–9
   Group Policy–based firewall client installation, 53–54
   ISA Server integration with, 5–6, 27–28
   Proxy Server upgrade, 74
   stand-alone vs. array members, 201–2
Active Directory Schema console, 29
Active Directory Users and Computers, 53
add-ons, 18
Add/Remove Programs
   Feature Pack 1 uninstall, 41
   H.323 Gatekeeper installation, 243
   Internet Connection Wizard, 68
   ISA Server uninstall, 42
   removing ISA Server from SBS, 71
Address Mapping page. *See also* server publishing rules.
   Citrix server publishing rule, 193
   DNS server publishing rule, 195–96
   HTTPS server publishing rule, 177–78
   RDP publishing rule, 192
   SQL server publishing rule, 190

administration, ISA Server, 3–20
   add-ons, 18
   caching mode, 4–5
   command-line utilities, 18
   firewall mode, 3–4
   ISA community, 18
   ISA Management Console, 12–17
   MMCs commonly used, 17
   product editions. *see* product editions
   remotely, 19–20
   wizards, 17
administrative requirements
   arrays, 203
   enterprise policies, 211, 213–18
   firewall clients, 54
   logging to database, 98
   Proxy Server upgrade, 74
Advanced Calling Option, NetMeeting, 248–49
Advanced tab, cache configuration, 37–38
Advanced view, ISA Management Console
   aborting sessions, 86–87
   overview of, 13
   resetting alerts, 93
   viewing alerts, 92
alerts, 88–93
   capturing with Windows 2000 event log, 90
   configuring, 91–92
   creating, 88–91
   e-mail messages, 89–90
   intrusion detection with, 275, 279
   resetting, 93
   running programs with, 90
   stopping Proxy 2.0 Server, 77
   viewing, 92
allow rules. *See* access policies
ALTADDR command, 194
antivirus software, 271
application filters
   disabling protocol definitions, 110
   inbound access control, 147, 166–69
   outbound access control, 141–44

Application Usage reports, 95
Array Membership tab, 38–39
array policies. *See also* enterprise policies
   allowing, 218
   back up and restore, 220–21
   configuring, 219
   enterprise policies, 212, 219–20
   overview of, 211
   policy elements and, 105
arrays
   creating and configuring, 202–7
   installing Feature Pack 1 on, 41
   membership, 27–30
   reports on, 94
   resolving requests within, 138, 152
   stand-alone vs., 201–2
   upgrading Proxy Server 2.0, 74, 77–78
The Art of Deception (Mitnick and Simon), 270
attacks
   firewalls and, 4
   intrusion detection and, 272–75
   preventing, 271
   types of, 270, 272
authentication
   basic, 132
   HTTP Redirector filter, 142
   incoming listener, 151
   Integrated Windows, 132
   outgoing listener, 136–37
   outgoing Web requests, 137–38
   publishing OWA server and, 187
   RSA SecurID, 285–86
authentication, Web publishing
   incoming, 151, 152
   installation modes, 147
   prerequisites for, 149
Automatic Discovery, 33–35
autorun, 22

B

BackOffice word, 67
back-to-back perimeter network. *See* perimeter networks, back-to-back
Backup Enterprise Configuration dialog box, 215
Backup Route tab, Web proxy clients, 50
backups
   array configuration, 220–21
   array members, 205
   enterprise configuration, 215
   Proxy Server 2.0, 73, 75
bandwidth priorities
   associated rules, 104
   defined, 15
   overview of, 117–18
bandwidth rules
   Bandwidth Rules folder, 15
   configuring, 128–31
   creating, 129
basic authentication, 132
batch files, 54–55
bidirectional affinity, 230

C

CA (Certificate Authority), 177
Cache Array Routing Protocol. *See* CARP
Cache Configuration, ISA Management Console, 16, 39–40
cache configuration properties, 36–38
cache mode, 35–40
   comparing with other modes, 24–25
   installation requirements, 7–8
   installing ISA Server on SBS, 60–61
   intra-array address, 38–39
   link translation, 160
   load factor, 38
   overview of, 4–5
   properties, 36–38
   schedule content downloads, 39–40
   size, 36
   Web publishing and, 147
call routing rules, 245–48
   e-mail address rule, 247
   IP address rule, 248
   phone number rule, 248
CARP (Cache Array Routing Protocol)
   configuring, 223–26
   defined, 223
   Web proxy client configuration, 50
Certificate Authority (CA), 177
certificates, Web server, 177
checklist, security, 278–79
Chkwsp32 command, 18
Citrix server, 192–94
client address sets
   associated rules, 104
   Exchange server publishing, 183, 186
   overview of, 109–10
   server publishing and, 162
   Web publishing and, 149
Client Configuration, ISA Management Console, 17, 49
Client Type address, 122
clients, 45–58
   Citrix, 194
   firewall clients, 51–57
   network infrastructure dependencies, 57–58
   overview of, 45
   publishing Exchange server, 183
   remote connections with VPN, 234–37

enterprise policies | 291

    SecureNAT clients, 46–48
    server publishing prerequisites, 162
    session types, 86
    Web proxy clients, 48–51
cluster parameters, configuring, 227–28
command-line utilities, 18, 85
Computers folder, ISA Management Console, 14
configuration, ISA Server, 30–40
    Automatic Discovery, 33–35
    cache, 35–40
    Local Address Table, 31–32
    Local Domain Table, 32–33
    overview of, 30
connectoids, VPN client, 236–37
content groups
    associated rules, 104
    defined, 15
    overview of, 112–14
Control Panel, firewall client configuration, 55–56
Credentials tab, reports, 94

D

databases, ODBC, 98–100
dedicated servers, 271, 282
demilitarized zone (DMZ). *See* perimeter networks
denial of service (DoS) attacks, 270
deny rules. *See* access policy
Deploy Software dialog box, firewall client, 53–54
description field, Bandwidth Rules, 129
destination name
    e-mail address rules, 247
    IP address rules, 248
    phone number rules, 246
destination sets
    defining, 104
    overview of, 107–8
    publishing Web servers, 149, 174–75
DHCP (Dynamic Host Configuration Protocol), 58, 69
dial-up connections, 69
dial-up entries
    associated rules, 104
    defined, 16
    overview of, 114–17
dictionary, link translation, 160–61
Direct Access tab, 50–51
distributed caching, 5–6

DMZ (demilitarized zone). *See* perimeter networks
DNS (Domain Name System)
    client dependencies, 57–58
    dynamic services for SBS, 69
    intrusion alerts, 89
    LAT and, 32
    publishing DNS server, 194–97
    publishing Exchange server, 183, 185
    publishing OWA server, 187
    publishing servers, 162, 172
    publishing Web servers, 149
    Round Robin, 230
    securing network interface adapters, 280–81
    SRV records, 241–42
    WPAD entry in, 35
DNS Intrusion Detection filter
    configuring, 273–74
    defined, 141
    filtering incoming messages, 166–67
DNS Query packet filters, 196–97
DNS Query Server protocol definition, 195
DNS Zone Transfer Server, 195
documentation, updating, 271
Domain Administrators group, 211
domain integration, 207–9
Domain Name System. *See* DoS (denial of service) attacks, 270
downloads, scheduled, 5
dynamic DNS, 69
Dynamic Host Configuration Protocol (DHCP), 58, 69
dynamic packet filtering, 164, 165

E

Edit Alias window, 52–53
e-mail
    address rules, 247
    alerts, 89–90
Enable/Disable icon, 91
End User License Agreement (EULA), 23
Enterprise Administrators group, 74, 211, 213–18
Enterprise Initialization dialog box, 28–29
Enterprise Initialization Tool, 27–28
enterprise policies
    array policies and, 28–29, 212
    arrays, 212–13, 217–20
    back up and restore, 215–16
    configuring, 212–13

enterprise policies, *continued*
  creating, 214
  defaults, 218
  deleting, 216
  overview of, 211
  packet filtering and, 165
  permissions for, 216
  policy elements and, 105
  protocol rules, 124
  remote connections, 217
  site and content rules, 121
  upgrading, 28–29
enterprise technologies, 223–50
  Cache Array Routing Protocol, 223–26
  H.323 Gatekeeper. *see* H.323 Gatekeeper
  Network Load Balancing, 226–30
  Virtual Private Networks. *see* VPNs
EULA (End User License Agreement), 23
Event Viewer, 88, 92
events
  analyzing, 88
  logging, 90
  monitoring, 87–88
Events tab, alert configuration, 91–92
Excel Workbook (.xls) file, 96
Exchange 2000 server, 182–87
  disabling socket pooling, 173
  ISA Server and, 183–85
  Outlook clients and, 185–87
  OWA server and, 187–89
  publishing, 182–83
Extensions, ISA Management Console, 16

F

fax server, 70
File And Print Sharing, 278
files
  extensions, 113
  logging to, 98
  system attacks on, 270
File Transfer Protocol. *See* FTP (File Transfer Protocol) server
filters
  application. *see* application filters
  DNS Intrusion Detection. *see* DNS Intrusion Detection filter
  enabling H.323, 244
  firewall benefits of ISA Server, 4
  IP packet. *see* IP packet filters
  POP Intrusion Detection. *see* POP Intrusion Detection filter
  security checklist, 279
  URLScan 2.5, 282–85
  Web. *see* Web filters

firewall chaining, 134–35
Firewall Client Options dialog box, 55
firewall clients, 51–57
  Automatic Discovery for, 34
  configuration, 55–57
  functionality of, 45
  Group Policy-based installations, 53–54
  IIS Web-based installations, 52–53
  overview of, 51
  Proxy Server 2.0 vs. ISA Server, 80
  session type, 86
  silent installations, 54–55
  UNC-based installations, 51–52
  as Web proxy clients, 57
firewall mode, 4, 24–25
Firewall Service
  defined, 83
  logging transactions, 96–100
  monitoring, 83–85
  starting, 90–91
  stopping, 90
FTP Access Application Filter, enabling, 182
FTP access filter, 141–42
FTP (File Transfer Protocol) server, 178–82
  disabling socket pooling, 173
  ISA server and, 180–82
  packet filtering and, 179–80
  publishing in trihomed perimeter network, 265–66
FTP tab, cache configuration properties, 37
full installations, 243

G

gatekeepers. *See* H.323 Gatekeeper
gateways, H.323, 241
gateway-to-gateway VPNs, 231–34
General tab
  alert configuration, 91
  cache configuration, 37
  reports, 94
Getting Started Wizard, 17
GPO (Group Policy Object), 53–54

H

H.323 filter, 141, 167–68
H.323 Gatekeeper, 241–49
  adding to ISA Server, 244
  call routing rules, 245–48
  configuring, 244–45
  defined, 83, 223
  enabling, 244
  installing, 243
  monitoring, 84–85

NetMeeting clients and, 248–49
overview of, 241
prerequisites, 241–43
Service Management Console installation, 243–44
Hack Proofing Your Network: Internet Tradecraft (Syngress Media Inc.), 270
Hacking Exposed Windows 2000 (Scambray and McClure), 270
hardware requirements
ISA Server, 7–8, 21–22
ISA Server 2000 Enterprise Edition, 12
SBS 2000, 9
help, ISA Server
events, 87–88
link translation, 158
Urlscan.ini file, 285
hierarchical caching, 5–6
host parameters, 228
hotfixes, 26, 69
.htm (Web page) file, 96
HTTP (Hypertext Transfer Protocol) requests, 119, 282
HTTP Redirector filter
configuring, 47–48, 142–43
defined, 141
firewall clients accessing Web cache, 51
HTTPS (Hypertext Transfer Protocol Secure) requests
content groups and, 113
processing incoming, 153
publishing, 176–78

I

ICA protocol, Citrix, 193
ICSA (International Computer Security Association) Labs certification, 4
ICW (Internet Connection Wizard)
configuring ISA Server on SBS, 63–67
failure to start, 68
troubleshooting ISA Server on SBS, 68–70
Identification page, ISA VPN, 232
IIS (Internet Information Services)
firewall clients, 52–53
Proxy Server 2.0 upgrade, 78, 79, 81
publishing and, 172–74, 176, 181
SBS troubleshooting and, 71
IMAP4 clients, 184–85
information leakage attacks, 270
Install New Modem Wizard, 115

installation, ISA Server, 21–30
array membership, 26–30
Feature Pack 1, 40–41
overview of, 21–25
Service Pack 1, 26
uninstall feature, 42
Windows Server 2003 and, 26
installation modes, publishing, 147
integrated mode
configuration in, 30
installation in, 24–25
publishing in, 147
Integrated Services Digital Network (ISDN) adapter, 22
Integrated Windows authentication, 132
interface configuration, security, 278, 279–80
internal addresses, 61–62
International Computer Security Association (ICSA) Labs certification, 4
Internet Connection Wizard. *See* ICW
Internet Explorer, 49
Internetwork Packet Exchange/Sequenced Packet Exchange (IPX/SPX), 73
intra-array address, 38–39
Intra-Array Communication dialog box, 38–39
intrusion detection, 271–75
alerts and actions, 275
configuring, 272–75
overview of, 271
IP (Internet Protocol) Address Rule, creating 248
IP addresses. *See also* perimeter networks
LAT configuration, 30
Network Load Balancing configuration, 230
rule creation, 248
security, 278
IP Half Scan attack, 272–73
IP packet filters
array policies, 219
configuring, 128
creating, 126–27
deleting, 127
DNS Query, 196–97
enabling, 164–65
FTP services and, 179–80
incoming requests, 148
IP routing and, 166
logging transactions, 96–100
outgoing requests, 119

IP packet filters, *continued*
  publishing services in perimeter
    networks, 263–67
  SBS and, 65–67
  security checklist, 278
  trihomed perimeter network and,
    255–56
IP routing, 166, 245
IPSec NAT Transversal, 241
IPX/SPX (Internetwork Packet Exchange/
  Sequenced Packet Exchange), 73
ISA Management Console
  launching, 13
  monitoring services, 84–85
  monitoring sessions, 85–87
  nodes, 14–17
  remote administration, 19
  views, 13–14
ISA Server Control service, 83, 84–85
ISA Server Feature Pack 1, 40–41
ISA Server Service Pack 1
installation, 7, 26
  installation on Windows Server 2003, 25
  uninstall of Feature Pack 1, 41
  uninstall of ISA Server, 42
ISA Server 2000
  administering, administration, ISA
    Server
  as caching server, 4–5
  clients. *see* clients
  configuring. *see* configuration,
    ISA Server
  defined, 3
  as firewall server, 4
  installing. *see* installation, ISA Server
  monitoring. *see* monitoring
  reporting. *see* reports
  upgrade from Proxy Server 2.0. *see*
    Proxy Server 2.0
ISA Server 2000 CD
  Enterprise Initialization Tool, 27–28
  Installation Guide, 22
ISA Server 2000 Enterprise Edition
  arrays and, 211
  CARP support, 223
  comparing product editions, 5–6
  DNS configuration, 58
  enterprise policies and, 211
  overview of, 11–12
  stand-alone vs. array members, 201–2

ISA Server 2000 Standard Edition
  comparing product editions, 5–6
  DNS configuration, 58
  overview of, 10–11
  stand-alone, 201–2
ISA Virtual Private Network Configuration
  Wizard, 231
ISDN (Integrated Services Digital Network) adapter, 22

K

Keywords tab, SMTP filter, 168–69

L

L2TP protocol packets, 234–36, 239–40
LAND attacks, 272–73
LAT (Local Address Table)
  back-to-back perimeter networks,
    257–58
  DNS configuration, 57
  intra-array communication, 225
  ISA server installation and, 25
  ISA server installation on SBS, 61–62
  newly installed ISA Server, 31–32
  public address back-to-back perimeter
    networks, 260–63
  publishing, 172
  trihomed perimeter network, 255–56
LDAP (Lightweight Directory Access
  Protocol), 27–28
LDT (Local Domain Table)
  DNS configuration, 57
  newly installed ISA Server, 32–33
  Web proxy client, 50
licensing
  ISA Server 2000 Enterprise Edition, 12
  ISA Server 2000 Standard Edition, 11
  Small Business Server 2000, 9
Lightweight Directory Access Protocol
  (LDAP), 27–28
link translation, 158–61
  caching, 160
  dictionary, 160–61
  Link Translator filter, 158–59
Link Translation tab, Web publishing rule,
  159, 160, 160–61
Link Translator filter, 144
Live Stream Splitting, 144
load factor, 38, 225

Local Address Table. *See* LAT
Local Domain Table. *See* LDT
Local ISA VPN Wizard, 231–33
log files
  components, 96–97
  configuring, 97–100
  logging user activity, 70
  security checklist, 279
Log Summaries tab, 94
logon scripts, 54–55
Loopback Adapter, 261–62

M

Mail Server Security Wizard, 162
MBSA (Microsoft Baseline Security Analyzer), 271
MCUs (multipoint control units), H.323, 241
Message Screener
filtering incoming messages, 168–69
installing, 25
Microsoft
  Excel Workbook, 96
  Firewall. *see* Firewall Service
  H.323 Gatekeeper. *see* H.323 gatekeeper
  ISA Server 2000. *see* ISA Server 2000
  ISA Server Control, 83
  ISA Server setup program, 22
  Loopback Adapter, 261–62
  newsgroups, 71
  Operations Manager 2000, 88
  Outlook, 185–87
  Proxy Server 2.0. *see* Proxy Server 2.0
  Trustworthy Computing program, 269–71
  Web Proxy. *see* Web Proxy service
  Web site information. *see* Web site information
Microsoft Baseline Security Analyzer (MBSA), 271
Microsoft Windows. *See* Windows versions
Microsoft Windows Media (MMS), 143
MIME types, 113
MMCs, 14–17
MMS (Microsoft Windows Media), 143
modems, 22, 115
monitoring, 83–93
  alerts, 88–93
  defined, 83
  events, 87–88
  ISA Management Console, 14
  ISA Server services, 83–84
  sessions, 85–87

Monitoring Configuration, ISA Management Console
  creating reports, 94
  defined, 16
  generating reports, 93–94
  viewing alerts, 92
Msp2wizi.exe, 76
multipoint control units (MCUs), H.323, 241
multiserver management, 5–6

N

NAT (Network Address Translation), 68
net stop service command, 77
NetBIOS Over TCP/IP, 278
NetMeeting, 20, 248
  internal client, 248
  external client, 249
Netst command prompt, 18
Netstat utility, 81
network adapters
  interface configuration, 279–81
  ISA Server installation, 21
  ISA Server on SBS, 65
  LAT configuration, 32
  Network Load Balancing, 230
Network Address Translation (NAT), 68
Network and Dial-Up Connections
  creating, 114–16
  interface adapters, 280
  Network Load Balancing, 227
  SecureNat clients, 46
  VPN clients, 236–37
Network Configuration, ISA Management Console, 16
Network Connection Wizard, 115
Network Load Balancing, 226–30
  configuring, 227–30
  defined, 223
  DNS Round Robin vs., 230
  installing, 227–29
  overview of, 226
  prerequisites, 227
  server publishing and, 230
Network News Transport Protocol (NNTP) server, 174
New Alert Wizard, 89–91
New Bandwidth Rule Wizard, 15
New Connection Wizard, 115–16
newsgroups, Microsoft, 71
NNTP (Network News Transport Protocol) server, 174
nodes, ISA Management Console, 14–17
Notepad, 276

O

operating systems, 6–7, 61
Operations Manager 2000, 88
Outbound Web Requests Listener, 80
Outlook, 185–87
OWA server, 187–89, 282–85
OWA Web Publishing Wizard, 189

P

pass-through, VPN, 237–41
passwords, enforcing, 278
PASV (passive) mode, 180, 266
PCAnywhere, 20
performance
    ISA Server Web-caching, 5
    optimizing server, 140
perimeter networks
    overview of, 253
    trihomed, 254–56
perimeter networks, back-to-back, 256–63
    configuring, 259–63
    defined, 253
    FTP, 266
    ISA Server, 257–58
    limitations of, 263
    overview of, 256–57
    publishing services in, 263–67
    Web server, 264
Period tab, reports, 94
permissions
    array, 207
    fax server, 70
    H.323 Gatekeeper, 245
phone number rules, 245–46
Ping command prompt, 18
Ping Of Death attack, 272–73
PNM (Progressive Networks protocol), 143
Point-to-Point Protocol over Ethernet (PPPoE), 65
policies
    access. *see* access policy
    array. *see* array policies
    enterprise. *see* enterprise policies
    policy elements. *see* policy elements
Policies tab, arrays, 219–20
policy elements, 103–18
    bandwidth priorities, 117–18
    client address sets, 109–10
    content groups, 112–14
    destination sets, 107–8
    dial-up entries, 114–17
    Enterprise policies and, 105
    ISA Management Console, 15–16
    overview of, 103–5
    protocol definitions, 110–12
    schedules, 105–6
    types of, 103
POP Intrusion Detection filter
    defined, 141
    enabling, 275
    incoming messages and, 168
POP3 clients, 184–85
Port 80, 35
Port Rules tab, Network Load Balancing, 228–29
ports
    incoming Web requests, 152–53
    Network Load Balancing, 228–29
    open, 81
    outgoing Web requests, 80, 138–39
    port scan attacks, 181, 271, 272–73
    publishing Web site, 176
    remote client connections, 234–37
PPPoE (Point-to-Point Protocol over Ethernet), 65
PPTP protocol packets, 234–36, 237–38
private address back-to-back perimeter networks, 259–60, 263
product editions
    basic hardware and server requirements, 7–8
    comparing features, 5–6
    ISA Server 2000 Enterprise Edition, 11–12
    ISA Server 2000 Standard Edition, 10–11
    operating system compatibility, 6–7
    Small Business Server 2000, 8–9
Progressive Networks protocol (PNM), 143
properties
    alerts, 91–92
    cache, 36–38
    destination sets, 107
    Events tab, 92
    firewall clients, 56–57
    H.323 Gatekeeper, 244
    IIS Web-based installation, 52
    incoming listeners, 150–52
    logs, 97–99
    outgoing Web requests, 135–40
    protocol rules, 125
    reporting job, 93–94
    routing rules, 133–34
    SecureNAT installation, 46–48
    site and content rules, 121
    Web proxy clients, 49
    Web publishing rules, 155
    Web sites, 176

protocol rules
    access to H.323 protocol, 242–43
    configuring, 125
    creating, 124
    deleting, 125
    outgoing request order, 119
    publishing Exchange, 186–87
    security checklist, 279
protocols
    associated rules, 104
    Citrix ICA, 193
    defined, 15
    DNS server, 195
    Exchange server, 184
    HTTPS sites, 177
    overview of, 110–12
    prerequisites, 162
    RDP, 191–92
    SQL server, 190
Proxy Alert Notification Service, 77
Proxy Server 2.0, 73–82
    backups, 75
    ISA Server upgrade, 76–79
    ISA Server vs., 80–81
    prerequisites, 73–74
    removing from array, 77–78
    stopping services, 77
    uninstalling, 75
    Windows NT 4, 74–76
Proxy Server Administration service, 77
public address back-to-back perimeter networks, 260–63
public IP addresses, 254–56
published servers, 81
publishing, 147–97. *See also* server publishing rules; Web publishing
    application filters, 166–69
    back-to-back perimeter networks, 258
    Citrix server, 192–94
    defined, 147
    DNS server, 194–97
    Exchange 2000 server, 182–87
    FTP server, 178–82
    HTTPS server publishing rule, 177-78
    installation modes, 147
    OWA server, 187–89
    perimeter network services, 263–67
    prerequisites, 171–74
    processing incoming requests, 148
    Publishing folder, 15
    Remote Desktop, 191–92
    requirements, 8

routing and IP packet filters, 164–66
rules, 219
secured Web sites (HTTPS), 176–78
server, 161
SQL server, 189–91
Terminal Server, 191–92
Web server, 174–76

Q

Query Analyzer, 99

R

RAM
    forward caching, 7
    high-performance Web caching, 5
    publishing, 8
    Windows Server platform and, 6
RDP (Remote Desktop Protocol)
    definition, 191–92
Real Time Streaming Protocol (RTSP), 143
remote administration, 19–20
Remote Desktop, 191–92
Remote ISA VPN Wizard, 231, 233–34
reports, 93–100
    defined, 83
    generating, 93–94
    logging alerts, 90
    logging transactions, 96–100
    saving, 96
    types of, 95
    viewing, 95
Resolve Requests Within Array Before Routing check box, 138
restores
    array configuration, 205–6, 220–21
    enterprise configuration, 215–16
Rmisa.exe tool, 42, 71
Round Robin, DNS, 230
ROUTE ADD command, 22, 172, 183
Route Add command prompt, 18
Router Scope option, 46–47
routing, 166, 172
Routing and Remote Access Service. *See* RRAS
routing rules, 131–35
    configuring, 133–34
    creating, 131–33
    deleting, 133
    firewall chaining, 134–35
    incoming requests, 148
    outgoing requests, 120

RPC filter
  defined, 141
  filtering incoming messages, 168
  publishing Exchange, 185–87
RPC Publishing Wizard, 185–87
RRAS (Routing and Remote Access Service)
  gateway-to-gateway VPNs, 234
  remote client connections, 235–38
  troubleshooting, 68
RSA SecurID, 285–86
RTSP (Real Time Streaming Protocol), 143

S

saving, reports, 96
SBS (Small Business Server) 2000, 59–72
  common procedures, 68–71
  configuring, 63–67
  features of, 5–6, 8–9
  installing, 60–63
  limitations of, 59–60
  overview of, 59
  removing, 71
  resources for, 71
  troubleshooting, 68–71
scalability
  comparing product editions, 5–6
  ISA Server 2000 Enterprise Edition, 11–12
  ISA Server 2000 Standard Edition, 10
  Small Business Server 2000, 8
Schedule tab, reports, 94
Scheduled Content Download
  CARP and, 226
  configuring jobs, 39–40
  defined, 83
  monitoring, 83–85
  overview of, 5
  starting, 90–91
  stopping, 90
schedules
  associated rules, 104
  defined, 15
  overview of, 105–6
scope field, Bandwidth Rules, 129
scope options, SecureNat, 46–47
screened subnets. *See* perimeter networks
scripted attacks, 270
SecureNAT clients
  Citrix server and, 193
  configuring, 47–48
  DNS requirements, 57–58
  firewall chaining, 134–35
  functionality of, 45
  installing, 46–47
  Network Load Balancing and, 229
  published servers and, 81
  session types, 86
  as Web proxy clients, 57–58
SecurID, 285–86
security, 269–88
  attacks and, 270
  checklist, 278–79
  disabling services, 281–82
  enterprise administration, 216
  firewalls and, 4
  intrusion detection, 271–75
  network interface adapters, 279–81
  permissions, 216
  references on, 286
  running ISA Server on a dedicated server, 282
  Security Configuration Wizard, 275–76
  Security reports, 95
  templates, 276–78
  Trustworthy Computing program, 269–71
  URLScan 2.5, 282–85
  Web authentication with RSA SecurID, 285–86
Security Configuration Wizard, 275–76, 276–78
Security Mail Publishing Wizard, 184–85
server publishing
  Citrix server, 192–94
  configuring, 161–64
  DNS server, 194–97
  Exchange server, 182–87
  FTP server, 178–82
  HTTPS server, 177–78
  installation modes for, 147
  Network Load Balancing and, 230
  OWA server, 187–89
  RDP, 191–92
  SQL server, 189–91
  SSL tunneling and, 158
  Terminal Server, 191–92
  Web server, 174–76
server publishing rules
  back-to-back perimeter networks, 258
  Citrix, 193–4
  DNS server publishing rule, 196
  configuring, 162–63
  defined, 15
  HTTPS server publishing rule, 178

DNS, 195–96
OWA server publishing rule, 188–89
publishing Exchange, 186
RDP, 192
SQL server, 190–91
Server Publishing Wizard, 17
service packs, 7, 26
service records (SRV), DNS, creating, 241–42
services
   disabling unneeded, 271, 278, 281–82
   monitoring, 83–85
   providing ISA Server functions, 83
   starting, 90–91
   stopping, 90
sessions
   aborting, 86–87
   defined, 85
   determining type of, 86
   monitoring, 85–86
site and content rules
   order for outgoing requests, 119
   overview of, 121–23
   publishing Exchange, 185
   security checklist for, 278
size, cache, 36
Small Business Server 2000 Setup Wizard, 60–63
Small Business Server ICW (Internet Connection Wizard), 63–67, 68
SMTP (Simple Mail Transfer Protocol) clients, 184–85
SMTP filter, 141, 168–69
SMTP (Simple Mail Transfer Protocol) server
   disabling socket pooling, 173–74
   publishing in trihomed perimeter network, 267
   sending e-mail alert messages, 89
social engineering attacks, 270
socket pooling, 172–74, 180
SOCKS V4 filter, 141, 143
software requirements
   ISA Server 2000 Enterprise Edition, 12
   ISA Server installation, 21–22
   Small Business Server 2000, 9
SQL Server, 98–99, 189–91
SRV (service records), DNS, 241–42
SSL (Secure Sockets Layer)
   bridging, 157
   certificates, 147, 153
   port, 139
   publishing sites, 176–78
   tunneling, 158

stand-alone ISA Servers
   characteristics of, 201–2
   configuring. *see* ISA Server, configuring
   installing, 21–26
   multidomain configuration/trust relationships, 208–9
   Standard/Enterprise Editions installed as, 6
   uninstalling, 42
static packet filtering, 164, 255–56
streaming media filters, 141, 143–44
Summary reports, 95–96
System DSN, 99–100

T

Task Bar, 55
Taskpad view, ISA Management Console
   aborting sessions, 86–87
   overview of, 13
   resetting alerts, 93
   viewing alerts, 92
TCP port, 138
TCP/IP (Transmission Control Protocol/Internet Protocol), 21
technical attacks, 270–71
Telnet command prompt, 18
templates, security, 275–78
Terminal Services, 19, 191–92
terminals, H.323, 241
terminology, upgrading Proxy Server, 74
tiered policy, 5–6
Tracer command prompt, 18
Traffic & Utilization reports, 95
Transmission Control Protocol/Internet Protocol (TCP/IP), 21
trihomed ISA Server perimeter network
   configuring, 255–56
   defined, 253
   interface configuration, 254–55
   limitations, 256, 263
   overview of, 254
   publishing services in, 263–67
Trojan Horses (scripted attacks), 270
troubleshooting, ISA Server on SBS, 68–71
trust relationships, 207–9
Trustworthy Computing program, 269–71

U

UDP Bomb attack, 272–73
UNC (Universal NamingConvention), 51–52
Uniform Resource Locator (URL), 50
uninstallation
ISA Server, 42

ISA Server Feature Pack 1, 41
Universal Naming Convention (UNC), 51–52
upgrades
  from Proxy Server 2.0. *see* Proxy Server 2.0
  Small Business Server, 59
  Windows NT 4.0, 207–8
  Winsock clients to firewall clients, 80
URL (Uniform Resource Locator), 50
URLScan 2.5, 282–85
  configuring Urlscan.ini file, 284
  disabling URLScan Web filter, 284
  installing, 283
  overview of, 282
Urlscan.ini file, 284–85
User Manager, 110
users, logging activity, 70

V

views
  alert, 92
  events, 87–88
  ISA Management Console, 13–14
  reports, 95
  sessions, 85–87
Virtual Network Computing (VNC), 20
viruses (scripted attacks), 270, 271
VNC (Virtual Network Computing), 20
VPN Client Wizard, 234–36
VPNs (Virtual Private Networks), 231–41
  client connectoids, 236–37
  defined, 223
  gateway-to-gateway, 231–34
  ISA Server as, 231
  pass-through, 237–41
  remote clients, 234–37

W

Web filters
  authentication with RSA SecuID, 285–86
  inbound access with, 158–61
  overview of, 144
Web page (.htm) file, 96
Web proxy clients
  Automatic Discovery for, 34
  configuring, 49–51
  DNS requirements, 57–58
  firewall/SecureNAT clients configured as, 57
  functionality of, 45
  installation, 49
  overview of, 48–51
  session types, 86

Web proxy rules, 131
Web Proxy Service
  defined, 83
  logging transactions, 96–100
  monitoring, 83–85
  starting, 90–91
  stopping, 90
Web publishing, 148–61
  accessing secured sites, 157–58
  disabling socket pooling, 173
  incoming Web requests, 149–53
  installation modes, 147
  overview of, 148
  prerequisites, 149
  SSL bridging and, 157–58
  Web filters, 158–61
  Web server, 174–76
Web publishing rules
  back-to-back perimeter networks, 258
  configuring, 155–56
  creating, 154–55
  defined, 15, 147
  deleting, 155
  disabling, 156
  enabling, 156
  link translation and, 159–61
  OWA server, 188
  processing order, 148, 156–67
  Web sites behind ISA server, 175
  Web sites on ISA server, 176
Web Publishing Wizard, 17
Web requests, incoming
  CARP, 224–25
  DNS server, 195
  HTTPS site, 177
  overview of, 149–53
  publishing servers and, 162
  SQL server, 189
Web requests, outgoing
  CARP, 224
  configuring, 135–40
Web servers
  overview of, 174–76
  in trihomed perimeter network, 264
Web site information
  add-ons, 18
  antivirus software, 271
  event analysis, 88
  Feature Pack 1, 283
  firewall clients, 51, 54
  hotfixes, 26
  ISA community support, 18
  ISA Server reports, 100
  Loopback Adapter, 262

newsgroups, 71
PPPoE configuration, 65
Proxy Server 2.0, 76, 81
remote administration, 19
reporting, 100
RSA SecurID, 286
SBS, 9, 59, 69, 71
security, 269, 271
service packs, 26
supernetting, 255
upgrading Windows NT4, 75
Urlscan.ini file configuration, 285
Web Usage reports, 95
Weekends schedule, access policy, 105
Windows NT 4.0, 74–76, 207–8
Windows Server 2003
 domain configuration/trust relationships, 208–9
 ISA Server installation, 26
 memory/processor support, 6–7
 network dial-up connections, 115–16
 Network Load Balancing and, 230
 socket pooling, disabling, 173
Windows 2000
 domain configuration/trust relationships, 208–9
 ISA Server installation, 22
 logging alerts to Event Log, 90
 network dial-up connections, 114–15
 Network Load Balancing, 230
 socket pooling, disabling, 173–74
 upgrading Proxy Server, 73, 74–76
WinNuke (Windows Out-Of-Band) attack, 272–73
WINS, 280–81
Winsock clients, 80–81
Winsock Proxy Service, 77
wizards. *See also* specific wizard names
 ISA Server, 17
 ISA Server VPN, 231
 publishing, 147
Work Hours schedule, access policy, 105
World Wide Web Publishing service, 77
worms (scripted attacks), 270
WPAD (Web Proxy Autodiscovery Protocol), 33–35, 50

About the Authors

Jason Ballard

Jason Ballard is an information systems specialist for Toyota Motor Manufacturing North America. He specializes in various Microsoft products that provide Internet connectivity, network architecture, directory services, and server-based computing. Jason received a bachelor's degree in business administration from the University of Kentucky, is an MCSE+I on Microsoft Windows NT 4.0, an MCSE and MCSA on Windows 2000, and a Microsoft Certified Trainer (MCT). In addition, Jason holds certifications from Citrix and CompTIA. He provides solutions to meet customers' expectations and goals involving products such as Windows Server 2003, Windows 2000, Windows NT, Microsoft ISA Server 2000, Proxy Server 2.0, IIS Server, Sharepoint Portal Server, Exchange 2000 Server, and Citrix Metaframe.

In addition, Jason is an accomplished presenter and public speaker, having presented seminars and demonstrations for emerging technologies to a variety of audiences. Outside work, Jason enjoys many activities, including spending time with his family, running, cycling, participating in triathlons, and playing golf and basketball. You can reach him on the Internet at *www.tjballard.com*.

Bud Ratliff

Bud Ratliff is a senior project manager and systems architect at Koinonia Computing and specializes in providing document-based project design and program management for the Information Technology industry. He earned the Project Management Professional certification from the Project Management Institute and is an MCP+I and an MCSE on both Windows NT 4.0 and Windows 2000. An entertaining and proficient teacher, Bud is an MCT, holds a bachelor's degree in education, and enjoys helping individuals and groups explore new technologies.

Bud's focus on technology includes a deep technical knowledge of Windows operating systems, productivity tools, systems management and deployment tools, and techniques used in distributed computing environments. When not working on projects for his clients, Bud runs, bikes, fences, plays guitar, and travels with his family. You can reach him on the Internet at *www.budratliff.com* or e-mail him at consulting@budratliff.com.

Get a **Free**
e-mail newsletter, updates,
special offers, links to related books,
and more when you

register online!

Register your Microsoft Press® title on our Web site and you'll get a FREE subscription to our e-mail newsletter, *Microsoft Press Book Connections*. You'll find out about newly released and upcoming books and learning tools, online events, software downloads, special offers and coupons for Microsoft Press customers, and information about major Microsoft® product releases. You can also read useful additional information about all the titles we publish, such as detailed book descriptions, tables of contents and indexes, sample chapters, links to related books and book series, author biographies, and reviews by other customers.

Registration is easy. Just visit this Web pa and fill in your information:

http://www.microsoft.com/mspress/regist

Microsoft

Proof of Purchase

Use this page as proof of purchase if participating in a promotion or rebate o this title. Proof of purchase must be used in conjunction with other proof(s payment such as your dated sales receipt—see offer details.

Microsoft® Internet Security and Acceleration (ISA) Se 2000 Administrator's Pocket Consultant
0-7356-1442-3

CUSTOMER NAME

Microsoft Press, PO Box 97017, Redmond, WA 98073-9830